REEF SECRETS

REEF SECRETS

■ STARTING RIGHT ■ SELECTING FISHES &
INVERTEBRATES ■ ADVANCED BIOTOPE TECHNIQUES

ALF JACOB NILSEN
SVEIN A. FOSSÅ

MICROCOSM

t.f.h.
PROFESSIONAL
SERIES™

T.F.H. Publications
One T.F.H. Plaza
Third and Union Avenues
Neptune City, NJ 07753
www.tfh.com

This book has been published with the intent to provide accurate and authoritative information
in regard to the subject matter within. While every precaution has been taken
in preparation of this book, the publisher and author assume no responsibility for
errors or omissions. Neither is any liability assumed for damages resulting
from the use of the information herein.

ISBN13 9-781890-08767-8

ISBN 1-890087-67-X (hardcover); ISBN 1-890087-68-8 (softcover)

Printed and bound in China

06 07 08 09   3 5 7 9 8 6 4 2

Library of Congress Cataloging-in-Publication Data

Nilsen, Alf Jacob.
  Reef secrets: starting right, selecting fishes & invertebrates, advanced biotope
  techinques / Alf Jacob Nilsen, Svein A. Fosså.
    p. cm.
  ISBN 1-890087-67-X (hc.)—ISBN 1-890087-68-8 (softcover)
  1. Marine aquariums. 2. Coral reef animals. I. Fosså, Svein A. II. Title.

SF457.1 N55 2002
639.34'2—dc21   2002069572

Color separations by T.F.H. Publications, Inc.
Designed by Eugenie Seidenberg Delaney and Alice Z. Lawrence

Co-published by
Microcosm Ltd.
P.O. Box 550
Charlotte, VT 05445
www.microcosm-books.com

For our beloved children

Håvard and Siri Nilsen;
Gisle Kalpesh and Norun Ragini Fosså.

It is you who shall inherit the world.

■ ■ ■

ACKNOWLEDGEMENTS

T HIS BOOK COULD NOT HAVE become a reality without the help and support of many friends and colleagues. We would first like to thank Peter Wilkens and the many enthusiastic marine aquarists of Berlin and other parts of Germany who many years ago introduced us to "the new world of reef aquarium keeping." Through their pioneering work, we saw our first glimpses of what the coral reef aquarium might someday become.

Through the fascinating art of reefkeeping, we share hundreds of friendships worldwide. Although we cannot name each of you individually, we thank and acknowledge all who so generously continue to feed us their observations, new aquarium experiences and knowledge, their ideas and creative visions.

The promising state of the modern coral reef aquarium today is due to the experimentation of thousands of amateurs and their sharing of information throughout a global network of marine hobbyists.

Within the ranks of professional marine biologists and public aquarists are a number who have time and again provided us with advice and who have helped elevate the standards of home reefkeeping. In particular, we wish to thank Dr. Bruce Carlson, the former director of the Waikiki Aquarium, for his support, encouragement, and work to bridge the interests of professional and amateur marine aquarists.

We are also grateful to Scott W. Michael for once again letting us use so many of his magnificent photographs. Special thanks also to Larry Tackett, Denise Nielsen Tackett, Janine Cairns Michael, and Erling Svensen for their world-class underwater images.

Our editor and publisher, James Lawrence, and the staff at Microcosm receive our sincere thanks for enthusiastically helping make our concept for *Reef Secrets* a reality. Particularly, we acknowledge designer Eugenie Seidenberg Delaney, editors Alice Lawrence and Alesia Depot, and scientific reviewers Larry Jackson and Dr. Ron Shimek.

Last, but certainly not least, we extend deep gratitude to our dear wives, Lise M. L. Nilsen and Kristin Hystad Fosså, who— amazingly enough—continue to show patience and support for our many projects.

—*Alf J. Nilsen & Svein A. Fosså*
Hidra and Grimstad, Norway

CONTENTS

INTRODUCTION

*Bringing the Living Wonder of Tropical Coral Reefs
into Our Own Homes and Offices*

V ISITORS TO TROPICAL CORAL REEFS typically come up from their first dive or snorkeling experience stunned by the beauty and diversity of what they have just seen. Brilliantly colored fishes, corals, sponges, and all manner of strange invertebrates are everywhere. For those of us fortunate enough to get out and observe an unspoiled coral reef, the first visit creates a profound sense of awe that becomes a lifelong memory.

Sadly, however, the vast majority of people on Earth will never have the chance to see a coral reef. Even people living permanently in tropical island nations sometimes never know the beauty that lies beneath the waves off their own shorelines.

For tens of millions of people, the only way they can

Festooned with life, an Indonesian reef, **left**, serves as an inspiration for aquarists, naturalists, and divers alike. The Great Barrier Reef, **above**, is a hotbed of marine diversity.

experience the living biology of our richest marine ecosystem is by peering into a coral reef aquarium, either displayed in private homes, offices, or in zoos and public aquariums.

By offering a window on a sparkling world that is so unlike anything we encounter in our terrestrial lives, the saltwater aquarium provides a firsthand look at fishes, corals, plants, and countless fascinating, bizarre invertebrates. For some of us, it is a living science demonstration and a constant source of new sights and natural history lessons. For others, a reef aquarium is simply a thing of beauty, a rare focal point in the home, and a source of great enjoyment and relaxation.

Increasingly, marine aquariums—both public and private—are becoming a vital tool for making large numbers of people more aware of what coral reefs are and why we should know about them. For a variety of reasons—ranging from pollution to global warming—coral reefs are today considered even more threatened than the trop-

Reef scene in the Red Sea offers aquarists a tantalizing challenge: can we hope to replicate such scenes in home aquariums? Great advances have been made in recent years, with better equipment and a vastly improved understanding of natural conditions.

ical rainforests. In the worst-case scenarios of some scientists, today's coral reefs may be decimated in the course of just a few decades in this new century if tropical water temperatures continue their climbing trend.

Fortunately, all is not yet lost, and there is a growing urgency for us to help preserve the reefs by educating people who have no idea what coral reefs are or why we should care about them. As both educators and passionate aquarists, we have a sincere belief that the coral reef aquarium is a powerful and commonsense tool to use in spreading our knowledge of the beauty and value of these disappearing biotopes.

WHAT IS A CORAL REEF?

IT TAKES MORE THAN A FEW WORDS to explain the term "coral reef." A technical definition might be: a ridge of biologically created rock and calcium carbonate coral skeletons usually found in shallow tropical waters.

Beyond this, we also know that it is an extremely complicated ecosystem composed of an enormous as-

semblage of living organisms—algae, flowering plants, microorganisms, sponges, corals, worms, mollusks, crustaceans, echinoderms, sea squirts, fishes, sea turtles, and occasionally visiting mammals, including man—in other words, members of almost all known groups of living creatures co-existing in a balanced ecosystem. Many of the species that inhabit coral reefs still remain unknown to science.

We also know that the existence of tropical coral reefs depends on sea temperatures being in the range of 18 to 30 degrees C (64 to 86 degrees F) and water conditions being clean and clear. In fact, this ecosystem is unique in growing and thriving in a "nutrient desert," where access to vital elements such as nitrogen and phosphorous can be very limited. (Most other biological "hotspots" occur where nutrients are readily available to fuel plant growth.) The secret success of coral reefs comes from a strange and wonderful symbiosis between reef-building corals and tiny single-celled algae, called **zooxanthellae**, that live within the coral tissues.

Widely considered one of the world's finest amateur reef aquariums, this magnificent 11,000 liter (2,860 gal.) system created by David Saxby in London, England, demonstrates the potential of home aquarists to keep thriving corals and fishes in captive systems.

But a reef is not simply a tropical phenomenon. Deep-water reefs are found in most oceans, but these are built very differently from the tropical coral reefs. While tropical coral reefs grow relatively quickly, the deep-water reefs in colder zones grow extremely slowly. Off the coasts of Norway, for example, there are ancient, deep-water coral reefs that bear little resemblance to the shallow-water coral reefs of the tropics.

The allure of coral reefs for humans can be traced back many centuries, and saltwater fishes have been kept in captivity at least since the ancient Mediterranean civilizations in Egypt and Rome. However, until very recently, it was thought that reef-building organisms such as corals could not be kept in captivity at all. Some scientists went so far as to predict that corals would never be kept alive in aquarium settings. Certainly, no one had the vaguest notion that reef-building corals would ever thrive and multiply in a closed aquarium.

Until about the mid-1980s, it was common to keep a few colorful marine fishes and more or less colorful dead coral skeletons in an aquarium. Various chemicals were used to kill off parasites and cure fish diseases whenever needed—unfortunately all too often in many aquariums. Today the situation is very different. New technology and a better understanding of reef conditions and biology have made it possible even for relatively novice amateurs to construct and maintain closed aquarium systems that are capable of holding, growing, and propagating many of the animals found on the tropical coral reefs, including the reef-building stony corals.

While we are now able to keep a "living reef" in captivity, this does not mean that we have been able to copy nature perfectly. In fact, a captive reef has a number of obvious limitations—starting with volume of water and circulation that can never match that of a true reef—that are important for us to recognize and remember.

There are many organisms that have such specialized requirements that they, with our present state of knowledge, cannot be kept successfully. These should clearly not be purchased by amateur aquarists, and some should

Reefkeeping advances have largely come from dedicated amateur aquarists like Doug Robbins, kneeling, Tony Vargas, Terry Siegel, and Greg Schiemer (left to right) of New York City.

An unparalleled educational tool, the marine aquarium is the closest many people will ever come to seeing a live reef creature. Many private aquariums have hundreds of visitors each year.

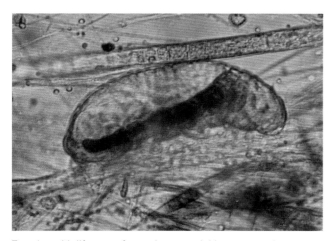

Teeming with life, a reef aquarium can yield many surprises, including new scientific discoveries. This "water bear" (Phylum Tardigrada) was first discovered not in nature but in an aquarium.

simply not be collected and offered to the public. As we will explain throughout this book, the reef aquarist has a world of choices to make in stocking his or her aquarium. With better information, it is possible to avoid the mistakes of the past in which so many animals unsuited to aquarium conditions were purchased and died.

Having spent decades learning these things the hard way, we cannot stress too strongly the importance of two traits for anyone who wants to keep a healthy, beautiful coral reef aquarium: curiosity and patience.

One of the things that keeps people involved with marine aquariums is the fact that you can never "know it all." Be ready to immerse yourself in books and articles that expand your knowledge of marine biology and husbandry practices. Listen to what other successful aquarists have to say.

Secondly, try to conquer the general impatience that seems to infect so many aquarists. It is, unfortunately, far too common to see people buying marine animals first and asking necessary questions afterwards. All too often, the unresearched specimen turns out to be impossible to feed, grows far too large, or is so aggressive that it destroys the peaceful balance of the hobbyist's tank. A responsible aquarist consults a guidebook or asks more experienced aquarists before bringing home a new animal. Always ask the question: Can I keep this animal alive and well in my particular system? Will it live harmoniously with my other animals? (Most good aquarium shops have a set of reference books and will be happy to let you look or even join you in the search for more information.)

The general purpose of this book is to present—in a simplified and understandable way—the key elements in a modern coral reef aquarium, relating them to the conditions in nature that we are trying to replicate or replace: water conditions, circulation, lighting, substrates, aquascaping, and feeding. We are increasingly interested in the notion of creating marine biotope aquariums and have offered some ideas that we hope will spark your interest and creativity.

We will also attempt to help you as a marine hobbyist to choose desirable and appropriate invertebrates and fishes for your aquarium. We have included almost all of the organisms most commonly offered for sale to marine hobbyists, and have dealt with them in a manner that will help you in selecting the correct animals for your personal aquarium—and avoiding the ones that are hard to keep alive or that will not fit into your particular

Even small, simply equipped, and relatively inexpensive aquariums can become beautiful reef displays: this miniature Dutch system houses live rock, a lush growth of green and red macroalgae, and a colorful African Flameback Angelfish (*Centropyge acanthops*).

system. The matter of keeping our animals alive and healthy relates to the last chapter, which is a discussion of the role of marine aquarists in the health of coral reef ecosystems—a subject that no intelligent and involved hobbyist can afford to ignore.

REEFS & REEFKEEPING

WITH THE NATURAL BIOTOPE—wild coral reefs—coming under increasing threats from warming events and human impact, attacks on anyone seen to be exploiting the resources of reefs have also increased from many directions. Questions have been raised about the potential harm done to reefs by harvesting for the marine aquarium livestock trade. Some environmental groups have even called for bans on such collecting.

What will the future bring? Does the coral reef aquarium have a future? Yes—we are optimistic. We see that technical progress continues to be made by marine aquarists and that enthusiasts are rapidly increasing their skills and expanding their knowledge. We are increas-ingly able to provide animals with long, healthy lives in our aquariums, and even to reproduce many of them.

Aquaculture of giant clams, corals, and reef fishes for the marine aquarium trade is becoming a reality. Furthermore, the coral reef is possibly the most productive of all marine biotopes. With care and thoughtfulness, collection of reef organisms for the aquarium trade should be a most sensible use of natural resources. Sustainable use of the reef resources benefits local tropical communities economically and gives them added reasons to protect their reefs.

Recent cooperative initiatives between the aquarium trade and nature conservation organizations, including the Marine Aquarium Council, give us optimism about the future. The goal is to educate collectors.

We believe that marine aquarists will play a vital role in helping to stop destructive fishing practices, support sustainable harvesting plans, and educate their families, friends, and the general public about the living wonders, beauty, and value of coral reefs.

CHAPTER 1

LIGHT, DARKNESS & SHADOWS

Illuminating the Reef Aquarium: Look First to Nature

L IGHT IS LIFE. ONLY A FRACTION OF THE energy emitted from the sun reaches Earth as light and heat, but it is this energy that keeps our planet alive. The sun makes our Earth inhabitable by life forms by providing acceptable temperatures and providing energy for the production of nutrients.

Thanks to an incredible biochemical trick that evolved in simple plants more than three billion years ago, the power of the sun can be used to transform water and carbon dioxide into carbohydrates that fuel all life on Earth. This vital reaction is known as **photosynthesis** and it is made possible by the light-absorbing com-

Even well below the surface, the sun shines brightly in sparkling waters and is the driving life force for a reef ecosystem that exists in clean, clear, nutrient-poor waters. **Above:** a vivid purple *Acropora* sp. stony coral exposed to intense light in shallow water has developed colorful UV-light protective pigments.

pounds of the cells, especially the green chlorophylls. Only plants and algae are able to use photosynthesis to fuel their growth. Because these plants and algae utilize sunlight directly and are the essential first link in all food chains, they are called **primary producers**. On tropical reefs, seagrasses and algae—including many forms that attach to the substrate as well as microscopic cells drifting in the water column—are the primary producers, an indispensable component of the reef ecosystem.

Contrary to popular belief, these primary producers are also a vital component of the coral reef aquarium. Here they adapt to the artificial illumination that is available in any given tank, but they will be more or less successful depending on a number of factors that the aquarist can control. In order to achieve a well-balanced and functioning coral reef aquarium, we need to take care of the primary producers, and to have at least a basic familiarity with the role of light and photosynthesis. In fact, the choice of lighting for a reef aquarium is a cru-

A stunning field of table-shaped *Acropora* spp. corals covers a portion of Harrier Reef along the outer Great Barrier Reef. Somewhat protected from powerful UV radiation by their location partway down the reef slope, corals grow prolifically here.

cial decision in determining the types of animals that can exist and, we hope, thrive in that system.

Some of the most desirable animals kept by reef aquarists are not plants or algae themselves but are able to carry out photosynthesis because they have microscopic algal cells living in their tissues. These cells are known as **zooxanthellae** or **algal symbionts** (organisms that live with other organisms). Example of coral reef animals that have the nutritional benefit of zooxanthellae living within their tissues are a great many of the corals, sea anemones, the giant clams, some sponges, and other invertebrates. These are termed **photosynthetic organisms**, and managing their health and well-being is one of the key secrets to succeeding with a reef aquarium. (See pages 209-215.)

NATURAL REEF LIGHTING

ANYONE WHO HAS VISITED THE TROPICS or explored a shallow reef flat during midday will know all too well how strong solar radiation can be near the Equator.

When we swim over the beautifully colored corals surrounded by equally colorful fishes and lose ourselves in the beauty, we all too often forget the time and end up with a sunburn. It takes only minutes for an unaccustomed body to be severely sunburned.

The irradiance at the equator, where the sun blazes directly overhead at noon, is several times stronger than that of temperate shores. It is the ultraviolet light known as UV-B that causes sunburns. There are some important lessons in the glare of the tropical sun for all marine aquarists to learn and use.

Why, for example, do the delicate polyps of corals not get burned? They are found in the wild in brightly lit shallows, permanently attached to the same spot. Some corals are even exposed to open air during very low tides, but still they are able to cope with the burning UV radiation.

The answer comes in knowing why people who live in these areas are less inclined to get burned, or why even we Northerners can gradually adapt to stronger irradi-

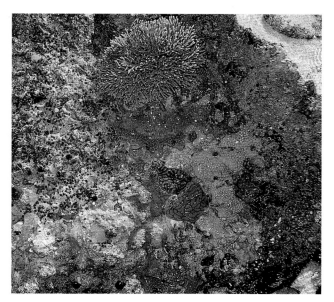

Apparently devoid of life, the top of a slab of rock on the Great Barrier Reef is exposed to extreme levels of UV-radiation daily.

The bottom side of the same rock is found to have various sessile organisms flourishing in the protected shade.

ance if we allow ourselves time to tan gradually, rather than burn. Humans in the Tropics have higher concentrations of the protein melanin, a dark protective pigment, in their skin. For natives, the melanin content may be genetic, while fair-skinned types develop protection by repeated exposure to the sun.

Similarly, corals found in shallower water are protected by the presence of protective pigments and granules that act much like sun lotion. The pigments can be seen as pink, violet, bright blue, or fluorescent colors in the animals. Without this chemical protection, the corals would suffer severely and die.

Further illustrations of the effect of strong light on reef animals is seen in the **sessile** organisms, such as sponges, bryozoans, and sea squirts, that live attached to the substrate without protective pigments. Just like the corals, they cannot escape the sun's potentially harmful radiation. Do they live here in the shallows at all? Yes, but you have to search in shaded spots, such as darkened holes, crevices, and under rocks, to find them. Turn a few boulders over and there they are. While the upper side of a reef boulder located in shallow water can appear lifeless, the underside flourishes with all sorts of animal life. If we forget to place the boulder back in its

> ### NATURAL SHADE
> Creating shady spots in the aquarium provides a more interesting scene, while at the same time offering natural shelter to certain animals.
>
> ■ ■ ■

original position, the delicate life will be dead within a few hours due to radiation. Sunlight is life-giving on the reef, but it can also destroy life.

Why then have so many corals evolved to live in such strong radiation? If they were plants, most people would better understand their demand for light, but corals are indeed true animals. Although many species prefer to live a few meters deeper than on the very shallow reef flat and thereby avoid the most intense radiation, they still seek the light. Would it not have been more natural to live like the bryozoans and the sea squirts, in the shade and darkness and thereby avoid the burning sun? The landscape of the shallow reef could then have been left to the algae and seagrasses.

Indeed, many corals do live in the shade. Dive into a shaded cave and take a look at the gorgonians and delicate soft corals hanging from the underwater roof. But these are not reef builders.

The link between the sun and the all-important stony corals that form the reef is that the zooxanthellae within these corals need adequate levels of light to thrive and provide their hosts with the energy to live, grow, and reproduce. The delicate balance between too little and too much light is something that the reef aquarist

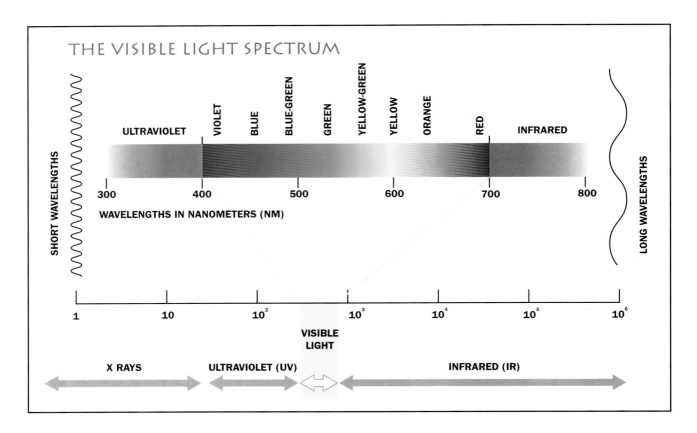

THE VISIBLE LIGHT SPECTRUM

SHORT WAVELENGTHS

ULTRAVIOLET · VIOLET · BLUE · BLUE-GREEN · GREEN · YELLOW-GREEN · YELLOW · ORANGE · RED · INFRARED

LONG WAVELENGTHS

300 · 400 · 500 · 600 · 700 · 800

WAVELENGTHS IN NANOMETERS (NM)

1 · 10 · 10^2 · 10^3 · 10^4 · 10^5 · 10^6

VISIBLE LIGHT

X RAYS · ULTRAVIOLET (UV) · INFRARED (IR)

must appreciate, because it can mean the difference between life and death in the aquarium.

LIGHT SPECTRUM

VISIBLE LIGHT IS ONLY A FRACTION of the electromagnetic spectrum, and what we see under an aquarium lighting hood is a mixture of blue, green, yellow, orange, and red colors separated by their wavelengths (see illustration, above). Some of these colors are more important than others for life in general, and marine plants and animals in particular. For example, chlorophyll in plants and zooxanthellae absorbs light best at wavelengths of 420 nm—corresponding to "actinic" blue lighting—and 670 nm in the red end of the spectrum.

Next to the blue light is the ultraviolet light, which is composed of long wavelength UV-A (important to many corals), medium wavelength UV-B (the radiation that causes sunburn), and short wavelength UV-C (which is deadly to all living tissue, but luckily largely blocked by the atmosphere). Next to red light is infrared radiation, also known as heat radiation.

The short wavelength blue light penetrates deepest into the ocean, while the longer red wavelengths are effectively absorbed by water. Exactly how far light pene-

trates depends on how clear the water is, but blue light always goes deepest. This is easily seen if you try to take underwater photographs in a few meters depth without using a flash. Although your brain sees beautiful colors, the photos will look blue when developed.

The surface of the water is seldom calm, but is broken by small or big waves. This curving of the surface causes the light beams to be bent and spread in all directions. The ripples also act as small lenses that can concentrate sunlight, producing **glitter lines** or concentrated rays of light typical in shallow-water situations.

The sandy bottom and the light surfaces of corals and rocks further reflect the radiation, spreading life-giving light to algae and animals living in crevices or under overhanging rocks and corals. The radiation on the shallow parts of a reef is in fact so strong that many algae prefer to grow in the semi-shade on the vertical sides of rocks or even under overhangs. In deeper areas, such as on a vertical reef slope at 20 m (66 ft.), algae can be the dominant group of organisms.

SYMBIOTIC ALGAE

THE TRUE REEF BUILDERS—the stony corals—greatly benefit from intense tropical solar radiation. In fact they cannot do without adequate levels of light. The reef-building corals are in a sense photosynthetic organisms. They are not plants, but they live in a vital symbiotic relationship with tiny plants, single-celled algae called zooxanthellae. The discovery of these photosynthetic partners in the 1880s revolutionized coral reef science and was perhaps the most important discovery in reef biology in the twentieth century. The practical applications of our knowledge of zooxanthellae have had a tremendous impact on the development of modern coral reef aquarium keeping.

Zooxanthellae are single-celled algae belonging to the dinoflagellates (Division Dinophyta), more specifically to the species *Symbiodinium microadriaticum* (often previously referred to as '*Gymnodinium microadriaticum*'). Today scientists believe that there is more than one species of zooxanthellae involved in symbiosis, and that

corals probably host different algae strains under different environmental conditions.

When planning a coral reef aquarium that will house photosynthetic corals and giant clams, it is essential to appreciate the basic biology of the zooxanthellae—or to at least know that they will be present—in the millions—as soon as the first coral or clam is introduced. Keeping the zooxanthellae alive is a must in order to make your photosynthetic specimens thrive and grow.

You may have noticed that many living corals look brownish. It is the symbiotic algae that cause the brown color. The tiny algae cells are found in the cells of the inner (endodermal) cell layers of the coral tissue where they are extremely numerous under favorable conditions (as many as one million algae cells per cubic centimeter tissue can be found). Like all plants, the zooxanthellae carry out photosynthesis and produce oxygen and organic

PHOTOSYNTHESIS AND CELLULAR RESPIRATION: THE BASICS

Photosynthesis is the biochemical reaction upon which all life on Earth depends. Only plants can carry out photosynthesis, which takes place in green chloroplasts inside plant cells. In photosynthesis, the inorganic compounds carbon dioxide and water react to form organic carbohydrate compounds (sugars) and oxygen. Light powers the reaction, which, simplified, can be written like this:

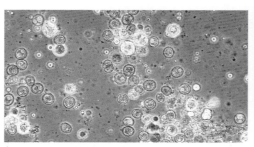

Zooxanthellae cells magnified 400X. These algal symbionts help drive the productivity of coral reefs.

utilized by all living organisms during cellular respiration.

In cellular respiration, all organisms burn nutrients to create the energy that sustains normal life activities. Cell respiration takes place in all living cells where nutrients react with oxygen to form energy—leaving water and carbon dioxide as waste products. This is the reverse reaction of photosynthesis:

$$6CO_2 + 12H_2O + light = C_6H_{12}O_6 + 6O_2 + 6H_2O$$

carbon dioxide + water + light = carbohydrates + oxygen + water

$$C_6H_{12}O_6 + 6O_2 = 6CO_2 + 6H_2O + ATP$$

carbohydrates + oxygen = carbon dioxide + water + chemical energy

Plants are the only organisms that can form organic compounds out of inorganic materials and are therefore called primary producers. The formation of one mole of carbohydrate requires 2,000-2,500 kcal light energy of which about 30% is bound in the carbohydrate molecules as chemical energy. This chemical energy is transferred into the food chain and

ATP (adenosine triphosphate) is an energy storage and transfer compound used in most biological systems. One mole of carbohydrates burned in respiration sets free about 672 kcal of chemical energy. The above reactions are very simplified, but the complete chemistry of photosynthesis and cell respiration can be found in most biology textbooks.

compounds (carbohydrates or simplified sugars) from water and carbon dioxide (see box, page 19). Corals, like all other organisms, need nutrients. They do indeed capture plankton with their polyps, but in addition to this, some of the nutrients and oxygen produced by the zooxanthellae are translocated to the coral. The algae, on the other hand, get a supply of carbon dioxide released from the corals as a waste product after respiration. The relationship between the coral polyps and their algae is mutualism (in which both parties benefit). The amount of nutrient produced by the algae is, however, very much dependent on light intensity. In too low light intensity, photosynthesis does not happen; in moderate light, the algae produce enough nutrients to keep their own respiration going; while in strong light, there will be a surplus of nutrients, which the corals can benefit from—hence the corals' need for light.

The light must penetrate through the outer layers of coral tissue (ectoderm) to reach the algae. In these layers are pigments that protect the algae from harmful radiation. If the light becomes too strong, the number of algae is reduced, causing a change in the coral's coloration. In decreasing light, the zooxanthellae population increases, causing a dark brown color to develop. It is common to observe that a coral that is brightly colored when first imported gradually turns brown when kept for a period of weeks or months in the aquarium. Insufficient light, or light of the wrong type, is the main cause of brown-looking corals. (Unnaturally high nutrient levels in the aquarium water may also contribute to the proliferation of zooxanthellae and thus make formerly color-

Hidden in the shadowy folds of a massive stand of scroll coral (*Turbinaria reniformis*) are a multitude of shade-loving organisms.

ful corals turn brownish.)

The intertwined biology of zooxanthellae and their hosts is very complex and not yet fully understood, but scientists are now actively studying these organisms to understand the mechanisms of coral bleaching in the wild. On the reef there are also other organisms that have symbiotic algae. Some sponges live in association with blue-green algae, and a few of these are commonly grown in the coral reef aquarium.

REACTIONS TO LIGHT VARIATIONS

CORALS, SPONGES, giant clams, and many other organisms are **sessile**, meaning that they live attached to the substrate. Most often they have an obvious structure that attaches them, like the pedal disc of anemones or the basal plates of corals. They have to be well adapted to the local environmental conditions that surround them. If their habitat changes, they have practically no ability to relocate to more favorable conditions, so they will suffer and in many cases die.

The same holds true in the aquarium. If you suddenly change the quality and/or quantity of light over your tank, you will most certainly observe a reaction among your sessile animals. Increase the amount of UV light drastically, and the corals that thrived so well and had developed such nice colors will bleach and perhaps even die. Decrease the amount of light, and notice how the colors and shapes of the corals change.

Motile, or mobile, organisms have better chances of influencing their local light conditions. They often have a body shape that allows them to move elegantly through the water (e.g., many fishes), or they have developed organs that can secure a rapid retreat if necessary (e.g., the tail of a lobster can provide quick and powerful propulsion when needed). If light conditions change and become unfavorable, the motile animals simply escape to other, more favorable locations. Unfortunately, they have very limited escape possibilities in the aquarium. If the light is too strong, perhaps even reaching harmful levels, even fishes cannot escape unless you provide them with necessary secluded and shaded retreats, such as caves. This is particularly important for nocturnal animals, which often have eyes that are sensitive to strong light. It is indeed necessary to understand natural conditions and how to recreate them as best we can if we want to have a successful coral reef aquarium.

NIGHT & DAY

THE MAJORITY OF HUMANS sleep during the night, perhaps dreaming about remote tropical beaches and colorful reef organisms. While we sleep, the scene on the reefs changes. The **diurnal**, or day-active, organisms go to sleep just as we do, while the **nocturnal**, or night-active, animals come to life. Corals that were closed during the day now open their polyps and hunt for prey. Shrimps and crabs that were hiding during the light hours now start their nocturnal feeding forays. Nocturnal fishes that sheltered in caves or deep-water habitats during the day now swim into shallow waters to hunt and feed, while elegant tube anemones that withdraw in their tubes during the day now open up in all their beauty. The coral reef at night is a place so full of life that it must be seen to be believed. When a new day dawns, the night hunters retreat and retract, and the scene is once again transformed for the day-active reef creatures. We ourselves wake up in our palm hut and run out for an early morning swim.

The shifting between night and day—or light and darkness if you like—is biologically important. While photosynthesis is always talked about as a reaction dependent on light, the truth is that parts of the chemical reactions take place only during darkness. Most plants and photosynthetic animals do best with a constant daily routine of alternating light and dark. In the Tropics, where our reef livestock originated, day and night are about equal, and a simple 12 hours of light and 12 of darkness is most natural for a marine aquarium. Every aquarium with artificial lighting should have a timer or timers to ensure that the daily photoperiod is regular and consistent.

Plankton and other tiny organisms that serve as food for plankton feeders migrate to the surface and open water during the night and thus become fair game for predators. Turn a flashlight during the night onto a well-established coral reef aquarium and you will observe a different life than that which you normally see. Point the light toward the surface of the tank, or place a small blue bulb just above the surface, and you will see tiny

Adapted to a nocturnal life and with days spent in the shadows, soldierfishes require protective aquascapes in the aquarium.

Lacking zooxanthellae, this *Dendronephthya* sp. soft coral needs very little light and feeds on tiny algal plankton cells.

planktonic organisms gathering in the light field. Keep a sea pen like the beautiful (but challenging) *Cavernularia* sp., and you will observe how it hides in the gravel during the day, but expands beautifully as soon as the light goes off and the night sets in. The aquarium does not sleep during the night, but its life takes on a different appearance.

LIGHT VARIATIONS IN THE AQUARIUM

GREAT ADVANCES IN REEF AQUARIUM KEEPING in recent years have come from our having access to more appropriate and powerful light sources. The conventional "cool white" fluorescent lights and simple incandescent light bulbs used for decades by struggling marine aquarists were woefully inadequate. Even the "plant lights" favored by many freshwater aquarists today provide poor results for most marine tanks. In short, the spectrum or color of the light is wrong and often too weak for most photosynthetic marine organisms.

Fortunately, a growing array of very good alternative light sources for artificial aquarium illumination is available on the market today. Most commonly used are fluorescent light tubes (with the proper color characteristics) and power compacts for smaller tanks, and metal halide lamps alone or in combination with fluorescent tubes for medium-sized and large tanks.

Technical discussions of the latest lighting types can

TABLE 1-1

COMMONLY IMPORTED NOCTURNAL INVERTEBRATES

GROUP / PHYLUM	COMMON NAME	SCIENTIFIC NAME
CNIDARIA	sea pens	*Cavernularia* spp. and *Pteroeides* spp.
	Red-polyped Gorgonian	*Swiftia exserta*
	Colorful Sea Rod	*Diodogorgia nodulifera*
	dead man's fingers	*Nephthyigorgia* spp.
	colonial anemone	*Isaurus* spp.
	yellow cup corals	*Tubastraea* spp.
ANNELIDA	bristleworms	Many genera with small and medium-sized species
MOLLUSCA	Black Limpet	*Scutus unguis*
CRUSTACEA	marble shrimps	*Saron* spp.
	Common Dancing Shrimp	*Rhynchocinetes durbanensis*
	reef lobsters	*Enoplometopus* spp.
	Australian Miniature Spiny Lobster	*Palinurellus wieneckii*
	small crabs	Many genera
ECHINODERMATA	feather stars	*Himerometra* spp.
	brittle- and serpent stars	*Ophiolepis* spp.
		Ophiocoma spp.
		Ophiarachna spp.
		Ophioderma spp.
		Ophiomastix spp.
	long-spined sea urchins	*Diadema* spp.
	sea urchins	*Echinometra* spp.

Proof that artificial lighting can be used to maintain beautifully pigmented corals, this 760 L (200 gal.) home aquarium created by Tracy Gray of Victorville, California, is lit by multiple metal halide lights (four 175 W bulbs and two 400 W bulbs with a 20,000 K rating). Such success with stony corals—maintaining vivid colors and healthy growth rates—was unheard of until very recently.

be found in other references and in online forums, but nothing compares with firsthand viewing of different types of lights in aquarium shops and other hobbyists' homes. Beginning aquarists typically begin with fluorescents and later switch to more intense metal halides.

If you want to have an aquarium resembling the very shallow reef flat housing colorful stony corals, you obviously must install strong illumination containing UV-A radiation. Metal halide bulbs are currently the favored choice of many reef aquarists for replicating the intense light energy conditions of such habitats. However, some successful coral keepers prefer VHO (very high output) fluorescent bulbs and keep their light-hungry specimens closer to the surface where conditions are brighter.

But even in the shallow, high-energy zones on the reef, there are patches with shadow. We have learned to build the aquarium aquascape in such a way that small overhangs and caves create local spots with less light. Creating a natural light field in the aquarium is determined both by the lights chosen and the way you construct the reefscape.

An interesting approach for the aquarist with some experience and a large tank is to construct a simulated reef flat that falls off to a reef slope. In such a system, the upper zone has very strong illumination (and perhaps more vigorous water motion), while further down the slope the water depth is greater and the illumination weaker, making it more appropriate for other corals.

REEF AQUARIUM LIGHTING CHOICES

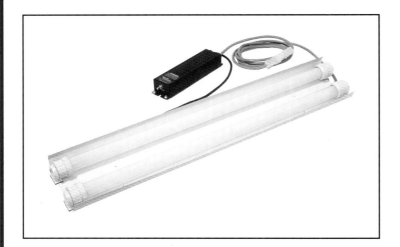

FLUORESCENT LIGHTS are the usual first choice of most new aquarists and they are available in various lengths, power ratings, and spectral outputs.
ADVANTAGES: more affordable to purchase and operate than metal halides; cooler operation.
DISADVANTAGES: may need replacement every 6-8 months for peak performance.

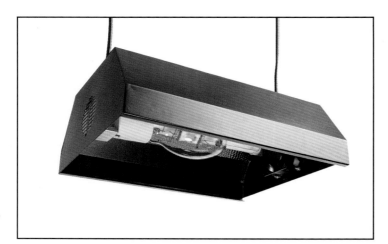

COMPACT FLUORESCENTS are a relatively new option for reef aquarists and are especially suited to smaller systems.
ADVANTAGES: higher wattage than comparably sized standard fluorescents. Good choice for micro- or nano-reefs.
DISADVANTAGES: easily broken if not properly handled and mounted.

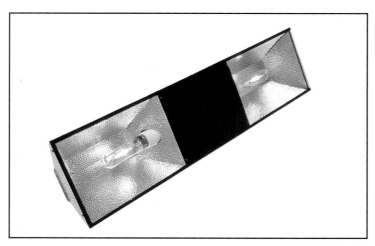

METAL HALIDES are the primary illumination source for many advanced reef aquarists and a necessity for large deep-reef aquariums.
ADVANTAGES: intense light for demanding shallow-water corals; produce a more realistic underwater scene, with typical "glitter lines."
DISADVANTAGES: expensive to buy and operate; generate considerable heat.

Lighting photographs courtesy of Drs. Foster & Smith.

Not every corner of the aquarium will be illuminated evenly—nor should it be. It is very possible to provide part of the tank with strong illumination and allow the other areas to enjoy partial or full shade. One can do this by placing metal halide or HQI lamps off center. Such a configuration makes it possible to keep organisms with different lighting requirements in relatively close proximity.

Unfortunately it is rare to find aquarists who think in an untraditional way with respect to illumination and decoration. We tend to use the same light period every day, with a set period of hours having full lighting without variation. This is not what happens in the wild. One effect that is almost never copied is the presence of clouds, but using computerized controllers may eventually allow us to vary the light intensity on our captive reefs throughout the period that the lights are on. Tidal fluctuations in the aquarium and/or surface movements also influence the light characteristics. By causing the surface to ripple periodically, for instance, we can create interesting variations in the light that are closer to those in nature and more interesting to look at.

We urge the aquarist to use his or her own creativity to build a light environment that best suits the type of fishes and invertebrates you wish to keep. Again, there is no single "best" way to light a marine aquarium—although the closer to nature the better. Indeed, a reef system may be blindingly bright or only dimly lit. One important thing to remember is that once you have an illumination level and spectrum that your animals are happy with, they will adapt biologically to this illumination. The population of symbiotic algae will stabilize and the corals will grow in a direction toward the light source. If you constantly change the setup, neither you nor your aquatic charges will ever settle down and make the most of the microenvironment that has been created.

When considering a purchase in an aquarium shop, how can we distinguish a nocturnal or shade-preferring organism from one that needs bright light? When you see all those beautiful fishes and invertebrates offered for sale, how can you know which ones to select for your specific aquarium? Sometimes this is easy, but not always.

CHANGING BULBS

Sudden increases in light levels affect most aquarium organisms badly. Take great care when you change the lights on a reef aquarium.

■ ■ ■

As the red light is rapidly blocked by water, "red" becomes an invisible color in deeper water. Therefore many organisms living here have a red body. When they are red they are invisible to other animals and therefore better protected against predators. Many shrimps, such as the beautiful Scarlet Cleaner Shrimp (*Lysmata debelius*), have this attribute. Many soldierfishes (*Myripristis* spp.) are also red. They normally live in caves in the deeper parts of the reefs and are nocturnal. How do we know this? Take a look at the big eyes, they are signs that these fishes are active during the night. "See but do not be seen" is their motto.

We have already mentioned pigmentation in corals. Generally speaking, colorfully pigmented stony corals live in high light intensity, and are dependent on this light to grow. One exception is the orange cup corals or sun corals (*Tubastraea* spp.). These have bright red or orange tissue and most often large, yellow polyps, which are only expanded during the night. As they are non-photosynthetic (not living in partnership with zooxanthellae) they need to get all their nutrients from captured plankton and hence the need for large, effective polyps. Table 1-1 (page 22) lists some of the commonly available invertebrates that are naturally nocturnal.

In soft corals, you can once again look for colors and shape. Photosynthetic soft corals are often fleshy and have brownish or yellowish colors due to the presence of symbiotic algae, the genus *Sinularia* being a common example. Soft corals that prefer weak illumination—deep or shady conditions—often have thin tissue, a delicate branching shape, and intense red, purple, or yellow colors as in the genus *Dendronephthya*.

Nature is, however, full of strange adaptations and surprises—it frequently seems that exceptions are more common than examples that follow the basic rules. *Dendronephthya*, for example, is sometimes found in the wild in brightly lit situations. For the newcomer to reef aquarium husbandry, however, it helps to know the rules (e.g., *Dendronephthya* typically does best in lower-light situations) before trying to break them. The Stocking Guide section of this book (pages 98-207) offers lighting guidelines for many species and groups. 🪷

CHAPTER 2

WATER QUALITIES & MOVEMENT

Creating and Maintaining the Best Possible
Seawater Conditions in a Reef Aquarium

PUT A CLOWNFISH IN A FRESHWATER GUPPY tank and it dies. Put a discus fish in your reef aquarium, and it dies, too. Put a healthy colony of staghorn coral in a tankful of sharks and it will die as well. Why? The reasons are differences in the "water quality"—an expression that is heard wherever two or more aquarists meet.

All water-based solutions have measurable qualities. The quality of the water we maintain in our reef aquariums has a vital influence on the well-being of the organisms we keep. We must seek the best possible water quality, which is best defined as "a solution of saltwater that is as close as possible to the composition of natural seawater."

But natural seawater is very complex in nature, and it is not an easy matter to define what a perfect solution

Azure waters of the Great Barrier Reef, **left**, are clear, clean, and starved of nutrients. Indo-Pacific sea fan, **above**, is dependent on water currents to sweep plankton into its tangle of branches.

for the reef aquarium really is. Even among scientists who have worked with the chemistry of the seas for decades, there is much divergence of opinion on the true chemical composition of "natural seawater." For the purposes of this book, we choose to simplify, ignore some lively controversies, and to focus on most the important aspects of water quality for you as an enthusiast.

WHAT IS SEAWATER?

WHY DOES THE SEA TASTE SALTY? Why is the water of the sea saline while that in streams, rivers, and lakes is fresh? The reason goes back eons to the time when the oceans of our planet were formed. The elements that make up our planet Earth dissolved in water, making the oceans a mixture of water and dissolved chemicals. The elements that build the landmasses are still today in an equilibrium that was created over billions of years.

The result is oceans that have a relative stable content of dissolved elements, which together compose

TABLE 2-1

ELEMENTS of SEAWATER IMPORTANT to the AQUARIST

Many trace elements are vital to living organisms even though they occur in minute concentrations. The trace elements noted here are often discussed among marine enthusiasts, either because they are problematic or because they are believed to be of utmost importance to the well-being of the reef aquarium. Copper, for instance, is a heavy metal and highly toxic to fishes and invertebrates, but incorporated in many medicines used against parasites. Iodine is often added to the aquarium and is important to many algae as well as invertebrates, but it rapidly becomes depleted in a closed system. Silicon is common in the sea (but yet not recognized as a major element), but can cause an uncontrolled blooming of diatomaceous algae in the closed marine aquarium.

ELEMENT	FORM IN SEAWATER	CONCENTRATION (mg/L)
Major Elements		
Chloride	Cl^-	19,354
Sulfate	SO_4^{2-}	2,712
Bromine	Br^-	67.3
Fluorine	F^-	1.3
Boron	B	4.5
Sodium	Na^+	10,770
Magnesium	Mg^{2+}	1,290
Calcium	Ca^{2+}	412
Potassium	K^+	399
Strontium	Sr^{2+}	7.9
Some Trace Elements		
Silicon	$Si(OH)_4$	2,000
Manganese	Mn^{2+}, $MnCl^+$	0.0002
Iron	$Fe(OH)_2^+$, $Fe(OH)_4^-$	0.002
Copper	$CuCO_3$, $CuOH^+$	0.0005
Iodine	IO_3^-, I^-	0.06

(After Spotte, 1979. *Seawater Aquarium, the Captive Environment*. John Wiley & Sons.)

roughly 3.5% of the volume. The remaining 96.5% is pure water—the colorless, transparent "universal solvent" made up of hydrogen and oxygen.

During evaporation from the oceans, only pure water rises into the atmosphere and returns to Earth as rain. This is why streams, rivers, and lakes are mostly fresh and the sea is salty. Let the water in your reef tank evaporate without refilling and the result will be a dramatic shift in the ratio of dissolved elements to pure water—or increased salinity. Remove saltwater from the tank and add only freshwater and the opposite occurs—the salinity drops.

Of the dissolved materials in seawater, two elements, sodium (Na^+) and chloride (Cl^-), dominate completely, contributing more than 3%, or almost 86% of the total solids. Sulfate (SO_4^{2-}) and magnesium (Mg^{2+}) add another 0.4%, while bromine (Br^-), fluorine (F^-), boron (B), calcium (Ca^{2+}), potassium (K^+), and strontium (Sr^{2+}) compose yet another 0.088%. These are the major elements of the sea and add up to 3.488% of the total dissolved nutrients. The remaining 0.012% is composed of dozens of **trace elements**—such as iodine, zinc, and manganese—which are found in minute concentrations, some of them vital to the health of oceanic life.

The quantification of elements is only one way of looking at the composition of the seas. The elements can be grouped in many other ways, such as importance to living organisms, nutrients vs. nonnutrients, or degree of depletion with increasing or decreasing depth. Table 2-1 lists the most important elements of the sea—from the aquarist's point of view.

For those of you who are lucky enough to live close to the ocean, nothing is better than using natural seawater for your aquarium. However, you need to check the salinity (see page 39) and be certain that the water is collected in areas where there is little pollution, usually away from harbors and densely populated shallow shorelines. We have used natural seawater collected off the coast of Norway in our own aquariums for years and have never experienced any problems.

Most of you, however, will be using artificial seawater, which is a salt mixture dissolved in freshwater. Synthetic seawater is a perfectly acceptable substitute, and it is used by public aquariums and leading reef aquarists around the world. Most basic marine guidebooks cover the subject of mixing and using artificial saltwater, and we will not deal with it here, except to say that what-

A colony of *Acropora millepora*, a beautiful species of staghorn coral, thrives in shallow, nutrient-poor waters of the Coral Sea. Cloudy water impedes stony coral growth, and high levels of dissolved nutrients would allow algae to proliferate and choke out such corals.

ever your choice of seawater, its quality is sure to change over time in your aquarium.

PATIENCE REPAID

One of the worst mistakes you can make in connection with a captive reef is to start stocking your aquarium as soon as you have filled it with water and completed the decoration. This is a real hazard and will lead you into a lot of trouble!

Patience is a difficult concept for new aquarists, but it is an absolute key to success. Fill your system with seawater, and be sure to let it clear and reach the proper pH and temperature before adding live rock or sand (see page 53-63). Complete the aquascaping and let the installed equipment run normally and allow at least 8 weeks—even better 12 to 24 weeks—before stocking.

During this waiting period, you must restrain the strong temptation to start populating your reef with fishes and invertebrates. Exceptions are algae-eating and detritus-processing organisms, which can be added ear-

lier, normally after some 4 weeks time. Why is this so important? The answer lies in the fact that water quality changes over time.

A brand-new aquarium appears very clean and sterile. In fact it is far too clean and far too sterile to support a large stock of animals. As time goes by, the first brown filamentous algae (diatoms) appear. The decoration usually gets a brownish look, and the walls of the tank start looking dirty. Do not be discouraged. This is the sign that the microorganisms in the aquarium have started to work.

Gradually, more and more algae appear. Green algae threads and slimy algae start to grow. If live rock has been used for aquascaping, you now enter a most interesting period with all sorts of micro- and macroalgae and strange animals popping up from the rocks. Rather than despairing over the situation, take your time, use a magnifying glass, and study the world of tiny organisms that seem to develop right before your eyes. Patience and observation, rather than daily use of a water test kit,

The collector cup of a protein skimmer gathers dark wastes extracted from aquarium water. Scale measures fluid removed.

A gigantic skimmer designed for commercial systems or very large aquariums. It is entirely possible to overskim a reef aquarium, so the skimmer size should be chosen carefully.

is a better approach to any new marine aquarium setup.

During this time, many beneficial changes are taking place that you cannot observe directly. What you see as algae growth is actually a result of biological activity from microorganisms that are proliferating in the new system. Every aquarium, no matter how clean it looks after you have filled it with water and completed the aquascape, contains organic materials that are subject to decaying processes that have a great impact on the quality of the water.

As the bacteria and other microorganisms build stable and dense populations, they chemically convert organic compounds to inorganic compounds, energy, and waste products through the vital biochemical reactions known as respiration and photosynthesis. Along the way, they release many chemical compounds, some that serve as plant nutrients, such as ammonia, nitrate, and nitrite—the first two being highly toxic to invertebrates and fishes. If you add fishes at this point, they will become stressed, be attacked by external parasites, and die. This is tremendously wasteful and discouraging to the aquarist. With patience, the loss of such animals can be avoided.

Once the levels of toxic ammonia and nitrite have subsided, many hobbyists begin to introduce herbivores to begin controlling the algae growth. Various snails, herbivorous hermit crabs, and perhaps one or a few hardy, grazing fishes such as tangs (*Zebrasoma* spp.) or rabbitfishes (*Siganus* spp.) can be added.

As the time goes by in a new saltwater aquarium, the water conditions become safer and steadier. The populations of various decomposing bacteria that are vital for the balance of the system have built up and stabilized, normally after about 12 weeks, although many variables come into play and can either speed this up or slow it down considerably.

At this point, the scenery in your tank will look very different than it did during the first couple of weeks. It is now time to carefully add more organisms. A typical progression then occurs: You let the filter system and skimmer run and start feeding your fishes and invertebrates. You change some water now and then, clean the skimmer, and replace the evaporated water. Now and then you add more animals, test out new sorts of food, and even start feeding with live plankton. The corals grow and everything is magical—until one day when you suddenly discover a slimy red carpet of algae developing on the bottom of your white coral gravel. The quality of the water has again changed to a point where the balance of the system has shifted. Luckily your algae never become a severe problem and you continue keeping the aquarium for years. The corals grow and the fishes thrive. However, the water quality constantly changes, and the solution you will have in your tank after 5 years is in most cases very different from what you started out with and very different from the quality of natural seawater.

WATER QUALITY OF CORAL REEFS

ALONG NORTHERN SHORES, including the coast of Norway where we live, the sea is generally rather rich in nutrients. By "nutrients" we mean chemical elements—mainly nitrogen (N) and phosphate (P)—that are vital to the plants and algae that are the primary producers, or the start of the oceanic food chain. Twice a year (spring and autumn) an upwelling of bottom ocean water very rich in nutrients causes planktonic algae to bloom. The planktonic algae in turn serve as food for myriad types of zooplankton that have a population explosion a couple of months after the first algae blooming.

One might reasonably think that the nutrient concentrations would be much higher over a coral reef, where the number and diversity of species and specimens are much higher than in temperate waters. However, the opposite is the case. In general, the water over tropical coral reefs is starved of nutrients ("nutrient poor"). Although the conditions vary from region to region, the general situation has long been described as a nutrient desert. In some oceanic reefs, such as in the Coral Sea

TABLE 2-2

NUTRIENT LEVELS ON SOME CORAL REEFS

LOCATION	INORGANIC NITROGEN (μM)		INORGANIC PHOSPHORUS (μM)	
	Ocean side	Lagoon side	Ocean side	Lagoon side
St Croix. US Virgin Islands	>0.283	>0.512	0.08	0.10
Salomon Atoll, the Maldives	0.98	1.20	0.43	0.67
Great Barrier Reef	1.02	1.26	0.26	0.26
Enewetak Atoll, Marshall Islands	0.349	0.912	0.174	0.169
Pago Bay, Guam	0.22	<0.45	0.21	0.16

Modified from D'Elia & Wiebe (1990), In: Dubinsky (ed.) *Ecosystems of the World, Vol. 25: Coral Reefs.*

[To convert ppm (parts per million = mg/L) to μM (micro molar = μmol/L), multiply by 1,000 and divide by the element's molecular weight.]

In general, coral reefs are regarded as nutrient-poor ecosystems. By "nutrient" we mean chemical compounds utilized as energy sources by photosynthetic organisms (in this context, algae). Nitrogen and phosphorus are the two most important algae-fueling nutrients. These compounds occur in many chemical forms in the sea: nitrogen as inorganic ammonium (NH_4^+), nitrite (NO_2^-), and nitrate (NO_3^-); phosphorus as inorganic phosphate (PO_4^{2-} or HPO_4^-). Both elements can also occur in organic forms when they are bound to carbon-containing compounds like proteins or amino acids. Aquarists typically measure nitrate and phosphate. If you measure 1.0 ppm nitrate (NO_3^-) in your reef tank, this will correspond to 16.13 μM, which is more than 16 times the amount of total inorganic nitrogen measured at the ocean side of Salomon Atoll in the Maldives. Or if you measure 0.5 ppm phosphate (PO_4^{2-}), this equals 5.26 μM, a concentration more than 12 times the value for natural seawater at the same atoll.

ADDING CALCIUM: A BRIEF PRIMER

Calcium is a crucial element for life in the ocean as well as in the coral reef aquarium. Calcifying organisms, such as stony corals, giant clams, and calcareous algae, extract dissolved calcium from the water and use the element to build their skeletons and shells. In the sea, calcium is found in a concentration of about 420 ppm (mg/L) in the form of calcium ions (Ca^{2+}).

Calcium can be added to the reef aquarium in a number of ways. One way is to make Kalkwasser—a saturated (s) solution in which calcium oxide (CaO) is dissolved in freshwater, forming calcium hydroxide, calcium ions, and hydroxide ions:

$$CaO_{(s)} \rightarrow Ca(OH)_{2(s)} \rightarrow Ca^{2+} + 2OH^-$$

Kalkwasser has two primary benefits for the reef aquarium: first, calcium ions are supplied; second, hydroxide ions are added that neutralize organic acids.

The Kalkwasser is mixed in a closed, nonreactive container and allowed to settle. The clear solution is added, drop by drop, to replace water that evaporates from the aquarium. It is important to note that the pH of saturated Kalkwasser is very high (extremely basic, at 12.45, actually). The rapid addition of a large amount of Kalkwasser can harm the aquarium severely—even killing all life in the tank. Kalkwasser is, furthermore, not a very stable solution, and will not stay saturated for long. Saturated Kalkwasser contains about 850 mg/L Ca^{2+}. Kalkwasser must be dosed carefully, either manually, by gravity with a control valve, or by a small dosing pump.

A safer method of adding calcium and buffering compounds is via a "calcium reactor" containing calcareous gravel ($CaCO_3$). The pH is lowered to approximately 6.5 by the addition of CO_2, dissolving the gravel and releasing calcium and bicarbonate ions.

Finally, so-called "two-part" ionic liquid solutions have become an easy, although not inexpensive, method of adding calcium and buffers (alkalinity plus various bicarbonates).

A small fragment of *Acropora* sp. staghorn coral collected in Fiji after several months' growth in author Nilsen's aquarium.

With constant access to dissolved calcium provided by Kalkwasser, the colony of *Acropora* shown above has grown substantially over a period of 25 months.

Turf algae of various types are important to the tropical coral reef system, but in the aquarium—where nutrient levels are much higher than in nature—the algae flourishes and must be kept under control by adding various algae-grazing fishes and invertebrates.

off the eastern coast of Australia, the level of nutrient is extremely low. Table 2-2 on page 31 shows the average levels of nutrient for some coral reefs. How such a diversity of plants and animals can exist in an ecosystem that lacks nutrients puzzled scientists for a very long time, and the answers are still being found. Part of the explanation lies in the symbiosis of stony corals with algae (see page 211), but the very intricate nutrient webs found on reefs are also fundamental in understanding how various food sources are cycled through the ecosystem.

NUTRIENTS IN THE AQUARIUM

IF WE TAKE A LOOK AT THE BREAK-IN period of a new reef aquarium from a biochemical point of view,

SKIMMER SIZE

While a protein skimmer is the single most important water cleaning device for most marine setups, it should be correctly matched to the aquarium volume and stocking density. Skimmers that are either too small or too large can create problems.

■ ■ ■

we can measure some important changes taking place by tracking the chemical element nitrogen (N).

Nitrogen composes about 75% of our atmosphere, and gaseous nitrogen is fixed (or converted from atmospheric nitrogen into a form usable by plants) in the ocean. The element is a vital plant nutrient and is part of most organic molecules, including proteins, amino acids, and products from animal excretion. When these compounds decompose, nitrogen is set free as inorganic ammonia (NH_4^+), which is toxic to animals.

Several groups of nitrifying bacteria continue the breakdown, first using the ammonia to form nitrite (NO_2^-, also very toxic) and then producing nitrate (NO_3^-, less toxic to fishes, but still dangerous to invertebrates). Eventually, denitrifying bacteria completes the

TABLE 2-3

COMPONENTS OF A SUCCESSFUL CORAL REEF AQUARIUM

COMPONENT	TASKS	MAINTENANCE	COMMENTS
WATER	This is the natural environment for our animals. As much as is possible, provide the necessary elements for the organisms kept.	Small but regular water changes are in most cases necessary, usually limited to a total of less than 10% a year in a well balanced tank.	Check parameters like salinity, pH, and temperature often, and keep a record of the values.
LIVE ROCK AND SAND	These important elements create natural decoration as well as providing a variety of micro- and macro organisms in the captive environment.	Do not move or rearrange the live rock aquascape once it is designed. Leave the rocks in peace and allow them to develop.	Good water motion around the rock is desirable.
PROTEIN SKIMMER	Removes dissolved organic nutrients before they are decomposed by bacteria and thereby keeps the system desirably nutrient-poor.	The skimmer needs proper and regular cleaning on a fixed schedule.	In tanks where a higher level of nutrient is desired, a biological filter can be used instead of a protein skimmer.
LIGHT	Light is mandatory for providing energy to the primary producers (photo-synthesizers) in the system.	Lamps and bulbs need to be replaced at least once a year; metal halide lamps even more often.	When new lamps are installed, an increase in UV-radiation can occur, which can be harmful to organisms. Observe their reactions closely.
WATER MOTION	Motion is necessary not only to move food particles and waste products but to simulate a key factor in the natural habitat.	Use powerful alternating or surging current water motion. Create your own water motion regime and maintain it.	We cannot duplicate the water motion found in nature, but most marine aquariums need better water circulation.
FILTRATION (OTHER THAN PROTEIN SKIMMER)	Removes dissolved waste products that the skimmer cannot extract.	Change activated carbon regularly. Change or clean mechanical filter medium often. Change phosphate-absorbing medium according to the schedule recommended for that product.	In most cases, filtration other than skimming is not needed. Activated carbon can be very efficient, but can cause nutrient depletion. Phosphate-removing media can be very efficient if phosphate is a problem.
CALCIUM	Add calcium to replace that used by calcium-fixing organisms, such as corals and clams.	Check the calcium concentration and the carbonate hardness of the water regularly and adhere to a regime of calcium and buffer supplementation as needed.	The use of calcium (Kalkwasser) was introduced by reefkeeping pioneer Peter Wilkens in the early 1980s and revolutionized marine aquarium keeping.
THE AQUARIST	Observe your living organisms and provide them the care and feeding they require. You have the sole responsibility for their well-being.	Be informed—learn about the natural habitat and the basic biological and chemical requirements of your plants and animals. Be patient.	Many new aquariums are ruined because animals are added too soon. Allow at least 8-12 weeks before animals other than detritus- and algae-eating organisms are added.

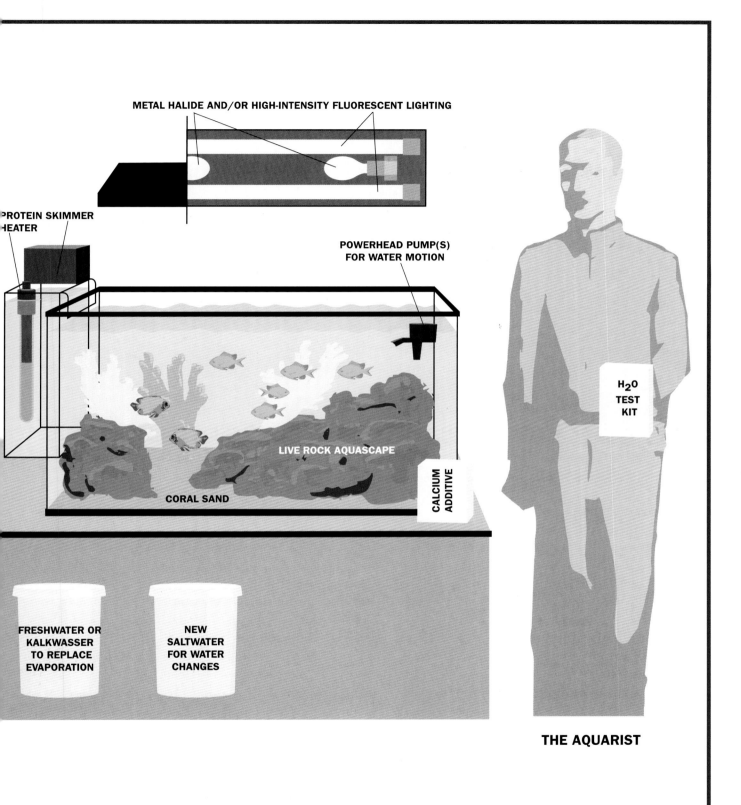

METAL HALIDE AND/OR HIGH-INTENSITY FLUORESCENT LIGHTING

PROTEIN SKIMMER
HEATER

POWERHEAD PUMP(S)
FOR WATER MOTION

LIVE ROCK AQUASCAPE

CORAL SAND

CALCIUM ADDITIVE

H₂O
TEST
KIT

FRESHWATER OR
KALKWASSER
TO REPLACE
EVAPORATION

NEW
SALTWATER
FOR WATER
CHANGES

THE AQUARIST

When water quality is right and circulation within the tank adequate, a beautiful captive reef can be the result, as shown in this large display system owned by Aqua Design, a company owned by Jan Olsen in Oldenburg, Germany. Note the growth of large stony corals.

cycle by producing nitrogen gas.

This nitrogen cycle taking place in the aquarium can be used as an indicator of the state of nutrient levels in a captive system. In general, a healthy coral reef aquarium should contain almost no ammonia and nitrite, and less than 1 mg per liter of nitrate. Ammonium, nitrite, and nitrate are all important algae nutrients. They supply algae with vital nitrogen, and if the concentration of nitrogen increases, the growth of algae in an aquarium will most likely explode. To avoid this, you need a stable population of various nitrifying and denitrifying bacteria. Such populations take time to build up and stabilize, thus our advice to have patience during the first few months after setting up a new aquarium. During the very first weeks, the level of ammonia, nitrite, and nitrate is usually high, but then decreases.

In order to keep the level of these nutrients low in the months and years to come, the denitrifying and nitrifying bacteria must continue to thrive, but at a level that is in balance with the size of your closed ecosystem.

In other words, you want to avoid any situation that produces a rapid excess of nutrients, which will cause nuisance algae to start overgrowing the aquarium.

You must be sure that not too much waste material (uneaten food or food scraps, dead plants or animals) are ever allowed to decay in the tank. If you can remove organic material before it enters the nitrogen cycle, it will avoid a spike in nutrient levels in the aquarium. This task is made much easier with the use of various filtering devices, especially protein skimmers or foam fractionators.

Other nutrient elements that can be studied are phosphorous (P) and carbon (C), which both have similar cycles in nature and in the aquarium.

INDICATIONS OF AN INCREASING NUTRIENT LEVEL

IF BACTERIAL ACTIVITY BECOMES TOO HIGH or the nitrogen cycle is not completed in your aquarium, you will be able to measure an increasing level of nitrate.

This situation can very well happen if you rely exclusively on biological filters. Biological filters (e.g., wet/dry or trickle filters) usually lead to increasing levels of nutrients and are only useful in lightly populated tanks or in aquariums where we want to keep organisms—such as sponges, ornamental worms, tunicates, or other filter feeders—that need higher nutrient levels.

Normally you will notice an increasing level of nutrients—by definition, a deterioration of the water quality—by an increase, sometimes an explosion, in the growth of algae. You may note that the water has become discolored and yellow-tinted. If the situation gets severe, stony corals are normally the first invertebrates to suffer. Many soft corals in such situations can expand their polyps and do well, but even they will suffer if the level of nitrate rises too high. If the nutrient level is so high that nitrite and ammonium are accumulating, most invertebrates will suffer and die, and fishes will become stressed and vulnerable to parasites and disease.

On the other hand, some animals will prosper only if the amount of food particles is higher than in normal reef tanks. These include many sponges and sea squirts, filter feeders that cannot survive without an almost continuous access to suspended organics and minute planktonic food. Also, the **ahermatypic** (nonphotosynthetic) stony corals, such as the genus *Tubastraea*, and soft corals and gorgonians without zooxanthellae, cannot thrive in a system lacking these nutrients. The delicate *Dendronephthya* spp., often imported but nearly impossible to keep alive, are examples of a group of corals that must have large amounts of **phytoplankton** (tiny, single-celled drifting algae) to survive. By contrast, most reef-building corals cannot tolerate high nutrient levels and prefer a nutrient-poor system where the amount of nitrate is less than 1 ppm (still much higher than on most coral reefs).

Although most reef aquarists today want to keep corals that have requirements for nutrient-poor water, we should point out that it is certainly possible to operate a different sort of reef aquarium—one that is richer in nutrients and contains a variety of beautiful micro- and macroalgae. Such tanks are often seen in Holland, where

the use of biological filters (which have vanished among aquarists in many other countries) is still relatively commonplace. It might be difficult to grow stony corals in such aquariums, but on the other hand, one sees a most remarkable profusion of other invertebrates, such as worms, sponges, and sea squirts, many of which develop from live rock.

FILTER TECHNIQUES

How can we assure that water quality stays optimal? Unfortunately, there is no easy answer to this question. Filtering equipment and techniques, feeding practices, number of animals, type of decorative materials, water changes, and additives all contribute to water quality.

If you decorate a small aquarium with a few pieces of live rock and populate the tank with only a few invertebrates and fishes, feed them carefully, and ensure proper water motion and aeration—then it is possible to maintain an unfiltered aquarium. This is the so-called "natural system" of the famous pioneer Lee Chin Eng of Indonesia, who demonstrated his minimal aquarium techniques in the early 1960s.

Another way to maintain proper water quality is to do regular **water changes**, replacing a portion of the system water every week or month. Experience has shown, however, that too-frequent water changes often have negative impacts on the system, such as causing instability and an uncontrollable growth of algae. Normally a water change of 5-10% a year is sufficient in a balanced reef aquarium. (Heavily stocked fish-only systems, which generate a great deal more waste, must be managed differently, with regular substantial water changes.)

Not many aquarists want to limit the number of animals in the spartan method of the "natural system," and therefore choose to install various filtering aids. One of the most useful devises in this connection is the **protein skimmer**, or foam fractionator. Protein skimmers come in a wide variety of brands, sizes, and types and have been debated and described over and over again. We will not take up that discussion here. However, it can be of little doubt that the introduction of the protein skimmer in the late 1960s was a small (almost silent) revolution in the

> ## WATER ADDITIONS
>
> When water evaporates from a marine aquarium, the salts remain. Evaporated water must be replaced by fresh water (with added calcium supplements, if this is your chosen method for replenishing calcium in the system).
>
> ■ ■ ■

hobby. Its true importance was not really understood before the mid-1980s, when other technical aspects of reef aquarium keeping were sufficiently mastered to allow us to see that skimming really mattered.

Skimming removes organic material before it is decomposed by bacteria and does in this way limit the level of nutrients in the aquarium. We now know that the skimmer also removes elements that are vital to the living organisms in the aquarium.

It is therefore important to install a skimmer that is of an optimal size related to the size of your aquarium. "The bigger the better" is definitely not advisable, as overskimming strips the system of vital elements. Skimmer design has improved greatly in recent years, but it is still important to clean and maintain the unit regularly to keep it performing efficiently.

Crystal-clear water is a characteristic of many reefs, as on this sheer fore reef in the Coral Sea. Skimming and the use of activated carbon help ensure water clarity in the aquarium.

with **live rock**. Live rock is more than decorative. It is an excellent biological filter that harbors beneficial bacteria, microalgae, and tiny animals—all vital to the biological balance of the system. We believe that good live rock used in combination with optimal and carefully maintained skimming is the best combination of filter techniques available and the best tool for assuring good water quality.

Filtration over **activated carbon** can sometimes be necessary as well. Activated carbon extracts compounds that cannot be skimmed off (mainly because they have no electrical charge), and is often used to remove the yellowish hue of aquarium water that contains dissolved organics. Activated carbon is very effective at rapidly increasing the clarity of aquarium water, but you should, in general, be careful with carbon filtration. Although it is efficient in

While protein skimmers remove organic material before decomposing bacteria can attack it, **biological filters** act in the opposite way. They utilize bacteria to break down waste products. In earlier days, it was common to install huge gravel filters next to the aquarium and let the water drain through sand beds or pass through submerged filter chambers filled with coral gravel. This can work fine for a period of time, but after a while the filter beds cannot cope with the nutrient buildup in the system, and they start releasing nutrient instead of removing it, causing algae to bloom and nutrient-dependent animals to proliferate.

Today the best biological filter is an aquascape made

removing organic compounds by absorption and adsorption, it is easy to overuse carbon—resulting in a negative reaction among certain sensitive animals.

The continuous use of small amounts of activated carbon is probably better than brief, periodic use of larger quantities. Heavy use of activated carbon can cause a sudden change in water quality. Most organisms are more sensitive to sudden changes than to those taking place over a longer period of time to which they can adapt.

We have firsthand experience of overusing activated carbon and causing a severe bleaching event among stony corals kept in one of our aquariums. The cause was not high temperatures (the common cause for bleaching), but the removal of dissolved organic compounds that had been absorbing UV radiation coming from powerful metal halide lamps. When these compounds were suddenly removed by carbon, the animals were hit with a fatal dose of UV radiation, against which they were unable to protect themselves.

Mechanical filtration, usually in the form of a canister filter that is run for a few days before it is cleaned, is sometimes useful in getting detritus out of the aquarium. The current trend is to eliminate constant mechanical filtration from the reef aquarium. Whether you need to use mechanical filtration or not depends on the population of animals kept, the amount of particulate material found in the aquarium, and the amount of food you add to the tank. In an aquarium with many large fishes, efficient mechanical filtration will often be required, while a tank housing sessile invertebrates and a limited number of small fishes can easily do without.

The key question now is, "How can I see if my filtration system is working?" Firstly, the system itself and all its organisms will tell you if you are on the right track or not. Is the aquascape relatively free of nuisance algae? Are your fishes healthy and with a low mortality rate? Are your corals showing good polyp extension? Are all your animals growing? In short, are things surviving? Are they thriving?

Secondly, it is wise to measure and log a few vital parameters of your system: salinity, temperature, and pH. These have a tendency to shift over time, with sometimes serious consequences. Again, the growth of algae is a good indication of the health of your system and the level of nutrients in the water. A healthy coral reef aquarium should have a diverse, but not dominant, growth of small algae (known as turf algae, page 209), which are vital for the balance of the system. Too little or too much algae or a sudden shift in the growth of algae, for instance the sudden proliferation of one species, can indicate that something is about to go wrong.

SALINITY

ONE OF THE MOST IMPORTANT parameters to check regularly is the salinity. Salinity is simply defined as "the total amount of solid material dissolved in 1 kg of sea-water" expressed in grams per kilogram (g/kg) or parts per thousand (ppt or °/oo). There are several ways to measure salinity, but it cannot be measured directly. Among aquarists, the most common method is to measure the density of the seawater, which refers to its mass per unit volume and is expressed as grams per milliliter (g/ml).

To measure the density, you need a hydrometer, available in many types, brands, and qualities. It is absolutely necessary to calibrate the hydrometer against a known solution with the correct temperature in order to ensure that you are measuring the real density of your aquarium water, because density is correlated with temperature. If the density reads 1.0250 g/ml at 20°C (68°F) it will read 1.0274 if the temperature rises to 25°C (77°F). To convert the density readings into salinity, you must use a table. A density of 1.0250 g/ml at 25°C (77°F) corresponds to 37.18 ppt, a very high salinity. For a reef tank at 25°C (77°F) the salinity should range between 32 and 36 ppt, corresponding to a density of 1.021-1.024 g/ml.

We have seen over and over again that salinity tends to decrease over time in coral reef aquariums. The reasons for this are many. A protein skimmer removes a lot of seawater, which is often replaced with freshwater or calcium-enriched water (see page 32). When we give away a coral or some coral fragments in a bag with some of the aquarium water, the loss is usually replaced—perhaps automatically—with freshwater. The salinity is decreased, not much to be sure, but over time the effects will become measurable. We have several times measured aquarium salinity levels of 25, which is almost 30% lower than the average salinity of natural seawater.

When the salinity decreases below 30, a normal reaction in the aquarium is an uncontrolled growth of slime algae. If you have problems with such algae, the first thing to do is check and double-check the salinity to make absolutely sure that it is within the normal range of a coral reef aquarium.

TRACE ELEMENTS

IF YOU EQUIP YOUR AQUARIUM with an efficient skimmer, periodically do filtration through activated carbon, change only a minute amount of water from time to time, and feed the animals sparsely, then your system can very well experience a depletion of trace elements.

While trace elements compose only a fraction of the total weight of elements dissolved in natural seawater, many trace elements are vital to living organisms in the sea. On the other hand, if present in a concentration higher than normal, many of these elements become highly toxic. Heavy metals like copper (Cu) and aluminum (Al) are examples of the latter. Trace elements should be present, but neither allowed to accumulate nor be exhausted or filtered from a reef aquarium.

For aquarists it is nearly impossible to test the amount of trace elements present, due to their minimal concentrations. Test kits are available, but for real accuracy, water samples must be handed over to experts with sophisticated equipment for such tests, which in most cases are prohibitively costly. Again, the best way is to observe the living creatures and take notice of behavioral changes.

A rule of thumb is that over time, using a typical set-up, combined with only modest water changes, trace elements—as well as most other elements—will become depleted. It is therefore necessary to add trace elements in the form of commercially available trace-element solutions. However, most of these solutions are vague or totally negligent in stating what elements you are actually adding. ("Magic" elixirs are alive and well in the marine aquarium trade.) From our experience, the best plan is to start out with a dose lower than that called for on the label and then observe the reaction in the aquarium for several days to a week before adding more. Under no circumstances should trace elements be added with a "the more the better" attitude. The opposite is, in fact, closer to the truth.

CALCIUM

Coral reefs are made from aragonite, a crystal form of calcium carbonate, laid down in the skeletons of reef-building corals. Calcium is a vital element on the reefs as well as in the coral reef aquarium. The concentration of calcium in the aquarium should be maintained as close to that of natural seawater as possible,

THE pH SCALE

Water (H_2O) is not only present in the molecular form of H_2O, but dissociates to the ions H^+ (acid) and OH^- (base). When H^+ and OH^- are equal, the water is neither acidic nor basic, but neutral with a pH equal to 7.0. A pH in the range of 0 to 6.999 is acid and has more H^+ than OH^-, while a pH from 7.001 to 14 is base with more OH^- than H^+. The amount of acid (H^+) is balanced against the amount of base (OH^-).

Each step on the pH scale is equal to a multiple of 10 in the concentration of H^+ to OH^-. A solution with pH = 5 contains 10 times as much H^+ as a solution with pH = 6 and hundreds of times more than a neutral solution of pH 7. In the reef aquarium, although the pH fluctuates throughout the day (slightly higher after a dark period), the value should remain in the acceptable range of 7.8 to 8.5.

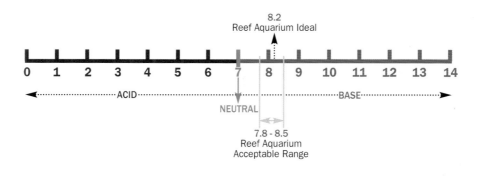

around 420 parts per million (ppm).

There are several ways to add calcium. Using calcareous water (Kalkwasser), a calcium reactor, or two-part (calcium and buffer) solutions are the most common methods used today. The chemistry involved in adding calcium to an active system is very complex and difficult for most nonchemists to follow. A simplified version is in the box on page 32. The reef aquarium literature has many books and articles that discuss the subject in great detail (see Further Reading, page 231).

pH

ANOTHER IMPORTANT PARAMETER to keep an eye on is the pH. Most aquarists are somewhat familiar with the pH-scale, which has values of 0 to14: 0-7 being acidic; 7.0 being neutral; and 7-14 basic. The pH, a term that actually means "the amount of H^+", is linked to the dissociation of the water molecule (H_2O) into positive hydrogen ions (H^+, acid) and negative hydroxide ions (OH^-, base). (See box on facing page.)

In natural seawater, the pH value is normally stable at around 8.2, meaning that there are about 12 times more base (OH^- ions) than acid (H^+ ions) present. The pH value of a coral reef aquarium should not vary out of the range of 8.0 to 8.5. A value around 8.0 is common in the morning (or after the dark period) when photosynthesis has been shut down, allowing the amount of CO_2 to increase in the system. With the lights on, photosynthesis uses CO_2 and the pH slowly rises to reach a maximum in the late afternoon, normally around levels of 8.5. The addition of Kalkwasser normally causes the pH to rise even beyond 8.5.

You can roughly check the pH value of your aquarium using a pH-drop test designed for aquarium purposes. However, such tests are not very accurate, having an accuracy of not more than 0.5 pH units. More expensive tests have a higher accuracy. The easiest and most accurate pH measurements are done with an electronic pH meter, a handy tool in common use by aquarists. It is important to remember that pH meters need proper calibration of the probe in order to be trusted.

ALKALINITY

ALKALINITY IS THE EXTENT to which a solution has excess hydroxide ions (OH^-), or in other words, how well the solution is able to neutralize acids, which is what we call "buffer capacity." The buffer capacity is measured in aquariums by testing the alkalinity directly or by measuring the "carbonate hardness" (KdH), which is the sum of bicarbonate and carbonate ions (the major buffering anions of seawater). The natural KdH of seawater is from 6 to 8.3 KdH, equal to 2.1 to 3.0 milliequivalents per liter (meq/L) alkalinity. To check the buffer capacity of your aquarium water, measure the KdH using one of the many test kits available. A value within the natural range is acceptable, but the method you regularly use to add calcium can greatly influence the KdH value that you measure. The use of Kalkwasser generally decreases the KdH, while the use of calcareous reactors and CO_2, normally increases the KdH.

The quality of the water of natural coral reefs is one of the secrets explaining the fantastic diversity of plants and animals living there. Maintaining good water quality is one of several challenges that the aquarist must meet. Here we have merely introduced the subject, and we urge you to read more to learn how to maintain the water for your captive reef. Some hobbyists love the technology and chemistry involved. Others watch their animals closely and simply use good husbandry and maintenance practices. Choose your own course, but never forget the importance of water quality.

WATER MOTION ON THE REEF

PROPER WATER MOVEMENT may be the most difficult physical feature to imitate in a small aquarium. Throughout most of the year, big waves crash more or less continuously on the reef edge, creating tremendous turbulence and water movement and pushing tons of oceanic water into the reef flat. Even with an unlimited budget, these are conditions that no aquarist will be able to replicate in a closed marine system. However, this does not mean that the movement of water in the coral reef aquarium is a factor that can be neglected or treated lightly. We must do what amateur aquarium enthusiasts have always done—find alternative ways to cope with the needs of our animals. In the typical home aquarium setup, water movement is inadequate or even neglected by hobbyists who are not aware of how important it is and how it can be accomplished.

There are several forces responsible for the water movement on coral reefs. The shallow reef zones are exposed to tides, which usually move water in and out of the reef flat twice in 24 hours. The fundamental causes of tides, which occur only in large bodies of water, are the

Eddies of current over a reef crest in the Solomon Islands suggests the power of water motion in the wild—one dimension of the natural environment that is not replicable in most aquariums. Incoming waves and tides bring massive, energetic water changes.

gravitational effects of the sun and moon on Earth and the rotation of our planet.

Tides can vary greatly, depending on the location, moon phase, and time of day. During extreme low tide, which occurs during the full moon, the tidal current can gain tremendous force. When the tide peaks or is at its lowest level, the tidal movement of water can come to a virtual standstill for several hours. During extreme low tide, the organisms on the shallow reef flat are often exposed to open air for a few hours, a period of time that is very stressful for sessile animals. The radiation from the burning sun can easily desiccate or burn the corals, which protect themselves by secreting mucus and generating internal protective pigments (see page 17).

The tidal forces also create a huge movement of wa-

TURNOVER RATE

As rule of thumb, the internal water circulation in a traditional reef aquarium should have a turnover rate of at least 10X the aquarium volume per hour. More is often better.

■ ■ ■

ter outside the reef flats. Tons of water are moving along the reef slope and reef edge every second. When huge volumes of water are being pushed into channels between reefs or entrances leading in and out of the lagoon, the current can be as powerful as the flow of a river. Every organism that lives here, including sea fans and many soft corals, needs to be able to attach itself properly. The tidal current is not constant, but rather rises, peaks, slows down, comes to a standstill, turns, rises, and peaks again—all in a daily, monthly, and yearly cycle.

There are also currents that are not directly linked to the tides, especially in deeper zones of the reef. Even though the current can be negligible on the surface, the situation at 10 or 20 m (33 to 66 ft.) can be very different. Here the movement of water may be strong and a real hazard to divers—but vital to the organisms who live at that depth.

Very different water movements are created by waves, which in turn are linked to the weather conditions. During tropical storms, huge waves build up, which on extreme occasions can lead to the near total destruction of the life of the coral reef. The reef structure and its life are, however, well adapted to tolerate normal wave action. Although the waves are large, they normally only move some boulders and break some corals growing on the reef edge, actions that must be regarded as entirely natural. The wave action along the reef edge pushes tons of new water into the reef flat and, like the tide, causes an important renewal of the water over shallow reef zones. In deeper waters, the forces of waves do not have the same impact. This can be experienced during a dive: it can be fairly quiet at 20 m (66 ft.), even though the waves on the surface are meters high.

BIOLOGICAL IMPORTANCE

WATER MOTION DOES MORE than affect the reef physically. It also is of an utmost importance biologically. The flow of water passing over the reef removes waste products created by biological decomposition, animal and plant respiration, and excretion. It also carries in important food sources and compounds from the surrounding oceanic waters, such as plankton and inorganic nutrients that will be consumed by algae. The sessile organisms of the coral reefs—the nonphotosynthetic gorgonians for example—are totally dependent on the current to supply them with food.

The current is also important when it comes to dispersing species. When sessile reef creatures such as corals release eggs and sperm for external fertilization, the larvae are transported to other locations where they can attach and secure the dispersal of their particular genotype. Also, asexually produced offspring (reproduction without fertilization), such as coral fragments or detached coral polyps, are transported by currents to new locations where they may find room to anchor and grow. Extreme currents, especially heavy wave action during big storms, can fragment branching stony corals, thus indirectly causing asexual reproduction and spreading of species.

Many corals secrete mucus, especially those exposed at low tide, and this coating is carried away when the tide rises again. This process also cleans the surface of the colony of attached detritus and bacteria. Many successful reef aquarists believe that this function, of washing away accumulating mucus and other wastes that build

---

TABLE 2-4

SOME ORGANISMS WITH SPECIAL WATER MOTION NEEDS

GROUP	GENUS / SPECIES
Sponges (Porifera)	Most species
Corals (Cnidaria; Alcyonacea)	*Dendronephthya* spp.
	Scleronephthya spp.
	Chironephthya spp.
Corals (Cnidaria; Gorgonacea)	*Diodogorgia nodulifera*
	Gorgonia spp.
	Ellisellidae; almost all nonphotosynthetic gorgonians
Sea Pens (Cnidaria; Pennatulacea)	All species
Corals (Cnidaria; Scleractinia)	*Tubastraea* spp.
Mollusks (Mollusca; Polyplacophora)	*Acanthopleura* spp., *Ischnochiton* spp., and others
Mollusks (Mollusca; Bivalvia)	*Spondylus* spp.
Echinoderms (Echinodermata)	All species of feather stars (Crinoidea)
	Shingle urchins, *Colobocentrotus* spp.

POWERHEAD CIRCULATION

POWERHEAD OUTFLOW

WATER CURRENTS

POWERHEAD INTAKES

Two or more powerheads or water return nozzles can be used effectively to create chaotic currents in an aquarium, especially when a wave timer is used to stagger the running of the pumps.

up on and around sessile corals and other invertebrates, is extremely important to replicate.

ADAPTATIONS TO WATER MOTION

THERE ARE MANY FORMS of animal adaptations to water motion. For example, most sea urchins feed on algae and are consequently most numerous in shallow water areas where there is plenty of food. But how do they hold on? We recollect standing on the reef off South Beach on Rarotonga once when meter-high waves were hitting the reef edge with tremendous force. Here, the Slate Pencil Urchin (*Heterocentrotus mammilatus*) lives in small crevices using its thick pencil-shaped spines and numerous tube feet to attach itself, allowing it to graze unfazed by the crashing waves. The smaller urchin species, *Echinometra mathaei*, solves the holdfast problem differently. It bores a small tunnel or hole for itself where it is so well secured that it is almost perfectly protected from predators as well.

Feather stars (crinoids) are most apparent at night, attached to spots exposed to heavy currents. Such locations are ideal for catching plenty of the minute plankton on which they feed. A feather star's body is a mass of tentacles and tiny, comblike branches constructed for sieving as much current as possible. How, then, can they remain attached in tides and waves? In the free-living

feather stars, the stalk is greatly reduced, but a set of curved, sharp cirri has developed—analogous to the talons of a perching hawk. These are perfect attachment organs.

Most corals and their allies also need strong attachment adaptations. Many nonphotosynthetic sea fans grow to diameters of a meter or more and prefer to project from steep reef walls or live in underwater canyons where water motion is strong. Their tiny polyps are spread on a network of branches, and in order to let as much water as possible pass through the network, the colonies grow at right angles to the current, exposing them to a great deal of water motion. In order not to break, the gorgonians have developed a flexible skeleton, in some cases adding flexible joints to the structure that can bend in the current. Solid basal plates secure the attachment.

Host sea anemones are typically found on the upper-reef slope, often amid strong wave action. They have a fleshy body, which can sway with the water movement, but their large pedal disc holds them tightly to the substrate.

Pelagic fishes have developed an arrowlike body shape, perfectly designed for moving into the current. The streamlined barracudas and mackerels are excellent examples. *Pseudanthias* and *Chromis* species spend most of the day in the water column just off the reef slope, where they feed on passing plankton. A tiny compressed body combined with a large tail and excellent eyesight make them perfectly adapted to hover in the current, pick their plankton, and rapidly seek shelter among the branches of corals whenever a predator appears. The feeding habits of such fishes, particularly many of the beautiful anthias species, make them challenging to keep. Strong water movement and a rich, almost-continuous supply of tiny planktonic foods are needed.

CREATING WATER MOTION

PROPER WATER MOTION ALSO SERVES important functions in the coral reef aquarium. Just as in nature, it transports and keeps food particles suspended in the water column. The circulation also prevents detritus from accumulating on the aquascape, and suspends it until it is removed by various filter equipment.

Water motion ripples the surface and breaks up the organic film that always gathers on quiet water surfaces. Movement of the surface facilitates the exchange of gases

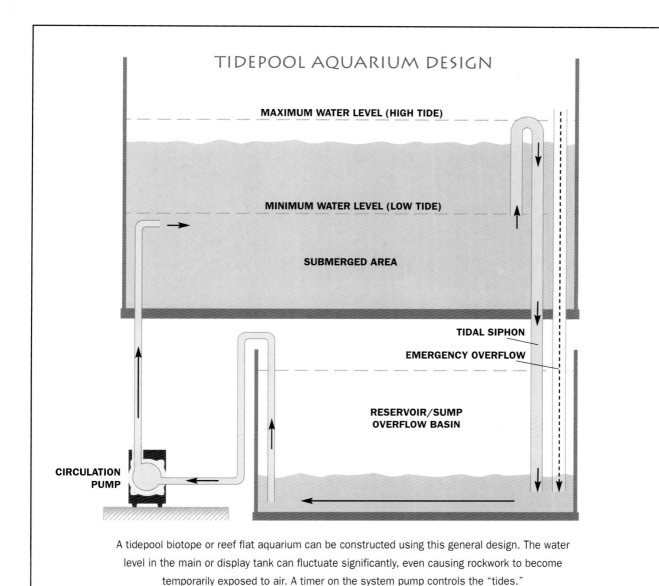

TIDEPOOL AQUARIUM DESIGN

MAXIMUM WATER LEVEL (HIGH TIDE)

MINIMUM WATER LEVEL (LOW TIDE)

SUBMERGED AREA

TIDAL SIPHON

EMERGENCY OVERFLOW

RESERVOIR/SUMP OVERFLOW BASIN

CIRCULATION PUMP

A tidepool biotope or reef flat aquarium can be constructed using this general design. The water level in the main or display tank can fluctuate significantly, even causing rockwork to become temporarily exposed to air. A timer on the system pump controls the "tides."

(e.g., carbon dioxide, nitrogen, and oxygen) between air and water.

Finally, water motion that simulates natural conditions allows captive organisms to behave as they do in the wild. By making the sessile organisms sway back and forth, the water motion creates an important aesthetic effect in the coral reef aquarium. The simple observation of thousands of experienced marine aquarists is that more realistic water motion leads to healthier fishes and invertebrates.

As a rule of thumb, it is often stated that you should have an internal water movement in your aquarium at least 10 times and up to 20 times the aquarium volume per hour. That is, in a 250 L (65 gal.) tank, the water circulating capacity of all pumps should total 2,500 to 5,000 L (650 to 1,300 gal.) per hour. This is, of course, an approximation, and the actual target depends on what reef zone you are trying to copy and what kind of animals you want to keep. A quiet sand-zone aquarium clearly requires less water motion than a reef-wall aquarium.

In general, most aquarists use powerheads and external circulation pumps to create a steady, perhaps alternating, water movement in their tanks. Circulation pumps come in many designs and sizes. Self-contained powerheads with a turnover of 1,000 to 4,000 L/h (260 to 1,040 gal./h) are commonly used because they require

Dr. Bruce Carlson inspects stony corals growing in an experimental outdoor tank in a nonpublic area of the Waikiki Aquarium. While director of the Aquarium, Dr. Carlson invented the "Carlson Surge Device" shown here and opposite to create strong, surging currents.

no plumbing. Usually the pumps are mounted near the surface of the aquarium, either above water or submerged, and the inlet is placed close to the bottom. These pumps start a water motion like that shown in the diagram on page 44. Increase the number of pumps and you tend to create chaotic and changing currents—a definite benefit in most situations. Sophisticated computers designed for aquariums as well as less expensive wavemakers and appliance timers are now readily available, making it possible to alternate the output of circulation pumps and thus create changing currents or even program the circulatory regime in detail.

If the aquarium is higher than about 60 cm (23 in.), you will have a difficult time moving the complete column of water by powerheads alone, and it is necessary to seek other solutions. Internal circulation pumps, including high-volume powerheads, can to a certain extent create currents in the larger tank, but they can hardly simulate waves or tides. Wave actions and tidal forces

are technically complicated to copy and thus mostly neglected by aquarists. Both factors are, however, biologically important to most of the reef organisms and we believe that much can be gained by attempts to simulate tides and waves in the captive reefs.

A tidal effect in the coral reef aquarium, where for instance some of the stony corals are partly exposed to open air for a short period of time, might elicit colors in the colonies other than those usually seen in captivity. One technical solution to the tidal problem is shown in the diagram on page 45.

Dr. Bruce Carlson, the former Director of the Waikiki Aquarium in Hawaii, developed an interesting wave-machine first used in connection with outdoor coral propagation tanks. The device consists of a container of water that is gradually filled with water from the aquarium and rapidly empties into the aquarium at regular intervals. The effect is a wave motion unlike the motions created by circulation pumps. You obviously need a lot

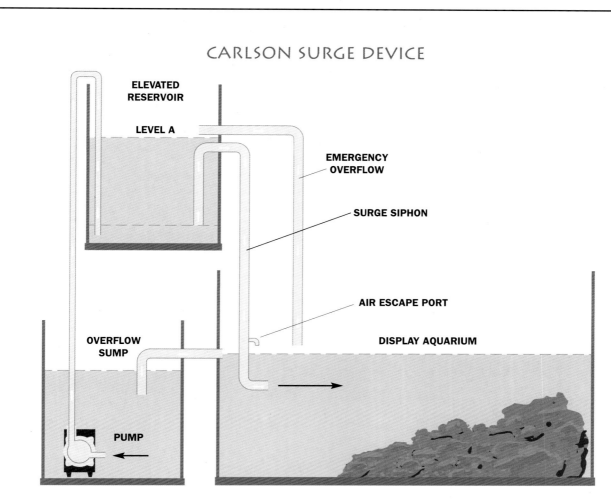

CARLSON SURGE DEVICE

ELEVATED RESERVOIR

LEVEL A

EMERGENCY OVERFLOW

SURGE SIPHON

AIR ESCAPE PORT

OVERFLOW SUMP

DISPLAY AQUARIUM

PUMP

This sophisticated system of siphons and overflows can be used to create powerful, rhythmic currents in a reef tank. Water is pumped from the overflow sump up to an upper reservoir where it automatically empties into the tank when it reaches level (A). The escape port prevents air-line block in the key siphon that empties the elevated reservoir.

of space over and around the aquarium to use this kind of wavemaking system, but the so-called Carlson Surge Device can be made smaller to suit your own setup.

Another way of generating waves and general water circulation in large tanks is through ellipsoid water agitators like the Swiss invention marketed as the Oloid™ agitator. This clamshell-shaped device can imitate natural water movements more closely than any other technology. It rotates on two axes and moves much like a paddle or the tail fin of a fish. With only a fraction of the power demand needed for traditional pump performance, the Oloid agitator is able to move large amounts of water by creating a flow with pulse-type movements that generate oscillations in the entire body of water.

Future possibilities for improving water motion in our coral reef aquariums are great. Amateur aquarists and inventors are likely to lead the way. Although the technical solutions are somewhat complicated and although you often need plenty of space to install the necessary equipment, we do encourage aquarists to be creative in seeking new solutions to the water-motion challenge.

An aquarium in which water motion shifts to and fro and where wave action is simulated would not only enhance the well being of the organisms, but would also contribute to the realism of the miniature reef. We think the visual rewards would be significant, and someday this sort of replicated wave action may even be accompanied by synchronized sounds.

CHAPTER 3

AQUASCAPING

Building a Small-Scale Ecosystem:
Combining Beauty and Biology in a Box of Water

CREATING A REEFSCAPE IN MINIATURE may seem to be the easiest challenge a new aquarist faces. Start with a good selection of decorating materials and a reasonable sense of balance—and there you have it! Nothing could be further from the truth, as a large number of the animals we keep in our aquariums have very particular demands for appropriate physical surroundings. Aquascaping is still an exciting phase of setting up any new aquarium, but the smart hobbyist will approach this with some important biological facts in mind.

DEMANDING ANIMALS

SOME ANIMALS WILL NEVER ACCLIMATE to an aquarium without ample hiding places—caves, nooks, and crannies that give them the cover they have enjoyed

Perhaps a future dream for aquascapers, this dark canyon in Indonesia is filled with glorious nonphotosynthetic life. **Above,** the Bluespotted Jawfish must have a deep substrate.

on the reef. Others have little or no use for such shelter, but rather need plenty of open swimming and roaming space. Providing your fishes an appropriate reefscape—one that mirrors the habitat they have evolved in for millions of years—is the best way to ensure they will settle in and display their natural behaviors.

Some reef animals need soft bottoms in which to burrow, grub for food, or bury themselves at night. Those that build tunnels may do best only in an aquarium with a deep bed of sand. Even some stony corals come from sandy or muddy areas rather than the stony substrate that most other species tend to demand. Among these soft-bottom dwellers are the popular elegance coral (*Catalaphyllia jardinei*), the fast-growing velvet finger coral (*Montipora digitata)*, and the anemone mushroom coral (*Heliofungia actiniformis*), to mention just a few.

How you put together the various elements of an aquarium reefscape can significantly influence parameters such as light intensity, water flow, and turbulence. By planning properly, you can make stable foundations

In a more mature reef aquarium, the sessile animals themselves have grown into a living aquascape, obscuring the original live rock foundation. Patient aquarists plan for the expansion of their corals. This lovely system is the work of Ralph Boger of Germany.

for attaching specific corals in a favorable location.

Several of the nonphotosynthetic corals (corals without zooxanthellae) need dark or at least shady growing areas, as strong light can be detrimental to their well-being. If these challenging corals are among your favorites, you might consider constructing a large cave as a feature of your aquascape.

On the other hand, if you want to keep a lot of reef-building stony corals, such as some of the *Acropora* species, you should consider making the decoration as open as possible to leave plenty of suitable growing space for these highly light-dependent corals. Particularly in tall aquariums, it may be necessary to construct plateaus in the upper third of the tank, close to the light source, for those shallow-water corals that otherwise are difficult to supply with enough light.

The configuration of the miniature reefscape also influences the ability of certain animals to get the food they need. For those animals that greedily accept anything you feed, there may be no problem, but for food specialists, the composition of the decorations may be crucial. Detritivores, animals that feed on detritus and the various small life forms that live on such organic debris, are frequently particular about where they graze. Most detrivorous fishes and many sea cucumbers, for instance, sift through muddy and sandy bottom layers, while sea urchins prefer to take their detritus off rocky surfaces. Algae-eating animals, unless they accept substitutes like lettuce or spinach, will normally depend on hard substrates suitable for algal growth.

> ## HABITAT PLANS
>
> Take the habitat requirements of the livestock you intend to keep into serious consideration when aquascaping your aquarium. If your centerpiece species will need caves, open swimming spaces, or deep sand beds, be sure to plan ahead.
>
> ■ ■ ■

TABLE 3-1

ORGANISMS COMMONLY FOUND with LIVE ROCK

GROUP	GENUS / SPECIES	COMMENTS
SINGLE-CELLED ANIMALS	Homotrema rubrum	Small, red colonies with thick, whitish pseudopods.
SPONGES	Many species	Normally grow slowly; can take years to establish well-developed populations.
HYDROIDS	Myrionema sp.	Caution! A boring hydrozoan that can overgrow the tank completely.
JELLYFISHES	Polyp stage of Nausithoe	Very common on fresh live rocks; resemble small, brown tubes.
ANEMONES	Aiptasia sp. (glass anemones)	Can reproduce quickly by pedal laceration. Must be controlled to prevent overgrowth.
	Anemonia sp.	Small, brownish with lighter tentacle tips. Can reproduce quickly by pedal laceration. Must be controlled to prevent overgrowth.
STONY CORALS	Euphyllia glabrescens Psammocora sp. Porites spp.	Typically introduced as small polyps; discovered later, after the rock has been in the tank for a while and the polyps have started to grow.
WORMS	Free-living bristleworms	Many species are common. Nocturnal. Some can reach a considerable length.
	Scaleworms e.g., Lepidonotus sp.	A few cm long and dorso-ventrally compressed. Very common. Harmless.
	Terebellid worms	Buried in small holes in the rock; expose many thin, slippery, transparent or white tentacles on the surface. Harmless.
	Feather dusters	Bispira viola is common and can form huge populations in the reef aquarium. Harmless.
	Calcareous tubeworms, e.g., Vermiliopsis sp.	Build small, white, spiral-shaped tubes. Red or orange tentacle crowns. Harmless.
	Peanut worms (Order Sipunculida)	Live in holes in the rocks; can even drill holes. Very common and important decomposers of live rock. Nocturnal. Harmless.
MOLLUSKS	Many different species, especially small snails from the genera Stomatella and Mitra as well as countless species of algae-eating snails. Boring-mussels from the genera Pholas and Lithophaga are also common.	Mitra snails feed on other mollusks. Stomatella spp. are algae grazers. The boring mussels are found in holes in the rocks; only the edge of the mantle is seen.
CRUSTACEANS	Amphipods and copepods	Establish large populations and are important food supplies for many organisms.
	Crabs	Many species; some are harmful, but most do little damage. Some can grow to a considerable size. Hairy coral crabs can be detrimental to corals.
ECHINODERMS	Several small brittle and serpent stars	Many reproduce successfully in the reef aquarium. Asterina sp., a tiny sea star, is a harmless algae grazer that can multiply enormously.

Fast becoming extinct, early marine aquariums were decorated with dead coral skeletons and often regularly or continuously treated with chemicals deadly to all invertebrate life.

Creative aquascaping may employ inert sunken objects, such as these clay urns—authentic for a Mediterranean scene and an appropriate home for several moray eels.

Although some reefkeepers scorn macroalgae, it can be used to very pleasing effect, as in this large tank with a central sand bed between a high wall at left and smaller rocky mound to the right.

Bottom-dwelling pipefishes (*Corythoichthys* spp.), and mandarinfishes (*Synchiropus* spp.) feed mainly on small benthic crustaceans that rarely are common in an aquarium unless it is provided with live rock or a bottom layer of very coarse substrate or coral rubble. While artificial decorations, such as dead coral rock or limestone combined with replica coral casts, can be an interesting alternative for fish-only tanks, they are clearly a poor choice for small, picky eaters that will starve to death without a prolific population of microfauna that need a naturally complex aquascape.

BUILDING A REEFSCAPE

IN THE END, THE UNDERWATER SCENE you design ought to be put together to suit the sort of animals you intend to keep. The larger the tank, the simpler this task will be, as a large aquarium can more easily contain many different microhabitats that will suit a variety of animal groups. In a reasonably large tank, we can combine some open space and swimming channels with caves, rocky nooks, steep slopes, and ledges where corals can be placed. The smaller the aquarium, the more important it is to plan exactly what livestock it will house. Small tanks can be just as beautiful and interesting as big ones—and they are certainly cheaper to buy and maintain—but they cannot be aquascaped or stocked in a haphazard way.

When all the more critical demands of the animals have been covered, one should focus on what kind of reef scenery one wants to recreate. For years, the average reef aquarist has copied what too many others have done before, and more often than not we have ended up with rather stereotypic tanks built with a solid rock wall against the back of the aquarium. There is little variation in the topography and few aesthetic focal points.

Even conceding that there are such walls on natural reefs, it is unfortunate that so many aquarists fail to see how uninteresting such tight heaps of rock really are. By envisioning a miniature section of a reef, one can find many interesting and appealing models for an aquarium interior: a sand zone, a shadowy cave, a reef gorge, a rocky pillar, or a micro atoll—the opportunities are legion. In many cases, though, a combination of elements typical of different zones will prove to give the most appealing impression and also make it easier to fulfill the differing needs of a variety of animals.

Also keep in mind that tight piles of rock tend to

A freshly imported piece of Indo-Pacific live rock, the basis for creating natural looking and biologically stable reef aquariums. In small to medium-sized tanks, live rock may be the only building material needed, while in large systems a hidden framework may be used.

block good water circulation. The result is stagnant areas where debris in the form of fine detritus, the remains of food, animals, and dead algae can accumulate and rot in an oxygen-poor environment. Furthermore, a reefscape with varying heights and various holes and tunnels in the rockwork will provide excellent cover for an interesting population of fishes.

No matter what configuration you choose and what substrates you use, do remember that it is very important to let the material remain undisturbed once the aquascaping is completed to your satisfaction. Restlessly regrouping and altering the look of the tank for weeks or months on end will only harm the system. Live rock, for instance, needs a long time to adapt to its new setting and to start to "grow." Many tanks never achieve their full beauty and biological richness due to aquarist impatience.

LIVING CREATURES

When working with live rock, always remember it is a living material that should be kept wet, well oxygenated, and at correct temperatures (20-28°C/68-82°F) at all times to avoid damage to the fauna and flora living in and on it.

■ ■ ■

LIVE ROCK

LIVE ROCK HAS BECOME a crucially important material for the modern coral reef aquarium, but what is it really? The term itself sounds utterly contradictory: rock can hardly be living. A more precise label could perhaps have been simply porous sea rock, coral rock, or reef rock. However, we are stuck with the term live rock, and, fittingly, the most interesting and valuable quality of this material is not the geological part, but rather that it comes to us teeming with myriad forms of life both on and inside the rock.

Any porous rock that is put into a biologically rich

Harvesting coral rock from an exposed reef flat, these villagers engage in an age-old practice of collecting loose calcium carbonate material from the reef for small-scale construction projects. Coral reefs generate new stony material at a prodigious rate, and small-scale collection for the aquarium trade by local fisherfolk is generally considered a sustainable use of this resource.

marine habitat will be rapidly colonized by a variety of those animals and plants that live in the area. Place a piece of bare limestone in the shallows on or near a reef, and you will soon find representatives of many orders of life forms on and in the rock, ranging from an abundance of bacteria and unicellular organisms to algae, sponges, worms, bryozoans (moss animals), mollusks, crustaceans, and echinoderms—to mention just a few.

Coral reefs themselves are composed of highly porous rock, containing large and small fissures and holes as well as millions of microscopic pores. This rock is a renewable resource, constantly built by the activity of calcium-binding organisms, such as stony corals and calcareous algae, that lay down calcium carbonate at an enormous rate. For example, it has been calculated that the calcium carbonate production of stony corals in Australia's Great Barrier Reef alone is in the range of 50 million tons per year.

Live rock also has tremendous aesthetic appeal that few artificial materials can match. Even with a very lim-ited eye for such things, the aquarist can easily use live rock to build realistic formations that closely resemble a natural reef.

LIVE ROCK SOURCES

MOST OF THE LIVE ROCK that enters the aquarium market is eroded coralline rock collected in or around natural coral reefs. Much of it is rubble created by violent tropical storms. Loose-lying small boulders and pieces that easily can be picked without traces of any breakage are preferred. In some pieces it may be clearly visible that corals have built much of it, but many chunks are so old and so strongly eroded (semifossilized) that any coral structures are very difficult to recognize. Rock with heavy calcareous algae encrustation, where a large proportion of the rock actually is of algal origin, is in particular demand.

Live rock can also be farmed, usually by putting down fossilized coral rock or any other porous natural or artificial nontoxic material in designated inshore areas accessible to convenient harvesting. Commercial farming of live rock is presently carried out in Florida and in Fiji.

In our view, however, it is difficult to see any major reason for farming this renewable resource that is in such abundance in nature, unless its "farming" can be done to produce a better or more economical product. Careful management plans for the harvest of natural live rock seem a much more reasonable tool for ensuring a low-impact industry that can provide much higher income for local communities than the same rock resource gives when collected for building purposes, lime burning, and other traditional uses.

The first live rock to hit the aquarium market is believed to have originated from Indonesian coral reefs. In the late 1960s and early 1970s, the Jakarta aquarist Lee Chin Eng, remembered for his "natural method" of aquarium keeping, tried to introduce live rock, which he termed "reborn coral," into the markets of the United States and Europe. Several exporters of aquarium animals soon started to offer the material under various names.

We remember imports of live rock into Norway as early as 1975, but only as very small pieces at ridiculously high prices. Live rock found its first enthusiastic market in the Netherlands, where the material was incorporated as an important part of what came to be known as Dutch mini-reef systems. In the rest of Europe, and possibly also in America, a sudden increase in the interest for live rock came after the Interzoo 1980 pet trade show in Wiesbaden, Germany, where Indonesian exporters showed aquariums completely decorated with live rock.

WHY USE LIVE ROCK?

TODAY WE CAN HARDLY IMAGINE a marine aquarium without live rock, as it has become a reliable element in creating a natural-looking and biologically healthy aquarium environment. The principal reason for using live rock is to introduce the natural micro- and macrofauna that are associated with the rock into our captive systems. This infusion of beneficial bacteria and small reef organisms has a very positive impact on the stability and biologi-

Calcareous algae developing on live rock after months in a reef aquarium.

Delicate feather duster worms (*Bispira viola*) may arrive on live rock.

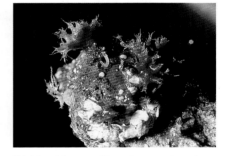
Bright red forams (*Homotrema rubrum*) commonly appear on live rock.

Harmless tiny sea stars (*Asterina* sp.) may come in on live rock and multiply greatly.

This torch coral (*Euphyllia glabrescens*) grew out of live rock in a Norwegian tank.

Snails from the genus *Stomatella*, center, are common hitchhikers on live rock.

An example of hidden PVC frames supporting a wall of live rock, held secure with plastic cable ties (view from rear of tank).

The same reef structure shown in the photo above, but from the aspect of the front of the tank. PVC frames allow excellent water circulation and economize on the cost of rock.

Live rock glued to the back glass of a large German aquarium using polyurethane foam. This technique works well, but the rock should be kept damp while the foam sets and dries.

cal diversity of a marine aquarium system.

The varied and diverse bacterial fauna that thrive on the enormous surface areas in the porous rock, combined with the other faunal elements and algae, make the rock a very effective and stable biological filter. On and inside the live rock, the complete breakdown and decomposition of organic wastes is accomplished with no moving parts: aerobic reactions take place on the surface of the rock, and more or less anaerobic reactions, including denitrification, occur in the interior. Thanks to the constant biological activities of different organisms in the rock, an aquarium with live rock becomes much more stable and diverse than one without.

Furthermore, one should not forget that many of the organisms associated with live rock are highly interesting in their own right. As can be seen in Table 3-1 (page 51) and in the photographs on page 55, many fascinating creatures can enter your aquarium on live rock. Besides being interesting, quite a few of these animals and algae will also serve as important food sources for many of your aquarium animals. Actually, we now know that many fishes and other animals require a tank with well-established live rock to survive. Animals that have specific needs for live rock fauna for food are noted in the Stocking Guide beginning on page 98.

HOW TO USE LIVE ROCK

IN ORDER TO ACHIEVE THE OPTIMAL biological effect of the live rock, we recommend that you use approximately 0.15 to 0.2 kg per liter (roughly 0.33 to 0.44 pounds per liter, or 1.5 to 2 lbs. per gallon) of live rock in a reef aquarium. A suitable amount of rock for a 100-liter (26-gal.) aquarium may thus be 15 to 20 kg (33 to 44 lbs.); in a 4,000 liter (1,040 gal.) tank you would need some 600 to 800 kg (1,320 to 1,760 lbs.). These are, of course, very approximate figures, and the exact amount will depend on the density of the rock and how you plan to arrange it. If the rock is very heavy you may need more to get the desired effect, aesthetic as well as biological. If it is very light, you may get by with less.

Your personal capability to build an attractive aquascape without simply building a compact pile of rock will also influence the amount of material needed. Before you start to aquascape, we recommend that you look to nature. Study underwater photos from coral reef biotopes, remember underwater scenes that you may have seen, and be creative. You do not have to copy oth-

Many grazing fishes, such as this large adult Blueface Angelfish (*Pomacanthus xanthometopon*), show higher survival rates and better acclimation to captivity in aquariums with well-establish live rock aquascaping that provides both cover and live prey items. On the other hand, a large grazer such as this can decimate desirable plant and invertebrate life in a typical reef aquarium.

ers. See Chapter 4 for aquarium biotope suggestions.

Be forewarned: freshly imported live rock will have an adverse effect on the stability of an aquarium and should never be added to an established tank stocked with animals. In the first few weeks, new rock goes through a period of "die off" or "curing," in which some organisms on and in the rock will perish and decay, creating ammonia and considerable amounts of debris.

When a reef aquarium is first set up, this is of little importance, as the maturation process of the live rock coincides with the overall break-in period of the aquarium. You should expect to get a temporary rise in organic load on the aquarium system, which may be small or significant—depending on how well cured the rock was before it went into your aquarium.

Many dealers take pride in selling "cured" live rock, but be prepared to pay more for higher quality and for having someone else deal with the strong odor of curing

rock. We actually prefer to cure our own rock in the display tank, allowing the high nutrient levels to cultivate the development of interesting life from the rock.

In any case, as with all new aquarium setups, you should expect initial organic pollution leading to a bloom in algae growth. Once again, we caution you to let the aquarium stabilize before you introduce any animals. (The ammonia and nitrite levels during live rock curing can easily kill many reef fishes and invertebrates.) Once the maturation of the rock has passed the most-active stages, you will see that various algae, including the desirable calcareous red or purple algae, start to spread and that more and more life forms appear, as if by magic, from the rock. Bear in mind, however, that the successive growth of algae from live rock can be a long and diverse process. The beloved red calcareous algae do not normally dominate until after 12 to 18 months, and are highly sensitive to bright light.

A rocky outcropping on a white sand lagoon bottom attracts a variety of fishes and other life and might serve as model for a creative aquascaper. Rather than build the usual high wall, the aquarist might construct an underwater island surrounded by sand or rubble.

THE LIVE-ROCK-ONLY AQUARIUM

MANY AQUARISTS ARE FAMILIAR with the fish-only tank, and the notion of a special aquarium setup for a particularly interesting species or group of species, like sea anemones with their symbionts, is not at all unfamiliar. We have another personal favorite that deserves mention: the live-rock-only aquarium.

The recipe is simple: set up a small aquarium—perhaps a mere 50 to 60 liters (13 to 16 gal.)—with nothing but high-quality live rock. Equip it with an inexpensive filter and heater, and let it stand in peace and quiet. Observe the interesting organisms that appear from the rock. In such a small aquarium, where getting a close look is no problem, you will have the ideal opportunity to study micro life forms that very few people ever see.

Some of the organisms that are known to have appeared from live rock are very seldom seen in the wild, including some that were new to science. Watch for all the marvelous sponges, hydroids, flatworms, bristleworms, peanut worms, sea spiders, barnacles, crabs, chitons, snails, mussels, moss animals, entoprocts, sea stars, brittle stars, and sea squirts —to name just a few.

HANDLING & TAMING LIVE ROCK

ONCE A QUANTITY OF LIVE ROCK has been brought home, time is limited. As quickly as possible, live rock must be placed in a tank or container of well-oxygenated, clean seawater. If it is left to dry out, or exposed to heat or cold, much of the valuable macro and micro life will be damaged and eventually die.

If you can, hand select rock of the sizes, shapes, and quality that will make it possible to build the decor you desire. Study the pieces one by one to get a rough idea of what building blocks you have at your disposal. (Fewer, larger pieces can be easier to assemble into a realistic reef than a greater number of small chunks.) If a cave or ledge is planned, for example, you may want to pick one or more broad, flat pieces to make construction easier.

Colonies of algae, sponges, or other organisms that look pure white, unhealthy, dead, or dying should be picked off or brushed away, but as many organisms as possible should be kept and protected as far as possible. It is these "stowaways" that make live rock such an incredibly valuable decorating material. Rumors among aquarists of terribly dangerous and voracious creatures entering the aquarium via live rock are frequently exaggerated. True, the odd coral- or fish-eating carnivore, such as some larger worms, a few crab species, or mantis shrimps, have been known to come in with rock. However, the most dangerous animals usually accompany their prey into the aquarium. If you are afraid of animals that will eat or damage your corals, it is much more important to scrutinize every new coral colony that is introduced into the tank.

There is a clear tendency among reef aquarium enthusiasts to be far too afraid of "harmful animals." Most animals introduced with live rock are relatively harmless and highly interesting from a biological point of view.

In most cases we recommend that live rock alone be used as the principal material for building the interior effects in a reef aquarium. This is in particular true for aquariums with corals and other sedentary invertebrates. Live rock may be combined with other materials to save costs, but the best results are often achieved when live rock only is used. To cut down on the amount of rock that must be purchased, and to create open space within the reefscape, we like to attach rock to a framework of acrylic or PVC tubing (see photos, page 56). Many methods can be used to hide the inert plastic supports under and behind the rock. This does take time and some acquired skills, and you may choose simply to build with rock itself.

Be sure that the reefscape is totally stable. Rock slides and collapses can easily kill prized specimens or even break the tank. Rock can be anchored in place whenever necessary with two-part underwater epoxy cement (which becomes inert after mixing and hardening), heavy monofilament fishing line, or long plastic cable ties sold in the electrical department of most hardware stores (black ties are less conspicuous). Never use metal screws or fasteners in the aquarium. (Even stainless steel will often corrode over time.)

Live rocks can easily be trimmed to fit into the aquascape by the use of a masonry saw, a hammer, and a chisel. (Be sure to wear eye-protective goggles when doing this work.) A standard percussion drill can be used to bore holes for cable ties or for prefabricating holes into which coral colonies can be secured later on.

DRY ROCK & ARTIFICIAL MATERIALS

IN SOME INSTANCES, COST CONSIDERATIONS or the need for a sterile environment may force an aquarist into using nonliving materials to build an aquascape. In a reef tank we generally recommend against it, because of the superior qualities of live rock, but sometimes there are few options but to use substitutes.

The most suitable rock material in such cases is usually some type of porous limestone, such as fossilized reef rock that is mined in many places in the world. Although normally less porous than natural live rock, in due course it can harbor much of the same fauna and flora if it is implanted with select pieces of good live rock. Once calcareous algae have covered the rock surface, such limestone structures look remarkably similar to "the real thing."

Very impressive constructions can be made from fully artificial materials, such as Styrofoam or polyurethane foam. Prefabricated decorations or decoration elements are available from many manufacturers, and the best of them look quite nice. Most artificial materials have one considerable disadvantage, though: they lack the porous surface that is important as a settlement medium for the bacteria and microorganisms that aid in maintaining good water quality. If you must use artificial decorations, other biological filter media may have to be employed somewhere in the system.

CORAL SKELETONS & CORAL CASTS

FROM MOST MODERN AQUARISTS' point of view, the days of coral skeletons as aquarium decorations are long gone. That doesn't imply that you cannot use them any

---

SUBSTITUTE BED

Sessile invertebrates—such as tube anemones and sea pens—that need a particularly thick bed of anchoring substrate can be satisfied with a section of suitably sized, sand-filled acrylic pipe. This avoids having to establish a deep overall substrate in the aquarium.

■ ■ ■

Aquarists can closely observe the fascinating commensal relationship between shrimp or prawn gobies (*Amblyeleotris* spp.) and almost-blind alpheid shrimps that form a lasting bond and share a burrow. They must have a deep bed of fine sand and bits of coral rubble.

more, but rather that in most cases you have better and more natural-looking alternatives. Even a basic fish-only tank will be a more stable system with live rock forming at least part of the decor. Hardy live corals, such as mushroom corals (*Sarcophyton* spp.) or finger leather corals (*Sinularia* spp.) can also grace such systems with wonderful effect, while being relatively immune to damage by fishes.

Occasionally, one may want to use dead or artificial decorations only, in order to facilitate chemical medication or a heavy organic water load through excessive feeding of large carnivorous fishes, such as sharks and rays.

Not all that long ago, coral skeletons, the dead and bleached remains of once flourishing corals, were the single most important decoration used in marine aquariums. As recently as 15 or 20 years ago, the aquarium literature was full of recommendations on how to treat and use skeletons. Today we prefer to recommend that the aquarist who wants nonliving coral shapes in his or her aquarium use the commercial casts of corals that are readily

available in hard and soft plastic materials. These artificial corals are lighter, have brighter colors, and a smoother surface that is less harmful to the fish as well as much easier to clean than the porous skeletons of dead corals.

BOTTOM SUBSTRATE

ONE FREQUENTLY DEBATED ASPECT of reef aquarium decoration and husbandry is whether or not to use a bottom layer of sand or other particulate matter. Opinions vary from no bottom substrate at all to the use of thick, layered sand and gravel bottoms. These arguments seem endless, and they can confuse many aquarists.

One true distinctive feature of a coral reef is the coral rock formations that are dominant over large areas. Thus, unless you actually want to keep animals that are directly dependent upon sand zones, there is no obvious direct need to include sand or gravel in an aquarium interior. On the other hand, the rock formations of a natural coral reef are also interspersed with both small and large sandy patches or even expansive sand flats. (In principle, you could make a "reef aquarium" that was nothing but a sandy, flat bottom.) Unless you specifically want to reproduce a portion of a reef where sand would be fully out of place, patches of sand are aesthetically interesting and create focal points that emphasize the rest of the interior. White substrate also serves to reflect light, beneficial to photosynthetic organisms and brightening the overall appearance of the tank.

Equipped with chemosensory barbels that are thrust into sand or holes to detect prey, goatfishes are active foragers that need a large expanse of soft sand. Note smaller wrasses gathering to snatch prey exposed by this species, *Parupeneus macronema*.

BIOCHEMICAL PROS & CONS

AMONG THE NATURAL PROCESSES going on in a particulate bottom layer is the biological decomposition of organic compounds. Much as in live rock, sand can harbor macro- and microorganisms and bacteria that take an active part in water purification processes. Under aerobic (oxygen-rich) conditions, nitrification—the oxygenation of nitrogenous compounds into nitrate—takes place. Where oxygen is lacking, as in very thick sand layers, the anaerobic process of denitrification happens. In theory, the combined nitrification and denitrification in a sand bed could function as a superior biological filter, eliminating all nitrate produced in an aquarium.

In contrast to the biological processes in live rock, sand does, however, have a couple of important drawbacks that make this breakdown of organic wastes less predictable:

• Sand is unstable and movable. In other words, large organisms can easily shift the bottom substrate around, thereby mixing aerobic and anaerobic layers and making it difficult to maintain stable biological decomposition processes.

• Sand is easily clogged, foremost by detritus. In stagnant sand beds, sulfide produced by anaerobic bacteria easily accumulates. In rare cases, this may pose a poisoning risk for the aquarium organisms, but even long before that it will seriously inhibit nitrification.

Neither of these possibilities is necessarily a reason to stop most of us from using a sand bottom. Thin layers of sand—up to 3 to 5 cm (1 to 2 in.) thick can be kept sufficiently stirred and oxygenated by water movement alone. Coarse gravel can be used safely in thicker levels than fine sand. If you keep animals that dig much into the substrate, such as sand-sifting fishes, burrowing crustaceans, or sea cucumbers, the bottom layer may be two to three times as thick without fear of having anaerobic patches develop.

Some authors advocate even thicker beds of substrate. A reverse-flow undergravel filter (which pumps water up through the bed of substrate) can work, or some adaptation of the famous Jaubert "plenum" system can be adapted. Others advocate the use of deep sand beds that function with heavy populations of interstitial fauna (worms, crustaceans, and other detritivores) that keep the bed "working." (See Further Reading, page 231.)

By using so-called "live sand"—coral sand that is biologically active thanks to an array of different bacteria and micro- and macroorganisms that live in it—the stability of the biological processes in the sand bed is enhanced. As we know from live rock, the multitude of organisms in live sand work to create more stable conditions than nearly sterile sand that has to be colonized by various organisms over time. If you are starting with dry coral sand, it is a good idea to crush some live rock into small pieces (less than 2 cm) and mix these into the gravel, once the sand bed has been created in the filled aquarium. This will inoculate the substrate with many

While some hobbyists prefer bare-bottomed tanks, a layer of white coral sand offers a more authentic look and definite biological advantages, as in this lovely home system owned by Raul Romero and designed by Jeff Turner of Reef Aquaria Design in Parkland, FL.

valuable micro- and macroorganisms.

Are the biological processes of a sand substrate really necessary to establish a functioning aquarium environment? If the aquarium is decorated with live rock and/or equipped with a suitably efficient biological filter, a bottom substrate is not necessary from a technical viewpoint. Aesthetics are in the eye of the beholder, while the imperative to provide certain animals with a soft substrate naturally depends on whether or not you intend to keep these creatures.

ANIMALS THAT NEED A BOTTOM SUBSTRATE

Sand zones associated with coral reefs are the natural habitat of a large number of animal species that are commonly imported for sale in aquarium shops. As noted earlier, several coral species—such as elegance coral (*Catadaphyllia jardinei*)—that rarely occur in the wild other than on sand or mud flats, and frequently among seagrasses, are popular among aquarists.

Similarly there are quite a number of anemone species that thrive on sand, such as the very popular giant carpet anemone (*Stichodactyla gigantea*) and the appropriately named sand anemones of the genus *Phymanthus*. All of these have a number of natural symbionts, in particular beautiful shrimp and crab species, but also fishes like the anemonefishes of the genus *Amphiprion*.

However, it is the animals that actively dig into the bottom substrate for protection or shelter, or that sift through the sediments in search of food, that are particularly dependent on a layer of soft sand in the aquarium. Tube anemones (*Cerianthus* spp. and relatives) and sea pens (*Cavernularia* spp. and relatives) are typical examples of animals that need a very deep substrate in which to bury their "feet." Without a proper, thick bottom layer of sand or very fine gravel, such animals will topple over from lack of support. If, for some reason, it is difficult to achieve an overall thick bottom in a particular aquarium, these animals can be given support by placing them in sections of acrylic pipe filled with sand.

One group of animals that has become increasingly common in the aquarium trade over the years is the genus *Alpheus*, which includes the nearly blind pistol shrimps, or snapping shrimps. These small, lobsterlike crustaceans dig burrows and channels in sand where they normally live commensally with certain gobies, the so-called prawn gobies, partner gobies, or watchman gobies, primarily in the genera *Amblyeleotris* and *Cryptocentrus*. Neither the shrimps nor their goby partners will do well in the aquarium unless they have a substrate of a depth corresponding to the length of the larger partner (at least some 6 to 8 cm [2.3 to 3.1 in.]). The aquarist who purchases these fishes and shrimps has an obligation to provide the animals with the substrate they need, but he or she will be amply repaid by the opportunity to observe one of the most fascinating partnerships on the reef.

SAND-STIRRING SPECIES

THE BEST WAY TO AVOID the problems of sand beds becoming clogged with debris is by introducing animals that revel in stirring up these sediments. For instance, some gobies—such as the *Valenciennea* species —do an excellent job of churning the bottom substrate. Practically no grain of sand is left unturned as they search for tiny animals that can be unearthed from the substrate and eaten. Similarly, goatfishes or mullets (e.g., *Parupeneus* spp.) actively grovel in the bottom, whirling up detritus along with the tiny invertebrates that they eat. Goatfishes are not easy to keep well-fed, however, and all but the most experienced aquarists should avoid them. Most digging and burrowing fishes and invertebrates will have a similar positive effect where thick bottom substrates are used.

Many serpent stars are excellent detritus feeders that also aid in turning over bottom sediments. As an added benefit, many species of serpent stars are very beautiful. We may see them only fleetingly, as they tend to hide during the day, but they do perform an important service. Not only is detritus moved about, but any dead animals that otherwise would be likely to foul the water are also sure to be sought out and eaten by these scavenging in-

vertebrates that patrol hidden recesses of the aquascape.

Other echinoderms also act as detritus feeders, notably several of the sea cucumbers that are available to aquarium keepers. In the reef you may find large numbers of detrivorous sea cucumbers feeding on sandy substrates or among rocks and rubble. They move around both on and in the sand and inside porous rocks. Most sea cucumbers, while not the most beautiful creatures, also do a very good job in the aquarium, feeding on and stirring up detritus. Several of the *Holothuria* spp. are both hardy, efficient, and readily available in the trade. Most of the detritus-eating sea cucumbers seem to do reasonably well in captivity provided they are given an aquarium with a diverse fauna of microscopic detritus-dwelling organisms on which they can feed.

Some expert marine aquarists absolutely reject the idea of keeping sea cucumbers, which can cause major poisoning events that kill fishes and other invertebrates. If threatened, or injured by a mechanical device, such as a water pump, a sea cucumber can evert parts of its digestive system and release potent toxins that can wipe out a whole tankful of livestock.

LIVING AQUASCAPES

AS YOU BUILD a miniature reef, it is easy to forget that the live animals you introduce may eventually grow to impressive sizes. In particular, the large sedentary animals, such as corals and anemones, will be just as important for the appearance of the aquarium interior as the rocky foundation on which they grow.

Before filling the aquarium with live rock and sand, try to picture how the grown coral colonies will appear in a year or two. Many species grow rapidly and will need enough space in which to expand. Corals that are destined to grow rampantly or to get very large usually look better in the back half of the tank, rather than in the foreground, where they will block your view. This is an exercise that many reef biologists could never have envisioned a few years ago—growing a captive coral reef.

Enjoy the thrill of this enterprise, use your imagination, and hope that the animals you place in the reef will behave and grow the way you expect them to. ✿

DIGGER BENEFITS

If your aquarium has a thick bottom substrate, always consider adding some digging fishes and invertebrates to facilitate turnover of the sediments. This will help prevent pockets of decay or anaerobic activity that can cause difficulties.

■ ■ ■

CHAPTER 4

BIOTOPES

Modeling Aquariums on Ecological Niches on and Around the Reef

W HEN CORAL REEF AQUARISTS ARRIVE at a tropical beach or a coral cay for the first time, they typically hurry down to the water in order to get a closer look at corals in their natural environment. But wait . . . all that appears is some sandy bottom, some swaying algae, and seagrasses. A little farther down the shore, huge mangrove trees are growing out of a muddy substrate. Where are the corals? There are a few mudskippers, but nothing that looks like a pristine reef environment. If anything, this scene is dirty and it smells like a swamp.

Fear not. You are standing on the brink of a most interesting habitat, and the reef with its beautiful corals lies just a short distance beyond the shore. Tomorrow you can don your mask and start looking at the reef. For now, take some time to explore some fascinating shallow-wa-

Small mangrove trees can be grown in open-topped aquariums, **left**. Dense mangrove growth at the end of a Cuban beach, **above**, with small seedlings sprouting in the foreground.

ter zones that more marine aquarists deserve to know about and appreciate. Known as intertidal or littoral zones, these areas are not only the source of much of the livestock that graces our home aquariums, they are biologically rich and full of interesting plants and animals.

THE BEACH ZONE

LIFE IN THE BEACH ZONE IS TOUGH. Low tides regularly leave the habitat exposed and dry, causing great fluctuations in temperature. During low tide, small tidepools can form in which the temperature and salinity can reach extremely high levels. Organisms living in this zone must be adapted to the variable conditions in order to survive here. Some animals and plants are almost perfectly suited to this habitat, while others are washed inshore and will be fortunate to escape with their lives. On the other hand, the innermost zones of a reef offer protection from large predators living on the reef edge and reef slope.

On oceanic islets, the beach zone often consists of

A typical mangrove-covered shoreline in Fiji sports a thick fringe of aerial roots curving down into the soft substrate. Many young fishes and invertebrates use this biotope as a nursery, growing in a habitat that effectively keeps large, roving predators away.

clean coral sand and hard rock formations known as "beach rock." Along the shores of continents and inshore islands, the beach zone often consists of rather muddy sand covered with seagrasses and algae. Mangrove trees, perhaps one of the common *Rhizophora* spp., grow on the frontier between the land and the sea, stretching their roots gracefully into the ocean.

These plants have evolved a range of adaptations for living their life between the tides. The arching aerial roots can be covered with invertebrates such as sponges, tiny corals and anemones, bryozoans, and sea squirts, together forming a unique marine community. The mangroves drop their seeds into the sea, where they drift to other locations, linking the littoral habitat to the coral reef. On the beach after storms we

UNUSUAL ZONES

Near-reef zones—lagoons, seagrass beds, mangrove swamps, tidepools—contain a number of interesting organisms that can be kept in captivity. Interesting, unconventional biotope aquariums can be modeled on these zones.

■ ■ ■

may find hundreds of seeds washed ashore, reminding us of how many of the plants of the tropical shores can migrate long distances to new shores and cays and start growing here.

On and within the muddy bottom, life flourishes, and soldier crabs, fiddler crabs, and mudskippers can be found by the hundreds. A few centimeters into the muddy substrate many mussels and worms are hiding. Dig a couple of buckets of sand and wash it through a fine mesh with plenty of seawater and you will reveal a wealth of organisms buried in the substrate. Most of these are snails—in some areas the bottom of the sublittoral zone can be almost covered with snails. Most of them are rather small, but occasionally bigger species, such as the poisonous cone shells (*Conus* spp.), are seen. Other mollusks, such as the jackknife clams and the tellin clams, also belong to the buried infauna. Both snails and mussels living in the substrate have large siphons that are stretched to the surface to sustain vital gaseous exchange.

Seagrasses are not algae, but flowering plants that often spread across extensive areas of sandy reef flat, binding particles of sand together with a creeping network of underground stems (rhizomes). Seagrass growth is essential in preventing erosion to nearby shorelines. *Syringodium, Halodule, Halophila, Thalassodendron, Cymodocea, Zostera,* and *Thalassia* are well-established genera of seagrasses, most of which are only found on muddy or sandy substrates, except for *Thalassodendron* spp., which can grow among corals and on hard bottoms.

In the seagrass beds we find a number of animals, some of which are perfectly camouflaged and well adapted to this environment. The substrate houses burying worms, brittlestars, starfishes, sea urchins, and conch shells. The knobbly starfish *Protoreaster nodosus* is sometimes very abundant in this zone in the Indo-Pacific. Many of the sea urchins found in seagrass meadows attach pieces of rocks, algae, and seagrass remains to their spines and become almost invisible. The Indo-Pacific giant carpet anemone (*Stichodactyla gigantea*) is common in this habitat, and we have occasionally even found the strange anemone *Phyllodiscus semoni*, which has a powerful sting and the remarkable habit of mimicking other animals in seagrass meadows. The anemones attract many symbiotic animals such as fishes, crabs, and shrimps that live within the protective cover created by their stinging tentacles.

The stony corals *Catalaphyllia jardinei* and *Montipora digitata* prefer inshore habitats and are frequently found among seagrasses. Attached to the blades of the seagrasses are various species of algae, tiny anemones and sea squirts, eggs of various mollusks, and juvenile sea horses. Many juvenile reef fishes also seek protection among the seagrass plants. Sea turtles love to feed in these seagrass meadows. All in all the seagrass beds are a rich habitat with many interesting organisms and a vital part of the greater coral reef ecosystem.

A SEAGRASS AQUARIUM

CAN WE CREATE A MANGROVE OR SEAGRASS community in an aquarium? The answer is an emphatic "Yes," but it is unfortunate that so few aquarists model

Small red mangrove crabs (*Sesarma* sp.) could be used to stock an unusual biotope system featuring inshore plants and animals.

Underwater view of a mangrove thicket that may harbor small fishes, sponges, upside-down jellyfishes, and other animals.

their tanks on anything other than "a slice of the reef."

In the common coral reef aquarium, a variety of colorful corals are kept with fishes, crustaceans, mollusks, and other invertebrates. It may come as surprise to learn that a seagrass aquarium can be just as colorful and diverse. The seagrass aquarium is definitely a class apart from a typical coral aquarium, but biologically just as interesting. In such a biotope, one has the opportunity to combine a set of organisms that can hardly be kept in a conventional coral reef setup. Here we have the possibility of observing the biology of a very special habitat, one from the shallow fringes of the coral reef community, and one we can even expand to be a most fascinating and unusual marine terrarium.

A seagrass or beach-zone aquarium can very well have a part of the terrain above water. Here we plant one

A seagrass aquarium at the Waikiki Aquarium makes an authentic display for a beautiful Elegance Coral (*Catalaphyllia jardinei*) that typically grows with its stony skeleton buried in soft bottoms where it can expand without competition from other corals.

possible, the aquarium should be located so that it can be viewed from all four sides. We use a deep bed of substrate, with a skimmer and a sump placed below the tank. If we wish to replicate tidal fluctuations in the aquarium (see drawing, page 45), the sump must be large enough to house the "tidal water."

With such a seagrass aquarium, we break the conventional rules and build a very different biotope that not only provides surprises to us as aquarists, but also proves irresistible to friends and visitors—you will have to use all your skill to keep the visitors' hands out of the water!

FANTASY SYSTEM: A REEF GORGE AQUARIUM

We dive in the Vadoo Channel between the North and the South Male Atoll in the Maldives, Indian Ocean. The current is very strong and we drift briskly along steep reef walls covered with sponges, sea fans, *Dendronephthya* soft corals, and orange cup corals by the thousands. We pass reef chasms and glide under rocky overhangs. Large schools of Lyretail Anthias (*Pseudanthias squamipinnis*) feed on plankton surrounding us in the strong current.

Like other diving aquarists, we have come back from such a trip dreaming about re-creating this sort of scene in a home aquarium. Imagine that you are lucky enough to have a large room available in the basement. This is almost essential, as you need to build a very large tank that must rest on the concrete basement floor, as it will weigh tons. You order a custom tank or build one from fiberglass, making it at least 100 cm long x 150 cm wide x 100 cm high (39 x 59 x 39 in.) with a volume of 1,500 liters (390 gal.). You use a thick front glass and—if the tank is made of fiberglass—mount a viewing window on the backside, as you want to look through the aquarium. You can walk around the tank, which is necessary in order to regularly clean the rear viewing pane. Behind this rear glass you mount a curved blue Plexiglas plate that will give the impression of looking into infinity.

or two mangrove trees, starting from easily available seedpods, and keep snails and other organisms naturally associated with mangroves. A group of fiddler crabs, for example, can be kept on the "shore." The substrate can gradually slope down beneath the waterline. Here we plant seagrasses and introduce a host sea anemone from the genus *Stichodactyla* and tiny specimens of anemonefishes (clownfishes) and a few anemone crabs. We partially bury a couple of live rocks in the sandy bottom and let the life from them develop over time. Several hermit crabs are introduced to control filamentous algae. Gradually we add more animals, such as tubeworms and snails. The file clams, *Limaria* spp., should be perfect for this habitat, giving you a chance to see these delicate animals, which are notorious for simply disappearing in typical reef tanks. Many different fishes would be appropriate for this sort of system, from solitary juvenile angelfishes to a group of beautiful Green Wrasses (*Halichoeres chloropterus*) that have evolved a color pattern to blend perfectly with seagrasses.

Ideally, a seagrass aquarium should be long, relatively shallow, and placed to be viewed partly from above. If

To aquascape the tank, you start by making two frames of PVC tubing, one on each side of the tank, on which to mount live rock. These will only be viewed from the front and will appear to be two reef walls rising from the bottom to the surface. Hidden within them is open space and a lot of room and refuge for fishes.

You let two 250-watt metal halide lamps illuminate the left side of the scene, while blue fluorescent light tubes mixed with a couple of daylight tubes illuminate the right side.

The bottom is filled with coarse coral gravel mixed with crushed live rock. A couple of large boulders lie on the bottom at the far back.

Two large skimmers connected to an external sump are in operation from day one, and huge pumps mounted outside the tank provide a very powerful alternating water flow. A large calcium reactor is coupled to a level switch and to the freshwater supply and refills the 25 liters (7 gal.) of water that evaporate daily. A powerful dehumidifier removes humid air from the basement.

A natural model for an Indo-Pacific reef gorge biotope would create a dramatic chasm of swimming space between two rocky walls. A school of Lyretail Anthias would be good subjects for the deep gorge, along with various other fishes and invertebrates.

The aquarium is filled with artificial seawater, all power and light systems started, and the aquarium is allowed to stabilize for 3 months with only the live rock and perhaps some herbivores. During this time, you carefully observe and log what happens in the tank as you plan how to stock this impressive biotope.

The first animals you add are as many as 50 brittle stars of several species. They thrive under the live rocks and appear mostly during the night. They are extremely useful detritus feeders that patrol the bottom for food remains and other organic waste products. You also add a few gobies and pistol shrimps, which immediately burrow into the sand and establish their small territories.

You select branching soft corals from the genus *Sinularia* as the major corals for your aquarium. You anchor them to the rocks in the upper half of the aquascape, in order to make them grow into the water column. Over time this creates an impressive decorative effect. You se-

lect various species of star polyps (e.g., *Briareum* spp.) to fill the spaces between the larger soft corals. These soon spread to cover much of the upper part of the rockscape, where the light is relatively strong.

A few cuttings of staghorn corals (*Acropora* spp.) establish themselves nicely, and after a year or two, you really have an attractive population of branching stony corals growing toward the surface. A couple of bubble corals (*Plerogyra sinuosa*) as well as some colonies of crystal coral (*Galaxea fascicularis*) are placed scattered in the lower reef wall (anchored with underwater epoxy cement or plastic screws). Your favorite coral in this section is the bullseye coral (*Caulastrea furcata*), which over time forms beautiful colonies and is easily spread to neighboring spots by small cuttings. They do very well here and expand greatly in the moderate light. On the bottom you place a few mushroom corals (*Fungia* spp.) and a couple of red button corals (*Cynarina lacrymalis*).

One of the reasons that your aquarium does so well is the system you have created to pump live plankton in the form of mysid and brine shrimps into the tank throughout the day. This is necessary as you keep a large

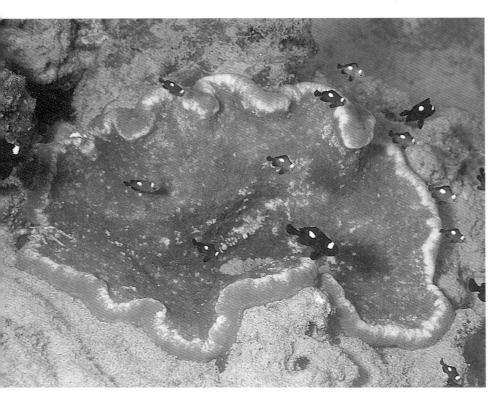

A large Pizza Anemone (*Cryptodendrum adhaesivum*) can make for an unusual centerpiece in a simple biotope setup. Various symbionts of the anemone complete the picture, including a group of juvenile Threespot Dascyllus (*Dascyllus trimaculatus*).

A PIZZA ANEMONE AQUARIUM

ON A HOLIDAY TRIP to Phuket, Southern Thailand, you start the day with a snorkel and set of fins, swimming in the warm water off Yachtclub Beach where your hotel is situated. This is certainly not a reef area, but nevertheless there are several reef organisms to be found. A Pizza Anemone (*Cryptodendrum adhaesivum*) with its many symbiotic animals is especially impressive.

This very sticky anemone is anchored in between coral boulders that are lying in sand and mud. Among its short tentacles are Spotted Porcelain Crabs (*Neopetrolisthes ohshimai*), a pair of White-patched Anemone Shrimp (*Periclimenes brevicarpalis*). A cluster of Sexy Shrimps (*Thor amboinensis*) stay just outside the rim of the anemone's disc. Several juvenile Threespot Dascyllus (*Dascyllus trimaculatus*) never stray far from their protective anemone host.

As you enjoy a spicy Thai meal that evening, you begin a plan for creating a replica of the Pizza Anemone scene in an aquarium. Once home again, you find an old tank that is not too large—only about 150 liters (39 gal.), but big enough for this purpose. You provide a pump for water movement inside the tank. A small hang-on protein skimmer mounted at the back corner of the aquarium is the major filtration. The illumination consists of three daylight tubes and one blue-actinic light. Calcium-enriched water (Kalkwasser) is used to refill water that evaporates, and you take great care to regularly check the pH and the salinity, as you know that anemones are sensitive to changing salinity.

You arrange two large pieces of fresh live rock to form a small crevice in which to place a colorful Pizza Anemone. The rocks reach nearly to the surface of the tank. You also crush some live rock and spread it around the bottom. Next comes a deep bed of coarse coral gravel mixed with roughly one-third fine coral sand. Along the sides and back of the small aquarium you plant some *Caulerpa* to provide beautiful curtains of macroalgae.

school of Lyretail Anthias (*Pseudanthias squamipinnis*) that absolutely thrive on frequent feedings of live food. A pair of Flame Angels (*Centropyge loriculus*) and a pair of Comets (*Calloplesiops altivelis*) are highlights of the relatively large population of fish in your gorge aquarium. Two pairs of Banded Coral Shrimps (*Stenopus hispidus*) and a Painted Spiny Lobster (*Panulirus versicolor*) are favorites of your visitors. The spiny lobster loves to hide in a hole in the reef wall with its long, white antennae projecting into the water column, and the first thing visitors always ask is: "What on Earth are those white things!?"

Your reef gorge aquarium continues to develop in an extraordinary display and all your efforts pay off the day you discover that several species of sponges are about to cover the surface of the live rocks where the light is weak. Countless amphipods and other microfauna populate the substrate. The cleaner shrimps are constantly producing eggs and even several of the fish species are exhibiting spawning behaviors. Now, after more than 3 years in operation, the aquarium has really settled down. It is its own miniature reef.

(You are prepared to prune the *Caulerpa* occasionally to prevent it from overgrowing the tank.) You add some brittle stars and several algae-grazing hermit crabs and let the setup run for 3 to 4 months. It is interesting to note the growth of algae and the appearance of unexpected organisms emerging from the live rock during this period of time.

Reflecting the scene back in Thailand, you come up with a stocking plan:

1	Pizza Anemone (perhaps the rare green color form)
1	pair of White-patched Anemone Shrimps
4	Porcelain Crabs
10	Sexy Shrimps
5-8	juvenile Threespot Dascyllus

The Threespot Dascyllus will only stay in the anemone as long as they are young, and you realize that you may want to swap them for new juveniles as they grow to adult sizes. A pair or trio of clownfishes would be an alternative, the natural choice being Clark's Anemonefish (*Amphiprion clarkii*)—most other clownfishes avoid this anemone. Unlike the damsels, the Clark's Anemonefish will form a pair or social unit of several individuals and become a permanent part of the biotope.

In Thailand, you noticed that several gobies with their pistol shrimp partners lived in holes in the sand not far from the anemone, and you eventually add two pairs of shrimp gobies (*Stonogobiops* spp.) and their commensal shrimps (*Alpheus* spp.). They will cautiously stay away from the anemone, but definitely make an interesting set of organisms in a unique and very special reef aquarium.

A RUBBLE ZONE AQUARIUM

BETWEEN THE REEF FLAT AND THE BEACH are various microhabitats that creative aquarists can rather easily replicate. This is a shallow area where many common aquarium animals are found, as well as the zone where live rock is often collected from the abundant accumulation of dead coral rubble. Over a bed of coral sand you find a varied cover of rubble, coral fragments large and small, and coral rock boulders in various shapes and sizes. The smaller, loose rocks are often turned over and tossed about by waves and currents, effectively preventing growth of larger invertebrates. Larger rocks or outcroppings may be very stable, allowing the growth of coral as well as algae. The accompanying image in just such a zone was taken on Agincourt Reef, part of the Great Barrier Reef, and shows a boulder approximately 1.5 x 1 meter (5 ft. x 3 ft.). It harbors a diverse gathering of flora and fauna—we counted no less than 12 different species of stony corals and 9 species of soft corals on this single rock.

The typical "everybody does it" way of decorating a reef aquarium has always been to pile small rocks up into a more or less solid wall. Although this certainly can give some interesting effects, it gets rather predictable seeing so many aquariums that follow the same scheme. Why not take a lesson from an actual reef, with a large boulder as the focal point, surrounded by smaller rocks, rubble, and sand?

Obviously, you want to work on a reduced scale that fits into an aquarium of some 400 liters (104 gal.); approximately 120 x 60 x 55 cm (47 x 23 x 21 in.). Perhaps you even start with a custom-made tank with a blue, curved back wall, which will enhance the illusion of a reef stretching endlessly into the background. The main structure of the aquascape is the boulder that you build from live rock on a framework of PVC tubing to allow for good water circulation. The backside of the boulder—invisible from the viewing side—is left open for easy access and cleaning. The boulder is given an irregular shape, approximately 60 cm (23 in.) long, and placed off center, some 20 cm (8 in.) from the left side and 40 cm (16 in.) from the right. The width of the boulder becomes about 35 cm (14 in.) at the widest so that room is left for 15 cm (6 in.) clearance to the front glass and 10 cm (4 in.) to the back wall. The height varies from a few cm (1-2 in.) in the lowest areas in front up to approximately 40 cm (16 in.) at the peak, leaving just a 15 cm (6 in.) water column above it.

Once the boulder has been constructed, you place some smaller rocks around it, before you fill in the bottom with a mixture of coral sand, coral gravel, live rock fragments, and other small rubble. You want to keep several digging animals in this aquarium, and the mixture of different sizes of substrate makes it possible for the animals to create stable burrows even with a fairly thin substrate. You fill the substrate up to a maximum of 5 to 6 cm (2 to 2.3 in.), to avoid problems with decomposition in the bottom layers.

This reef zone is very strongly illuminated in nature, and the stony corals and other species you will want

An irregular boulder surrounded by sand and coral rubble harbors a diverse assemblage of stony and soft corals and could easily be replicated by a creative aquarist. This system calls for simple aquascaping but very strong illumination and excellent water motion.

large boulder, but a few dispersed colonies are also attached to smaller rocks in the tank.

Another interesting invertebrate in this tank is the photosynthetic Ear Sponge (*Collospongia auris*) which you attach to a lower portion of the boulder. Various echinoderms are typical inhabitants of the rubble zone, so you include 5 to 6 sea cucumbers and 15 to 20 brittle and serpent stars. A large group of herbivorous hermit crabs and some snails will help keep the algae under control as well as making the aquarium interesting. Small sand-dwelling anemones, with their various symbiont partners, are another valuable addition that you cannot resist.

As for fishes, a group of 15 to 20 green or vivid blue damselfishes, perhaps from the genera *Chromis*, *Pomacentrus*, or *Chrysiptera* (preferably a single species) make an impressive display with interesting social interactions. Some digging shrimp gobies, *Amblyeleotris* and *Cryptocentrus* spp., with their partner pistol shrimps are perfect for this biotope. A colorful tang or surgeonfish is the last striking addition you make.

to keep need intense light. A 250-watt metal halide lamp is placed directly over the boulder for good effect. In addition, you install a 30-watt blue actinic fluorescent tube for dawn and twilight effects. Water movement in all areas of the tank is very important. To achieve this you install three to five pump outlets or powerheads with a total water turnover of 4,000 to 6,000 liters per hour (1,040 to 1,560 gal. per hour).

In stocking the rubble zone / boulder aquarium, a selection of small-polyped stony corals, such as *Acropora* spp. and *Pocillopora* spp., will make excellent focal points. For variation, you also want to include one or more brain or moon corals (*Favia* and/or *Favites* spp.). In addition, you include a few *Sinularia*, *Lobophytum*, and *Sarcophyton* spp. soft corals. The soft and stony corals will be fighting for space, affecting each other with growth-inhibiting chemicals. Therefore, you take care not to place them so closely together that they come into physical contact at first. Rather, you give them space to start to grow and allow the scenery to develop and change gradually as they spread and intermingle naturally in competition with each other. The majority of the corals are placed on the

A SMALL CAVE AQUARIUM

FOR INSPIRATION, WE TAKE A CLOSE LOOK at a small section of reef in the Maldives in the Indian Ocean. We are at about 10 meters (33 ft.) deep off the island of Kanifinolhu in the North Male Atoll. It is midday and the equatorial sun is burning fiercely. The water temperature is 28°C (82°F). Can this scene be mimicked in a marine aquarium?

In the foreground is a large, flat rock covered with dead branching corals overgrown by various fleshy algae. In the aquarium this might be replaced by live corals, if light conditions are right. The rock lies close to the front glass and is not very tall. Behind this rock is a rather large patch of fine coral sand mixed with a few pieces of live rock partly buried in the soft substrate. The sand flat stretches from the right front half of the aquarium to the back left corner and narrows as it flows to the rear.

In the far back corner, close to the bottom and behind the large live rock, a large colony of *Acropora* sp. grows. In between the branches of the coral are several symbiotic coral crabs—you can spot them easily as they are bright orange. The coral grows fast and is left plenty of room to expand.

The back part of the aquarium, behind the sand flat, is covered with large pieces of live rock arranged to form a deep cave close to the bottom. The cave opening is about 25 cm (10 in.) high, and the fine coral sand fills the bottom of the cave. From the cave opening to the back of the tank is about 35 cm (14 in.). A few branching stony corals—*Acropora* spp. and/or *Pocillopora damicornis*—grow on the rocks above the cave. Some fleshy algae that naturally occur in this depth and a few sponges have started to grow from the live rock. Close to the side wall is a large population of the soft coral *Sinularia dura*, a species that forms broad lobes in the moderate light reaching this zone. Toward the surface, on top of the live rocks above the cave, the small branching *Acropora microphthalma* grows densely. Among the branches, several pairs of Yellow Clown Gobies (*Gobiodon okinawae*) thrive and go through their spawning rituals. They need to hide themselves among the coral branches, as you also keep a rather large Spotfin Lionfish (*Pterois antennata*) that loves to feed on smaller fishes and crustaceans. This fish always attracts attention when friends come over for a visit. You keep a pair of Yellowheaded Sleeper Gobies (*Valenciennea strigata*), which are great diggers of the sand. They constantly take mouthfuls of sand while hunting for prey, continually stirring up nutrients for the corals while keeping the bottom layer clean. Your last fish is a Comet (*Calloplesiops altivelis*), a species that will naturally take up residence inside your cave. The large fishes prevent you from adding many crustaceans, but a pair of Banded Coral Shrimps (*Stenopus hispidus*) does very well in and around the cave. A troop of algae-feeding hermit crabs works to control the growth of filamentous algae.

This small cave scene is from the Maldives in the Indian Ocean, but it could be recreated to mimic a reef anywhere in the Tropics. Caves make fine settings for many fishes and crustaceans that thrive where shade and rocky shelter is always available.

Your tank volume is about 350 liters (91 gal.). As you want red calcareous algae to spread and cover the live rock, you have only used one metal halide lamp of 250 watts placed in the middle of your tank, rather than evenly illuminating the system with two or more bulbs. This gives enough light for the corals, and as they grow toward the surface, shady zones are created further down the reefscape and calcareous algae starts to flourish slowly over time. A blue fluorescent light tube provides pleasing, realistic effects in the morning and evening. Behind the decoration you have mounted a couple of powerful circulation pumps that provide vigorous circulation in the aquarium.

After about 2 years of careful tending, the aquarium has become a showpiece. The rocks have developed a diverse and exciting growth of algae and invertebrates, and you are finally repaid for not rearranging them as you were tempted to do from time to time. You have started to prune the corals and trade cuttings with your fellow aquarists. The rare satisfaction of creating a tiny replica of a coral reef tens of thousands of kilometers away in the Tropics is now yours to enjoy.

CHAPTER 5

AQUARIUM STOCKING

*Thinking Before Buying: Selecting Species Based on Compatibility,
Population Density, Aquarium Size, and Human Hazards*

RIEND OR ENEMY? MANY ANIMALS WILL instinctively know the difference between other animals they have no need to fear and animals that are likely to attack or harm them, such as predators and venomous species.

In nature, animals that are potential prey will try to stay out of reach or hide from their enemies, but in the confined quarters of an aquarium, the chances of evading trouble for very long are rather slim. Unless you have an extremely large tank, filled with escape routes and hideaways, the smaller or weaker species have poor prospects for survival. It is up to the aquarist to avoid such unfortunate situations simply by not placing incompatible animals into the same tank.

Choosing livestock for your marine aquarium is both a great pleasure and, at times, a vexing challenge. Pick the

Questionable choices: sea apple (*Pseudocolochirus* sp.), **left**, is a gorgeous animal but one that can poison an entire aquarium. The Regal Angel, **above**, needs expert care and feeding.

wrong animals and they may follow their natural instincts and eat each other or harass each other until one animal or the other starves or succumbs to the prolonged stress. Before buying any new animal for your aquarium, we urge you to consider a number of factors, including its potential ability to coexist with other species you already own or plan to acquire.

PREDATION

MOST ANIMALS SURVIVE by eating other live organisms—ranging from bacteria and plants to tiny invertebrates, fish fry, or even large animals. Sometimes the prey is substantially larger than the predator itself. If a given animal naturally targets any other organism that you want to keep in your aquarium, you have a potential problem at hand, unless the actual prey organism is particularly clever at protecting itself or reproduces so fast that it can keep up with a certain level of predation.

If you want to keep a lush growth of macroalgae in your aquarium, it will be difficult to house greedy herbivores, such as surgeonfishes or tangs (*Zebrasoma* spp.), in the same system. If you like to observe microfauna elements such as copepods, isopods, and worms, the many fishes—smaller wrasses, for example—that spend their waking hours picking over the substrate for exactly these prey items must be avoided. And certainly, most of the marvelous corallivores (obligate coral polyp eaters) among the butterflyfishes (*Chaetodon* spp.) are out of the question in a tank full of live corals.

In fact, many fish species need particular consideration before you combine them with other animals in a home aquarium. As most aquarists soon learn, there are many predators among the fishes that will not hesitate to eat other smaller fishes or invertebrates. In some cases, as with large groupers or lionfishes, it ought to be pretty obvious that many smaller reef fishes and ornamental crustaceans—damsels, clownfishes, pretty little shrimps—are potential prey. In the case of small, delicate fishes with tiny mouths, predation can be unexpected—for example, when they turn to snipping polyps from precious corals (Orangespotted Filefish, *Oxymonacanthus longirostris*) or biting scales and skin pieces from larger fishes in the tank (Bluestriped Fang Blenny, *Plagiotremus rhinorhynchos*). To avoid these expensive and sometimes cruel stocking mistakes (the prey cannot simply swim away from its predator), it is always imperative to check an animal's feeding habits before adding it to your tank. Once a new specimen is introduced into to a heavily aquascaped reef tank, it can be very difficult to remove, and a predator may do a lot of damage before you can catch it again.

If there is a consolation in making stocking mistakes, it is that every real aquarist—professional and amateur—has made such errors, and will probably be making more in the future. While there are rules about stocking, it is a fact that long established "truths" sometimes turn out to be wrong. Animals that have been kept by many other aquarists, without noteworthy difficulties, may suddenly begin creating problems in your aquarium.

A very good example of this once occurred when we placed a specimen of the Red Sea Mimic Blenny

SIZE PLANNING

Never buy any fish or invertebrate without knowing how large it can grow and how much space it will need. Be sure your aquarium size, filtering capacity, and other livestock will be appropriate. Large, predatory animals can destroy a balanced system.

■ ■ ■

(*Ecsenius gravieri*) into an established reef tank with several *Acropora* colonies. Although this blenny, like most of its close relatives, is known as a herbivore specializing in eating microalgae that it scrapes from the substrate, our fish immediately turned to eating the tissue of the *Acropora* corals in our tank, leaving very obvious wounds. It is uncertain whether this behavior was triggered by a desire to eat the zooxanthellae inside the coral tissue, or if it actually could have been the coral itself that was considered a food source. In later discussions with reef researchers, we learned that several species of the genus *Ecsenius* have been observed feeding on various coral species in nature. Still, most aquarists know these fishes as very good and peaceful algae grazers.

Similarly confusing cases are known from other fishes. Many aquarists have kept the beautiful Bicolor Angelfish (*Centropyge bicolor*) and regard it as an excellent companion for corals and other invertebrates. It typically feeds mainly on algae and tiny invertebrates that live between the corals and in the live rock, but in some cases, the very same species has turned out to be an avid nuisance that nips on both stony and soft corals, as well as on *Tridacna* spp. clams and many other sedentary invertebrates. We have seen one example in which a Bicolor Angelfish almost completely destroyed the coral population of an aquarium. What was once a healthy and beautiful reef aquarium turned into a coral graveyard because of a single fish.

Exactly the same can be said about the Flame Angelfish (*Centropyge loriculus*). In some tanks, this popular fish has destroyed most corals in a couple of days, while in other tanks it has lived for years and years without doing any harm whatsoever—like a true angel.

The question is whether the coral eating shown by these fishes is triggered by a factor inside the aquarium itself, or if it is a habit that some specimens may have already developed in nature. Chances are that the latter is the case, and that geographically separated populations of a species develop differing feeding habits. For the butterflyfish *Chaetodon kleinii*, which is often used as a grazer on glass anemones (*Aiptasia* spp.) in reef tanks, studies from nature show that specimens in Hawaii feed primarily on tiny crustaceans and zooplankton, while specimens in Micronesia fill their stomachs with polyps of *Sarcophyton* and *Litophyton* soft corals. The origin of the specimen can therefore be a major factor in deciding whether or not it will fit into any particular aquarium.

Unfortunately, published information on the natural feeding habits of most reef fish species is limited or even nonexistent. Here we believe that the observations of marine aquarists are important. The aquarium trade needs to become better at supplying information on where the specimens we buy were caught, and, in turn, aquarists need to keep records for future reference and use by others.

Fishes are not the only aquarium inhabitants that can show aggressive, predatory behavior. Many hobbyists have seen the same problems with crustaceans, primarily in certain coral-eating crab species that are occasionally introduced with live rock or new coral specimens, but also in species that are sold separately—for example, many of the large hermit crabs. Always investigate—in books, on the Internet, or in discussions with other aquarists and shop personnel—a new species before you buy a specimen for your tank.

AGGRESSIVE BEHAVIOR

AN ANIMAL DOES NOT HAVE TO BE an outright predator in order to harm its aquarium companions. In many cases, animals have developed defensive mechanisms to protect themselves, and these can be a major consideration when deciding if they fit into a particular aquarium setting.

In many fishes, the instinct to defend its territory against intruders is very strong. For example, this is typical in many dottybacks and hawkfishes. The aggression is often particularly strong toward specimens of the same species, but also toward any other animal that is perceived as a competitor—often because it has similar appearances or behaviors or because it feeds on the same resources. By constructing the aquarium aquascape in a manner that makes it possible to establish multiple territories (using space and visual barriers) it can be easier to keep such aggressive species together with species that they are inclined to chase.

Some animals are very aggressive feeders and drive away all other animals in order to keep available food resources for themselves. One often notices that very ac-

A Red Sea Mimic Blenny (*Ecsenius gravieri*) shown in the act of feeding on stony coral polyps. This fish had to be removed from a reef tank where it was causing serious harm to branching corals.

Detail of an *Acropora* sp. stony coral branch with white skeleton showing the damage inflicted by the Red Sea Mimic Blenny (*Ecsenius gravieri*), **top**.

The Green Brittle Star (*Ophiarachna incrassata*) is a threat to small fishes, as evidenced by this goby caught in a nighttime attack.

A brain coral becomes a mass of stinging tentacles that expand at night. Other corals placed too near will be stung in a battle for space. Many corals take on changed appearances after dark.

All sea cucumbers, such as this *Bohadschia graeffei*, can release the fish-killing poison holothurin if threatened or attacked.

The Sixline Soapfish (*Grammistes sexlineatus*) is cute as a juvenile but grows quite large and can excrete grammistin if it becomes stressed, toxic slime that may wipe out a whole tank.

tive animals steal away all food that enters the tank before the slower-moving animals have had a chance to get their share. Aggressive and quick feeders are often incompatible with slow, finicky feeders unless special precautions are taken. This is not something that can be ignored, as it frequently leads to death by starvation of the less-aggressive fishes (see Chapter 8, page 217).

TOXINS

MOST AQUARISTS ARE AWARE of the stinging properties of corals, sea anemones, and other cnidarians. Within special organs called nematocysts, or nettling cells, they are equipped with powerful toxins that may be injected into any animal with which they come into contact. The relative toxicity varies greatly between different groups and species, but some are capable of inflicting severe damage on other animals, including related corals or anemones.

Some sponges in the aquarium trade may release toxins if they die. It is not always easy to determine if a sponge is dead or alive when you buy it. We once recorded a so-called "Hard Blue Sponge" (*Xestospongia* sp.) releasing toxins that killed several soft corals in our aquarium. The fishes were, however, not harmed.

Sea cucumbers may cause major poisoning in the aquarium. They produce the very strong toxin holothurin, which is mainly concentrated in the intestines of the animals. The toxin may be released if the animal is injured, stressed, or dying, or if they expel their Cuverian tubules, which are sticky, stringy appendages found in some sea cucumber genera that can be forced out of their anal opening in a defensive move. Many aquarists have learned about the toxicity of sea cucumbers the hard way, and often too late, when every single fish in the tank suddenly has died from acute poisoning. Such situations often occur when the sea cucumber accidentally comes into contact with a stinging sea anemone or coral, when it has been sucked into a pump or filter and torn to pieces, or when it has burned itself on an unprotected heater. In addition, there are also reports of poisoning events coinciding with sea cucumbers spawning.

However, there is no reason to assume that a dead or dying sea cucumber always leads to poisoning. We have had experiences with a number of holothuroids dying in tanks with no damage whatsoever. Still, it is prudent to think twice before introducing such sea cucumbers into an aquarium with many prized fishes.

TABLE 5-1

SPECIAL COMPATIBILITY CONSIDERATIONS

NOTE: These are only examples of groups in which compatibility problems are likely to occur. The failure to list a particular group or species does not mean it poses no risks in its interaction with other aquarium inhabitants. Be sure to check the needs and habits of any species before introducing it into a tank. Consult the Stocking Guide section of this book (starting on page 98) or other literature carefully.

TAXONOMIC GROUP	PROBLEM	CONSIDERATION
FISHES		
Sharks and rays, Elasmobranchii	Predation	In general, sharks and rays require large aquariums and will feed on any invertebrate or fish they can catch. Careful research and planning is imperative before purchasing any of these animals.
Moray eels, Muraenidae	Predation	Most moray eels will eat any crustacean or fish (preference varies between species) slow enough to catch and small enough to swallow. Aggressive species may also inflict damage on fishes that are too large to be caught. Check the literature before making a purchase.
Frogfishes, *Antennarius* spp.	Predation	Frogfishes will eat any crustacean or fish small enough to swallow (up to half their own size or more). Slender fishes may be at risk even if they are as long, or longer, than the frogfish. Frogfishes are clever hunters and can catch even fast-moving species.
Seahorses and pipefishes, Syngnathidae	Vulnerability	These slow feeders must be kept in peaceful tanks with as little competition as possible. They are at high risk of being caught and eaten by anemones or severely burned by any stinging cnidarians.
Scorpionfishes, Scorpaenidae	Predation	Most scorpionfishes will eat any crustacean or fish small enough to swallow. They are patient, effective hunters and can catch even fast-moving species.
Dottybacks, *Pseudochromis* spp.	Aggression	Most dottybacks are aggressive defenders of their territory, especially toward fishes that bear some resemblance to themselves.
Butterflyfishes, Chaetodontidae	Predation	Many—but not all—species will eat stony corals as well as other invertebrates. Look up the eating habits of any prospective purchase.
Angelfishes, Pomacanthidae	Predation	Most angelfish species eat sponges, tunicates, and other sedentary invertebrates (including corals). Do not acquire an angelfish without knowing the habits and reputation of the species.
Hawkfishes, Cirrhitidae	Predation, aggression	These aggressive predators are likely to eat any crustacean or fish small enough to swallow. Most species will fiercely defend their territory from any intruder that bears a resemblance to itself.
Wrasses, Labridae	Predation	Many wrasses will eat a variety of benthic invertebrates, such as crustaceans, mollusks, and worms. Study the size, eating habits, and reputation of the species before bringing it home.
Blennies, Blenniidae	Predation	Although the vast majority of members of this family are peaceful herbivores, some species are aggressive predators on other animals, ranging from corals to fishes. Careful study of the literature is important prior to any purchase.

(continued on next page)

TABLE 5-1

SPECIAL COMPATIBILITY CONSIDERATIONS (CONT.)

TAXONOMIC GROUP	PROBLEM	CONSIDERATION
Mandarinfishes, *Synchiropus* spp.	Vulnerability	These slow, shy feeders should be kept in peaceful tanks with as little competition as possible, or in very large tanks where they can easily escape. They are at high risk of being caught and eaten by anemones.
Triggerfishes, Balistidae	Predation, aggression	These often-aggressive fishes may bite anything within reach. Most species can only be kept with large, tough fishes and stinging or distasteful cnidarians (anemones and corals).
Filefishes, Monacanthidae	Predation	Several species will eat stony corals and other invertebrates. Check the reference books before making a purchase.
Boxfishes, Ostraciidae	Toxins	Several boxfishes may release a very strong toxin (ostracitoxin) if the animal is injured, stressed, or dying. The toxin is potentially lethal to most companions in the tank. The toxicity varies between species. Check the literature before making a purchase.
SPONGES Hard Blue Sponge, *Xestospongia* sp.	Toxins	This beautiful and commonly imported sponge species has been known to release poisons when dying. The toxins can severely damage soft corals and other invertebrates.
WORMS Social Feather Duster, *Bispira brunnea*	Vulnerability	These small, delicate worms are often torn apart and eaten by brittlestars. Fishes, crabs, and other animals that prey on worms will also consider them an easy target.
CRUSTACEANS Mantis shrimps, Gonodactylidae	Predation, aggression	These aggressive predators have a notorious reputation for attacking tankmates that are perceived as prey or threats. Other crustaceans and small fishes are particularly vulnerable.
Harlequin Shrimp, *Hymenocera picta*	Predation	Feeds exclusively on sea stars; will harm and eventually kill any sea star in the aquarium. Can therefore be used to reduce/exterminate populations of the tiny *Asterina* spp. that sometimes proliferate in aquariums.
Anemone shrimps, *Periclimenes* spp.	Vulnerability	These fascinating shrimps are relatively safe once they have settled down in a host anemone, but during the introduction phase, they stand a very high risk of being eaten by any animal capable of catching them. The same may be said of many other small and medium-sized shrimps.
Hermit crabs, Diogenidae	Predation, aggression	Many large and medium-sized hermit crabs are highly predatory and aggressive, capable of inflicting damage on many invertebrates. There are also perfectly peaceful, herbivorous species. Study the literature closely before deciding on a hermit crab species for your aquarium.
Decorator Crab, *Camposcia retusa*	Predation	This indiscriminate carnivore is likely to feed on all available food in an aquarium—including corals and most other invertebrates.
Spider Crab, *Stenorhynchus seticornis*	Predation	Feeds extensively on tubeworms, but also likely to pick on many other sedentary invertebrates.

TAXONOMIC GROUP	PROBLEM	CONSIDERATION
ECHINODERMS		
Sea stars, Asteroidea	Predation	Many sea stars target various invertebrates, including sponges and corals, as part of their natural diet. Check the reference books closely before deciding on a sea star species for your aquarium.
Serpent and brittle stars, Ophiuroidea	Predation	Although the majority of serpent stars feed on detritus and carrion and are quite peaceful toward larger invertebrates, they may injure or eat delicate invertebrates like feather duster worms.
Green Brittle Star, *Ophiarachna incrassata*	Predation	Although this common brittle star is an opportunistic feeder that occasionally captures fishes, it is still relatively safe to keep in reef aquariums.
Sea urchins, Echinoidea	Predation	Most sea urchins are primarily herbivores, which may be a problem for a macroalgae community (particularly red coralline algae), and many will also ingest a variety of encrusting animals, like tunicates, bryozoans, and sponges. Some species even feed on corals. Study the literature closely before deciding on a sea urchin species for your aquarium.
Sea cucumbers, Holothuroidea	Toxins	The very strong toxin holothurin, which is concentrated in the intestines of most sea cucumbers, may be released if the animal is injured, stressed, or dying. Relative toxicity varies between species, but all may pose a risk to fishes.
CNIDARIANS		
Fire corals, *Millepora* spp.	Toxins	This and other hydroids have a strong nettling toxin that can cause problems for other animals. Must not be placed close to corals.
Tube anemones, *Cerianthus* spp.	Toxins	These anemones can inflict deadly stings on other animals. Should not be placed close to corals or other sedentary invertebrates. The tentacles may reach much farther than you initially suspect.
Sea anemones, Actiniaria	Toxins	Many species have strong nettling abilities and can inflict damage on other animals; they even eat slow-moving crustaceans and fishes. Beware: many anemones will actively move around the aquarium. Not all anemones are equally toxic. Check the literature before any purchase.
Elephant Ear Anemone, *Amplexidiscus fenestrafer*	Predation, aggression	This large disc anemone is capable of trapping even large and active prey, like fishes and shrimps, by forming a funnel that rapidly closes around the victim.
Crystal Coral, *Galaxea fascicularis*	Toxins	This coral's powerful stinging abilities deserve respect. Place well away from other corals. Beware: this species has extremely long sweeper tentacles that are extended during the night.
Hammer Coral, *Euphyllia ancora*	Toxins	The powerful stinging abilities of this coral deserve respect. Keep out of reach of other corals. Other species in the genus *Euphyllia* are less toxic, but care should still be taken when placing a colony.
Bubble Coral, *Plerogyra sinuosa*	Toxins	Powerful stinging tentacles extend at night. Locate at a safe distance from other corals.

(Think of it as aquatic Russian roulette if you choose to play this game.)

Boxfishes of the Family Ostraciidae and the soapfishes of the Family Grammistidae have similar capabilities of wiping out entire aquariums with their toxins. Here the chemicals are ostracitoxin and grammistin, respectively, but the risk is the same whenever one of these animals is stressed or injured: the release of the toxin can severely harm or even kill many of the fish's companions in a closed tank.

HARDINESS

ATTACKS FROM ENEMIES, whether they are the result of predation attempts or defense mechanisms, will have different effects on different animals. The natural, preferred prey of a predator will rarely have much chance of surviving in the same aquarium—although in rare cases the prey may survive if they outnumber the predators by a very large factor—for example, if you have a huge aquarium with lush coral growth, and only a couple of small fishes feeding on coral polyps.

Survival for many species depends on their ability to escape or hide from predators, their relative attractiveness as a food target, their stamina to endure continued attacks, and—very importantly—the abundance of more-suitable food for the predators. In other words, most animals will show varying degrees of ability to compete when placed in the company of an aggressive species. Animals that are slow feeders may not survive, while those that tend to go into hiding when faced with constant competition often do poorly or simply disappear in busy aquariums.

The loose term "hardiness" when used to describe certain fishes and invertebrates covers these traits and more. Animals that can take all sorts of competition and different conditions of water quality and lighting are often called "hardy." Those that are less hardy or more sensitive to aggression or varying environmental conditions need our special attention.

STOCKING DENSITY

As AQUARISTS, WE GET TO PLAY a godlike role, especially when we build a population of animals in a small closed world of our own making.

What is a population? A common biological definition is: "all the individuals belonging to a single species, or closely associated species, living in a specific geographic area." This means that all specimens of the Banded Coral Shrimp (*Stenopus hispidus*) found on the reefs surrounding the small Bird's Island off Viti Levu, Fiji, is the population of Banded Coral Shrimp at this spot. How many can that be? Impossible to say without actually counting—a few hundred, perhaps? Other groups, such as schooling anthias (*Pseudanthias* spp.) or *Chromis* spp., are found in the millions. The more specimens there are in a population, the higher the population density. On tropical coral reefs we find all kinds of population densities. Some organisms are there in countless aggregations, others as widely scattered individuals or pairs.

Why do some fishes form schools and cluster in such vast numbers? The simple answer is protection. If a school of fishes—such as jacks or trevally (*Caranx* spp.)—is being attacked by a shark, the odds of any particular individual surviving the attack is much better than if a single specimen met the shark alone. (Large predators have difficulty identifying a single target when presented by a school of prey fishes. Even if they can separate and take an individual, the bulk of the school survives.)

Some surgeonfishes, such as the Powder Blue Surgeonfish (*Acanthurus leucosternon*) normally live alone or in pairs on Indian Ocean coral reefs. Sometimes, however, this rather aggressive species forms large social groupings that swarm over the shallow reefs feeding on algae. Why? When feeding alone the fish is obviously highly vulnerable to attacks, but by forming large schools the feeding behavior becomes safer. The Striped Eel Catfish (*Plotosus lineatus*) forms extremely dense schools with thousands of juveniles packed together so tightly that they are probably perceived as one big fish by potential predators.

There are also several invertebrates that normally form dense populations in nature, such as the Common Dancing Shrimp (*Rhynchocinetes durbanensis*) usually found in large groups deep in caves and crevices.

> ## THINK YOUNG
> Fully-grown or "show" specimens of fishes and corals are more difficult to move and acclimate than juveniles and younger individuals of the same species. Grow your own show animals.
>
> ■ ■ ■

Some fishes, such as these flasher wrasses, seem to thrive in social groupings with members of their own species but will often do poorly in the aquarium if kept singly. Other examples of fishes better kept in groups are dartfishes, chromises, and cardinalfishes.

While a coral reef aquarium may be crowded with many different species of coral in a relatively small space, such scenery is uncommon in nature. Here the individual species of corals occupy a much larger area, often several square meters. Some species, such as fast-growing staghorn corals from the genus *Acropora*, can even colonize hundreds of square meters or form monospecific stands along large sections of a reef. A single wild colony of a table-shaped *Acropora*, such as the widely distributed Indo-Pacific species *Acropora hyacinthus*, can grow to a size much bigger than most reef aquariums and contain thousands of individual polyps and hundreds of symbiotic animals living among the branchlets. Too often, our tanks take on a hodgepodge look that misses the potential beauty and interest of a more realistic reef scene.

Although we will never be able to copy the natural "water-to-tissue ratio" of a coral reef in a closed aquarium system, we have one interesting option open to us: limit the mix of different species but increase the number of specimens. In other words, why not build an aquarium that contains just one or a very few species of corals and only one or two species of fishes? Here the corals will be allowed to grow very large and the fishes will be in dense populations more like those of their home reefs.

A DREAM REEF

As an imaginary example, you might start with a custom 750-liter (195-gal.) tank about 100 cm (39 in.) on each side, forming a square bottom. You have always fancied the fairy basslets or anthias (*Pseudanthias* spp.) so commonly found on Indo-Pacific coral reefs forming large aggregations around coral heads in the lagoon and on outer-reef slopes. You start by forming a reef pillar of live rock in the middle of the aquarium. The top of the pier stretches to 20 cm (8 in.) below the surface. The bottom of the tank is filled with a rather thick layer of coral gravel and you install a skimmer in a sump below the aquarium.

Often sold as charming little juveniles with bright black and white patterns, the Striped Eel Catfish (*Plotosus lineatus*) grow into drab, rather large adults. Additionally, their fin spines pack a venomous sting that is a potential threat to aquarists and tankmates.

Rather than stocking the tank with a dozen or even hundreds of different corals and fishes, you opt for two species of coral: one is a branching *Acropora* (perhaps a bright green or purple staghorn species) and the other is the table-shaped *Acropora latistella*. Both are readily available as small propagated colonies or as cuttings from other aquarists. Both species are fast growing. *Acropora latistella* forms plate-shaped colonies that project from the pier and the branching *Acropora* rapidly grows from the top of the pillar to the surface. The plates create different zones of light and shadow down the column. Several sponges and different species of macroalgae develop in the interesting patterns of light and shade. A metal halide lamp provides strong illumination at the top of the pillar and a pleasant light-pattern on the sandy bottom a meter down.

To stock the substrate you decide to use gobies and pistol shrimps. You select the Yellow Watchman Goby (*Cryptocentrus cinctus*) and add 6 specimens as well as an equal number of their commensal pistol shrimps (*Alpheus* sp.). Although the fish may have territorial battles—and a couple of them may lose and disappear—the survivors establish themselves nicely after a while. Soon they start living in pairs in association with the shrimps. The main attraction in this tank is, however, the fish: you introduce 60 fairy basslets, perhaps the common but beautiful Lyretail Anthias (*Pseudanthias squamipinnis*).

You have previously investigated aquarium stores to establish a supply source for providing live adult brine shrimp (*Artemia*) and frozen plankton and other foods several times daily, and the fishes thrive. Soon a dominant male develops and builds a harem of females.

You exercise restraint and do not recklessly add new fishes and corals—perhaps introducing some cleaner shrimps and coral crabs and an appropriate giant clam (*Tridacna maxima*), which becomes an attraction with its bright blue mantle exposed between the branching *Acropora* colonies.

After a couple of years you have a reef masterpiece: huge show corals and a remarkable captive population of anthias that might even reward you and your visitors with spawning behaviors.

A RED SEA CAVE

FROM A FRIEND YOU ARE GIVEN a rather small, rectangular aquarium of no more than 190-liter (50-gal.) capacity. You decorate the tank with live rock, building a single deep cave. Above the cave, it is 10 cm (3.9 in.) to the surface, and the rocks forming the opening of the cave stretch more than two-thirds of the way to the front glass. (You use hidden PVC pipe for supporting the structure and underwater epoxy for mounting the rocks.) The cave is absolutely solid and stable before any live specimens are added.

As a cave floor, you use crushed live rock mixed with a little bit of coral sand and scatter some bigger pieces of live rock here and there on the bottom. To illuminate the cave, you mount a small fluorescent light tube on one side of the aquarium where there is an opening in the rockwork, and a pleasant rather weak light fills the cave. When the tank has completed its 12-week break in period, it is time to start adding the organisms. On the top of the cave roof, toward a surface illuminated by full-spectrum and blue-actinic fluorescent tubes, you introduce several small colonies of Red Sea pumping *Xenia* sp. The species is fast growing and your plan is to let the entire top of the cave be covered with pumping *Xenia* polyps.

To continue the Red Sea profile, you also add one Orchid Dottyback, *Pseudochromis fridmani*, and one Bluestriped Dottyback, *Pseudochromis springeri*. You want sponges and calcareous algae to grow within the shadows of the cave, and you are willing to be patient as this is a slow process. Although from Australia rather than the Red Sea, the Yellow Assessor, *Assessor flavissimus*, is an excellent small fish and is naturally kept in small groups. You throw budgetary caution to the wind and add 15 of these lovely little assessors. You are surprised how well they establish themselves in the cave and how they swim with their abdomens toward the cave roof.

The Common Dancing Shrimp, *Rhynchocinetes dur-*

banensis, is a perfect fit for this small cave aquarium. You add a group of 25 specimens (there will probably be fewer males than females in the group). The shrimps soon group themselves on the roof of the cave, and together with the Yellow Assessors, they make a spectacular display, which now has become a real living biotope. You also add 20 black brittlestars that settle into fissures in the cave and between the crushed live rock pieces on the bottom. Their flexible arms project from their hiding places and make the bottom a lively scene. As a bonus, the brittle stars just happen to be excellent detritus feeders. A number of feather dusters (tubeworms from the genus *Sabellastarte*) are also added, and their colorful crowns prove to be true eye-catchers.

These fantasy tanks are just two casually imagined examples of potentially wonderful reef aquariums that contain few species but many specimens. By combining a knowledge of reef habitats and imagination, amateur aquarists can create many more interesting biotopes that take us beyond the unrealistic jumble of most reef tanks. (For other suggested biotopes, see Chapter 4.)

We believe that by increasing the density of same-species specimens (provided that the species can be kept in such groups) rather than the number of species, you will achieve a result that is much closer to the natural habitat.

AQUARIUM SIZE

ONE PROBLEM IN MAKING LIVESTOCK SELECTIONS is that aquarists frequently underestimate the space requirements of the animals. It ought to be obvious that a large fish needs a large aquarium, but many if not most of the specimens we buy are juveniles or immature adults, and it is not always obvious what their full space requirements will be.

The size of the aquarium you have absolutely dictates the animals you can keep, assuming that you are conscientious and acknowledge their need to thrive and behave naturally. In most cases, the aquarist is restricted in his or her choice of aquarium size by financial considerations and the available space in the room where the aquarium is to be set up. Thus it may be helpful to think about all our livestock choices by first establishing

> ## SMALL TREASURES
> It is certainly possible to create a successful and spectacular reef in a small aquarium. Bigger isn't always better.
>
> ■ ■ ■

Most moray eels, such as this Blackear Moray Eel (*Muraena melanotis*) are reasonably docile creatures, but aggressiveness and feeding habits differ from species to species.

Armed with deadly venom, the Stonefish (*Synanceia verrucosa*) is too dangerous to be kept in most home aquariums.

Foolhardy or careless hobbyists may be stung by captive lionfishes that can deliver a defensive wound that is very painful and occasionally requires emergency medical care.

what size tank we have to work with.

Unfortunately, there is a tendency—perhaps a mania—toward ever-larger reef aquariums. To counter this, we would be happy if we could persuade some people into buying aquariums smaller than what they actually have space for. Bigger isn't always better. For one thing, the aquarist often realizes too late that the costs involved in reef aquarium keeping are not trivial. You soon enough discover a world of expensive technical gadgets and enticing animals that you never knew existed, and it is better not to have emptied one's wallet completely when buying the tank. Furthermore, there are many, many animals that are much better kept and studied in a smallish tank where they are likely to be visible.

Whatever size aquarium you choose, there are a number of factors to consider before you bring an animal into it.

ADULT SIZE

MORE OFTEN THAN NOT, fishes and invertebrates are going to grow larger—sometimes *much* larger—than they appear when being offered in an aquarium shop. The beautiful Orbiculate Batfish (*Platax orbicularis*) may, for instance, be only some 5 or 6 cm (2 or 2.3 in.) long when you find it in the shop. After a year or two of heavy feeding, it may have grown to 10 times its original size, to a stunning half meter (1.6 ft.). For fishes that grow this big, and are active swimmers, you will of course need an aquarium that is much longer (and higher) than the adult size of the fish.

The only exception to this rule is when you intend to keep the animal only for the short term. Even then you must have a larger tank, or someone else with a large tank, ready to accept the fish as it grows.

Among the animals that tend to grow faster and get larger than the aquarist might expect are some species of giant clams. There are documented reports of *Tridacna squamosa* and *Tridacna derasa* growing from 2 cm to 60 cm (0.8 in. to 23 in.) in less than three years. One issue on the positive side here is that they don't need space to move around. In theory you could then do with an aquarium only slightly larger than the animal itself, but in practice most aquarists are uncomfortable looking at a large specimen crowding an undersized tank.

Most corals also tend to grow much larger than expected. Some common species of soft corals are known to reach colony diameters of more than 1 meter (3.3 ft.)

(e.g., *Sarcophyton glaucum* and *Sinularia flexibilis*), while many reach at least half that size. Exactly the same can be said of stony corals. When arranging small *Acropora* fragments, one should always bear in mind that they do get larger. Corals need space to grow.

Fortunately, however, most corals can be cut and shaped and kept from becoming too large with the aid of pruners, a knife, or a pair of scissors. Overly heavy trimming may, however, destroy the looks of the colony. Instead of relying on pruning, some reefkeepers prefer to keep coral species that do not grow large, or at least those that are slow growers.

Beginners also need to realize that some corals do not need much time to get considerably bigger than they appear in the shop. More than a few aquarists have been shocked to find that species such as the elegance coral (*Catalaphyllia jardinei*) and the plate or anemone mushroom coral (*Heliofungia actiniformis*) have expanded to many times their original size after only a few days at home. Under less than perfect conditions, these corals have a tendency to withdraw to a minimal size defined by the size of the skeleton. When they settle down in a well-balanced aquarium, they fill their tissues with water and expand dramatically. For instance, a mushroom coral with a skeleton of some 10 cm (3.9 in.) diameter will often expand to 30 to 40 cm (12 to 16 in.) in diameter, with 20 cm (7.8 in.) long tentacles.

Similarly, your newly acquired magnificent anemone (*Heteractis magnifica*) may appear small in the plastic transport bag, but remember that a fist-sized sea anemone often can reach 30, 40, or even 50 cm (12, 16, or 20 in.) in diameter when fully expanded. It is therefore necessary to use consideration when selecting and arranging sedentary invertebrates. Most species easily grow much larger than the size at which they are purchased.

POLLUTION POTENTIAL

SOME ANIMALS MAY NOT GROW to very large sizes, yet they can become a problem because they eat a lot. The Volitans Lionfish (*Pterois volitans*) is a good example. With slow-moving swimming habits and a maxi-

mum size of 30 cm (12 in.), it is well suited to larger home-scale aquariums. However, it is a heavy feeder that generates lots of waste and puts a strain on the filtering capacity of many systems. Before buying such a voracious species, you should consider whether your aquarium system has the capacity to deal with the pollution of a large predator. In a fish-only tank, the use of both powerful skimmers and efficient biological filters may become a necessity. If the filtration system is insufficient, you may end up with diseased fishes and unexpected deaths as well as serious algae problems directly correlated to the heavy nutrient load produced by your fish.

FREEDOM OF MOVEMENT

FISHES DO, OF COURSE, NEED SPACE to swim, and some invertebrates do also require room to move about. In particular, many schooling fishes are very active swimmers and need plenty of swimming space in order to lead healthy lives. The need for swimming and roaming space is not always directly linked to the size of the animal. Often, a small, active animal will need more space than a larger, more sluggish one.

Moray eels, for instance, often grow to lengths of 1 meter (3.3 ft.) or more, but they lead rather docile lives, confined to the immediate surroundings of their reef caves. For such fishes, the immediate concern is more its pollution-generating potential than its need for space. Even a meter-long moray can be totally comfortable in an aquarium of only 200 liters (52 gal). In contrast, the closely related snake eels, which have a nearly identical body shape, are active swimmers when they search for food and thus need a bigger aquarium.

HAZARDS TO HUMANS

WHILE WE HAVE GENERALLY FOCUSED on the well-being of the animals selected for the aquarium, there are some reef creatures that can pose a threat to the health and well being of you—the aquarist—and your family.

Generally speaking, no other form of animal keeping has as low a frequency of incidents involving human in-

---

ALLERGENS

Some commonly used feeder invertebrates (notably bloodworms and *Tubifex* worms) are known to contain allergens that can provoke annoying contact dermatitis and respiratory problems in many humans. Handle with care and minimize physical contact to avoid problems.

■ ■ ■

A beautiful Indo-Pacific urchin especially worthy of respect, *Tripneustes gratilla* has highly venomous tube feet, or pedicellariae, and must be handled with great care.

Fireworms, or polychaete worms, in the Family Amphinomidae can deliver a painful sting with thousands of delicate, sharp spines.

Hydroids in the genus *Aglaophenia* appear harmless but can deliver an extremely powerful sting that may hurt for days afterward.

juries as aquatics. Very few aquarists ever experience any kind of health difficulty because of their aquarium keeping, primarily because the really dangerous animals seldom enter the trade.

However, it is important for the well-informed aquarist to know that there are a few hazards that can affect him/her or other people, if proper cautions are not taken. Even animals that normally are safe can have negative effects on allergic or hypersensitive people, and handling an animal always implies a certain risk of being bitten, cut, or stung. Here is a review of some risks we all ought to recognize and respect.

ANIMALS THAT STING

MANY MARINE INVERTEBRATES use various toxins for catching prey and/or defending themselves from enemies, and it is among these that we find some real dangers for humans. Even though very few of the toxic reef animals will have more than a mild impact on most healthy humans, some are decidedly deadly.

For instance, the Box Jellyfish (*Chironex fleckeri*) was responsible for more than 70 deaths in Australia alone during the 20th century. In an aquarium, the Box Jellyfish would command respect, but not a huge risk, because one needs direct contact with many tentacles to be injected with a lethal amount of the stinging-cell toxin. This is not an animal normally collected for the aquarium trade, but it does illustrate that there are dangers in the sea. Moreover, some people can become very ill if they receive even mild toxic stings that are no more than a nuisance and irritation to most of us. Anyone with known allergies to animal stings should use great caution (and probably long-sleeved rubber gloves) when working in a reef tank or with reef animals.

ANIMALS THAT BITE OR CUT

EVERYONE KNOWS THAT LARGE SHARKS can be dangerous, but there are many smaller fishes, more likely to be kept in a home aquarium, which also can inflict nasty bites on a careless aquarist. Moray eels, even though they often are quite docile, can bite fiercely. Even though the bite itself may not be dangerous, it can be deep, leading to a high risk of bacterial infection that can then lead to secondary complications.

Some animals like surgeonfishes and mantis shrimps can also produce nasty cuts in human flesh without bit-

TABLE 5-2

POTENTIALLY INJURIOUS AQUARIUM INHABITANTS

NOTE: This table includes examples of aquarium inhabitants that we consider most likely to be harmful to an aquarist. By listing an animal we do not necessarily mean that all aquarists should avoid it. Neither does the failure to list an animal imply that it will never pose risks under particular circumstances. (Animals that are poisonous only if eaten are not included.)

TAXONOMIC GROUP	RISKS/SYMPTOMS	TREATMENT	PRECAUTIONS
SPONGES (Porifera)	Some sponges cause irritation and skin rashes, partly because of glassy spicules that pierce the skin, partly because of mucous toxins. Symptoms include itching, burning, and occasional redness.	Remove visible spicules. Topical application of household-strength vinegar may give relief.	Never handle unfamiliar sponge species without wearing rubber gloves.
FIRE CORAL (Cnidaria; Hydrozoa; *Millepora* spp.)	These coral-like hydroids can inflict powerful stings. Pain varies from a mild prickling sensation to a severe stinging pain and burning itch. Redness, swelling, and blisters may occur; occasional nausea. Cardiovascular or respiratory problems are very rare.	Apply household-strength vinegar or 20% aluminum sulfate in case unexploded stinging cells are still attached. Keep affected area away from more sensitive areas (face and eyes).	Never handle fire coral with bare hands. Always wear rubber gloves.
FEATHER HYDROIDS (Cnidaria; Hydrozoa; *Aglaophenia* spp. and *Lytocarpus* spp.)	Some of the fernlike hydroids that occasionally enter the aquarium trade have very strong and painful stings. Rashes, swelling, and blisters may occur. Rash may last for several days. Side effects, such as abdominal pain, cramps, and nausea, have been reported.	Apply household-strength vinegar or 20% aluminum sulfate in case unexploded stinging cells are still attached.	Never handle feather hydroids with bare hands. Always wear rubber gloves.
TUBE ANEMONES (Cnidaria; Ceriantipatharia; *Cerianthus* spp.)	Most species have only a mild effect on humans, because the stinging cells have difficulty piercing human skin. Occasional stings may occur, with burning pain, rashes, and small blisters.	Apply household-strength vinegar or 20% aluminum sulfate in case unexploded stinging cells are still attached.	Wear rubber gloves when handling unfamiliar species.
SEA ANEMONES (Cnidaria; Zoantharia; Actiniaria)	Most species have only a mild or no effect on humans, because the stinging cells have difficulty piercing human skin. Some species can cause burning pain, rashes, and small blisters. Anemone tentacles sometimes fasten to human skin with such strength that they are torn from the animal when the human draws away.	Remove any attached tentacles (use tweezers); apply household-strength vinegar or 20% aluminum sulfate to inactivate unexploded stinging cells that are still attached.	Wear rubber gloves when handling unfamiliar species.
STONY CORALS (Cnidaria; Zoantharia; Scleractinia)	Most species have only a mild or no effect on humans, because the stinging cells have difficulty piercing human skin. Some species can cause burning pain, rashes, and small blisters.	Apply household-strength vinegar or 20% aluminum sulfate in case unexploded stinging cells are still attached.	Wear rubber gloves when handling unfamiliar species.

(continued on next page)

TABLE 5-2

POTENTIALLY INJURIOUS AQUARIUM INHABITANTS (CONT.)

TAXONOMIC GROUP	RISKS/SYMPTOMS	TREATMENT	PRECAUTIONS
ERRANT BRISTLE-WORMS (Annelida; Polychaeta)	Several errant (free-living) bristleworms have fine, sharp bristles that can easily embed in human skin. Bristles may or may not contain venom. Contact can produce a rash, swelling, and numbness. Itching, burning, and pain may persist for many days. In severe cases, symptoms may include increased pulse rate, palpitations, fainting, and chest pains. The fireworms in the Family Amphinomidae (primarily *Eurythoe* and *Hermodice*) are particularly nasty in this respect. Some worms inflict painful bites as well.	Remove embedded bristles by using adhesive tape to peel them off. Apply methylated spirits, calamine, or other cooling lotion to calm the sting. In case of bites, wash the area with an antiseptic soap.	Never handle bristleworms with bare hands. Always wear rubber gloves.
MANTIS SHRIMPS (Arthropoda; Crustacea; Stomatopoda)	Mantis shrimps have large claws developed for raptorial feeding, similar to those found in the praying mantis insect. The inner edge of the claw usually has long spines or is shaped like the blade of a knife. The strike has, in some of the larger species, been estimated to have a force similar to that of a 22-caliber bullet. They have been reported to break thick glass aquarium walls. Aquarist's fingers can be badly bruised if the animal strikes.	Clean and disinfect wound thoroughly. Depending on the nature of the wound, it can be treated at home or may need medical attention.	Be very careful when working in a tank with large mantis shrimps. Any hand feeding must be done with long tweezers or a feeding stick.
CONE SNAILS (Mollusca; Gastropoda; *Conus* spp.)	All *Conus* spp. are venomous, and some (e.g., *C. geographus* and *C. textile*) can be deadly to humans. They use harpoonlike radula teeth to quickly inject their venom. Symptoms are immediate burning pains, followed by swelling and numbness. More serious symptoms are paralysis, which may become general, difficulties in swallowing and speaking, and vision problems. Heart failure and breathing difficulties or even stoppage may follow. There appears to be great variation in people's susceptibility to the venom.	Apply pressure bandage to the area that is stung to delay the spread of venom. Get victim immediate medical attention. If necessary, give artificial respiration and cardiac massage. Any victim likely to vomit should be put on his/her side to avoid choking.	Never keep cone snails in a home aquarium unless you are 100% certain you are dealing with a harmless species. Use heavy protective gloves or forceps if you ever need to handle a specimen.
BLUE-RINGED OCTOPUSES (Mollusca; Cephalopoda; *Hapalochlaena* spp.)	Blue-ringed octopuses use highly toxic venom to kill their prey quickly. This venom has caused human deaths as well. The bite is rarely felt and does not cause pain or swelling. The toxins affect nerve transmissions; the first symptoms may be numbness, blurred vision, and difficulty speaking. Paralysis, including respiratory paralysis, may develop.	Apply pressure bandage to the area that is bitten (if this can be located), in order to delay the spread of venom. Get victim immediate medical attention; watch closely for any need to give artificial respiration. Any victim likely to vomit should be put on his/her side to avoid choking.	Never keep a blue-ringed octopus in a home aquarium. Use heavy protective gloves and long-handled nets if you ever need to handle a specimen.

TAXONOMIC GROUP	RISKS/SYMPTOMS	TREATMENT	PRECAUTIONS
CROWN-OF-THORNS STARFISH (Echinodermata; Asteroidea; *Acanthaster planci*)	The sharp, heavy spines can puncture human skin and inject a toxin. The wound is intensely painful and produces swelling, redness, heat, and numbness. Stings from many spines at once may result in vomiting. Secondary infections often develop. Spine tips can break off in the wound, resulting in late complications that may require surgery.	Any embedded spines or parts thereof should be removed. Immersing the affected body part in 50°C (122°F) water can help break down the toxins. Avoid scalding the skin. Clean and disinfect the wound.	Never handle a Crown-of-Thorns Starfish with bare hands. Always wear thick protective gloves.
LONG-SPINED SEA URCHINS (Echinodermata; Echinoidea; *Diadema* spp.)	The very long, sharp spines easily penetrate human skin and break off. No toxin has been isolated from these sea urchins, but the wound is intensely painful, which suggests that there is venom present. Swelling and secondary inflammation may occur.	Any embedded spines or parts thereof should be removed. Clean and disinfect the wound.	Do not handle long-spined sea urchins with bare hands. Always wear gloves.
COLLECTOR URCHIN (Echinodermata; Echinoidea; *Tripneustes gratilla*)	This urchin species has venomous pedicellariae among its spines. Most are too small to puncture human skin, but extended contact or contact with tender skin (such as on the inside of an arm) may lead to a severe sting. Aching pains and localized swelling and redness are the immediate symptoms. More severe effects, like decreased blood pressure and heart rhythm disorder, are uncommon.	Immerse the affected body part in 50°C (122°F) water to break down the toxins. Avoid scalding the skin. Applying 20% aluminum sulfate may also help.	Never handle Collector Urchins with bare hands. Always wear rubber gloves.
FLOWER SEA URCHINS (Echinodermata; Echinoidea; *Toxopneustes* spp.)	These urchins are the most dangerous to humans. The large, open, flowerlike pedicellariae are highly venomous, and the painful stings may lead to severe symptoms, including collapse, paralysis, and/or breathing difficulties.	Immerse the affected body part in 50°C (122°F) water to break down the toxins. Get victim immediate medical attention. If necessary, give artificial respiration and cardiac massage.	Never handle flower sea urchins with bare hands. Always wear rubber gloves.
SHARKS AND RAYS (Chondrichthyes)	Although sharks and rays of reasonable "home aquarium size" are hardly dangerous to humans, bear in mind that they can still inflict serious bite wounds. Secondary infections may occur.	Clean and disinfect wound thoroughly. Depending on the nature of the wound, it can be treated at home or may need medical attention.	Take care when working in a tank containing a shark or ray. Never hand feed these animals without the aid of long tongs or a feeding stick.
MORAY EELS (Osteichthyes; Anguilliformes; Muraenidae)	Although morays are not typically dangerous to humans, they can still inflict serious bite wounds. Contrary to popular belief, morays do not have a venomous bite, but secondary infections, due to dirty teeth, are common.	Clean and disinfect wound thoroughly. Depending on the nature of the wound, it can be treated at home or may need medical attention.	Take care when working in a tank with moray eels. Never hand feed without the aid of a feeding stick.

(continued on next page)

TABLE 5-2

POTENTIALLY INJURIOUS AQUARIUM INHABITANTS (CONT.)

TAXONOMIC GROUP	RISKS/SYMPTOMS	TREATMENT	PRECAUTIONS
LIONFISHES (Osteichthyes; Scorpaeniformes; *Pterois* spp. and *Dendrochirus* spp.)	All scorpionfishes are more or less venomous, but the beautiful lionfishes are of particular concern because of their popularity with aquarists. The spines in the dorsal, anal, and pectoral fins are equipped with venom glands. Stings give immediate burning pains, often followed by inflammation of lymph glands, breathing difficulties, vomiting, and muscular spasms.	Immerse the affected body part immediately in 50°C (122°F) water to break down the toxins (soak for 30 to 90 minutes, or until the pain is reduced). Get victim immediate medical attention. If necessary, administer artificial respiration.	Take the utmost care when working in a tank with lionfishes. Never hand feed without the aid of long tongs or a feeding stick.
STONEFISHES (Osteichthyes; Scorpaeniformes; *Synanceia* spp. and *Inimicus* spp.)	Stonefishes have the most powerful fish venom known. The apparatus (connected to the dorsal fin spines) they use to inject the venom into the victim is also very sophisticated and effective. Symptoms are similar to those described for lionfishes, but are much more dramatic. <u>Human deaths</u> <u>have</u> <u>occurred</u>. Even in less serious cases, the recovery period may last two to three months.	*Immediately* get victim medical attention. If necessary, administer artificial respiration.	Never keep stonefishes in home aquariums. Use heavy gloves if you ever need to handle a specimen.
SURGEONFISHES (Osteichthyes; Perciformes; Acanthuridae)	All surgeonfishes possess one or more sharp, lancelike spines on the sides of the base of the tail. When the fish becomes excited or bends its body (depending on the species) the spine can be extended at right angles. With a quick movement of the tail, large specimens are capable of inflicting deep and painful wounds. Secondary infections may occur.	Clean and disinfect wound thoroughly. Depending on the nature of the wound, it can be treated at home or may need medical attention.	Take care when working in any tank housing large surgeonfishes and when netting and moving them.
RABBITFISHES (Osteichthyes; Perciformes; Siganidae)	Dorsal, pelvic, and anal spines are associated with venom glands. Stings can give symptoms similar to (but usually weaker than) those described for lionfishes. Stings are less likely to occur because rabbitfishes normally lack the curious nature of lionfishes.	Immerse the affected body part immediately in 50°C (122°F) water to break down the toxins (soak for 30 to 90 minutes, or until the pain is reduced). Professional medical attention may become necessary.	Take care when working in a tank with rabbitfishes.
TRIGGERFISHES AND PUFFERFISHES (Osteichthyes; Tetraodontiformes; Balistidae and Tetraodontidae)	These fishes and several of their relatives (boxfishes, filefishes, porcupinefishes) have strong beaklike teeth and powerful jaws. Large specimens can inflict serious bite wounds. Secondary infections may occur.	Clean and disinfect wound thoroughly. Depending on the nature of the wound, it can be treated at home or may need medical attention.	Take care when working in a tank with large trigger- and pufferfishes. Never hand feed without the aid of long tongs or a feeding stick.

ing. Unless it's a very large fish or shrimp, the chances of receiving a deep wound are slight, but it is better to avoid cuts in the first place. See Table 5-2 (pages 89-92) for likely risks of being bitten or cut in the home aquarium by any particular group of animals.

BACTERIAL INFECTIONS

ALL KINDS OF WOUNDS THAT PUNCTURE the skin may provide an opportunity for bacterial infections. Any wounds should, therefore, be carefully cleaned and disinfected. If lasting redness and/or swelling occurs, it is important to seek medical attention.

Apart from secondary infections, one bacterium species in particular has been reported as a cause of disease in aquarists: *Mycobacterium marinum*. It is a common bacterium in aquariums, where it can cause so-called **fish tuberculosis**—a disease that typically breaks out during weakened states of health brought on by poor water conditions. The disease often runs a lingering course, with one or a few fishes dying once in a while, but it can also strike as an epidemic. Symptoms may include bloating of the body, emaciation along the dorsal ridge, sunken belly, scale loss and lifted scales, open skin lesions, popeye, spinal curvature, jerky swimming, abdominal organ displacement, reduced reflexes, and appetite loss. Only autopsy can give a positive diagnosis.

Incidents of infection by *Mycobacterium* in man are very rare and not dangerous, but we find the need to describe it here because the symptoms are often unfamiliar to medical practitioners.

When the bacterium infects the skin of humans, it causes localized microscopic nodules (granulomas) to form. The granulomas occur at sites of skin trauma (scratches, cuts) within 2 to 3 weeks of exposure. The nodules slowly increase in size to become visible and may ulcerate. Multiple granulomas may form in a line along the lymphatic vessel that drains the site. These lesions will usually spontaneously heal in several months, but anti-tuberculosis drugs will speed healing. To avoid infection, use rubber gloves when working in the aquarium, especially if you have open wounds or lesions on your hands.

> ### SAFETY CONCERNS
>
> Remember that a few reef animals may be hazardous to human health, even when kept in an aquarium.
> If you own such animals, always take measures to keep children and others from reaching into the tank.
>
> ■ ■ ■

ALLERGIES

ALLERGIC REACTIONS MAY take different forms. In some people it may be similar to hay fever, with nose and eye irritations, tears, and sneezing. Others may develop skin swellings, itches, and edema. If swelling occurs inside the mouth or throat, there can be risks of suffocation. Very severe and life-threatening allergic reactions can involve anaphylactic shock, in which the person collapses with sweating, breathing problems, a fall in blood pressure, and fading consciousness.

Aquarium keeping is not known to involve many allergy risks, but particularly with toxic animals it is important to know that venoms that are harmless to most people can be deadly to others. Mild allergies are more common in relation to fish foods than to live animals.

In particular, allergic reactions to bloodworms (chironomid larvae) are quite common and seem to take two primary forms—a contact dermatitis and a respiratory response. The contact form, usually resulting from handling the frozen product, can result in itching, swelling, cracking, and peeling and/or blistering of the skin of the hands or swelling of the fingers. The respiratory response, which is more common when handling dried food products containing bloodworms, can be immediate or delayed by a number of hours. Usually the symptoms include some combination of runny nose, watery eyes, sneezing, and varying degrees of respiratory difficulty. The reaction may merely be a mild nuisance to many, but in some people it can cause acute respiratory distress or asthma, leading to a trip to the hospital.

The allergen in the bloodworms is probably the red hemoglobin-like protein erythrocruorin that gives the worms their characteristic color. The same protein is found in smaller concentrations in many other invertebrates (e.g., *Tubifex* worms) which are also used as fish food.

If you have any hint that you are developing a sensitivity to bloodworms or other food products, handle them with great care, minimize any required physical contact, and be alert to developing symptoms and problems. Better yet, switch to another fish food that doesn't pose a personal risk. ✿

CHAPTER 6

STOCKING GUIDE

A Concise Encyclopedia of Fishes and Invertebrates
Commonly Available to the Marine Aquarist

IFE ON EARTH HAS EVOLVED FOR MORE
than 3.5 billion years with continual species appearances and extinctions. Humans have iden-
tified more than 1 million different species of
animals—many more remain to be found and described.

To get an overview of the complex life on Earth,
scientists have recently grouped all described organisms
into five kingdoms, including the Animal Kingdom,
which is further subdivided into 36 phyla, or major divisions. The most widespread and commonly recognized
phyla are Porifera (sponges), Cnidaria (hydrozoans,
anemones, corals, and equals), Annelida (segmented
worms), Crustacea (crustaceans), Mollusca (mollusks),
Echinodermata (starfishes, sea urchins, sea cucumbers,
and equals), and Chordata (vertebrates and tunicates).
The phyla are further subdivided into several categories,
or taxa, where class, order, family, genus, and species are
the most commonly used divisions.

A species is assigned its scientific name (the two-part
Latin designation of genus and species) when it is sci-
entifically described. This is done according to fixed rules
designed to assure that any name identifies only a specific
interbreeding group—a single, recognizable species.
Nonscientists, among them aquarists, often prefer to call
familiar organisms by common names, popularized labels
that are easier to recognize for the untrained ear.
However, a common name is not bestowed under any
sort of rules and regulations. Anyone may create a common name for an organism and put it into public use.
This is especially common in the aquarium trade, where
many species have several common names, with variations from country to country, region to region, and even
aquarium shop to aquarium shop. (Consider the stony
coral *Heliofungia actiniformis*, a single species that is var-
iously called the plate coral, anemone mushroom coral,
disk coral, or long-tentacle plate coral.)

Leaf Scorpionfish (*Taenianotus triacanthus*), **left**, is innocuous
looking but actually a voracious predator. Slightly sinister in
appearance, the brittle star, **above**, is a harmless detritivore.

Juvenile Harlequin Sweetlips (*Plectorhinchus chaetodonoides*) is a perfect example of a fish that has immediate appeal to aquarists, but it is not easy to feed and grows into the brute shown below.

Adult Harlequin Sweetlips (*Plectorhinchus chaetodonoides*) is the mature version of the juvenile above. It grows to 70 cm (27 in.).

Seahorses (*Hippocampus* spp.) need special feeding and placid tankmates. As with all fishes, know their needs before buying.

Common names often breed confusion, while scientific names are clear and universally accepted and understood. In this book, we use both groups of names: the scientific names that are as up-to-date as possible, and common names as much in accordance with common practice in other literature and among English-speaking hobbyists as possible.

Nevertheless, either name, although it may serve to identify the organism, says very little—or nothing at all—about the organism's way of living, its required environmental conditions, or where it can be found. Take, for instance, the so-called Longnose Filefish (*Oxymonacanthus longirostris*). Neither the scientific nor the common name tells you that this fish lives among the branches of stony corals and feeds almost exclusively on live *Acropora* coral polyps—obviously vital information to have if you are considering the purchase of this beautiful fish for your aquarium. For this you need a guide written by and for aquarium keepers. (If they are honest, they will tell you to avoid this fish, which virtually never survives in captivity because of its specialized diet.)

A good aquarist can never have too many livestock guidebooks, and in the following Stocking Guide, we focus on what we consider the knowledge you might need when evaluating most commonly available species and groups as prospective aquarium specimens.

The selection of animals is based on our experiences with organisms that are readily available in the trade, and a desire to present typical representatives of the major groups or taxa. With this representative selection, it is our hope that you will come to appreciate how important it is to consult one or more livestock guides before buying an unknown species and bringing it home to your aquarium. By checking against this directory and looking into the other guides we recommend in Further Reading (page 231), you will save lives, save money, and avoid the anguish of having an animal perish under your care.

HOW TO USE THIS GUIDE

OUR GOAL IN CREATING this simplified directory of common invertebrates and fishes is to provide a book you can bring with you when shopping for animals and quickly determine whether a particular species or group is right for your system. With this information on hand, you will be better able to choose the right organisms for your home aquarium. Each page presents four animals. Each animal is presented with one photograph and a box containing selected information for that specific organism (and closely related organisms in the same genus). The box provides the following information:

The **heading** gives the scientific name, a brief hierarchy showing its systematic position in relation to other taxonomic groups, and one or more common names. It also lists the maximum size as well as information on the natural distribution, or range, of the species.

Specific points of interest and husbandry advice for the species are highlighted as appropriate, with different areas of concern or interest for different groups:

Lighting requirements are noted when necessary, especially for photosynthetic species that may need bright conditions for survival and growth.

Circulation (water motion) is of special concern for some animals, and this is detailed when appropriate.

Water Quality is noted for animals with special demands for clean water or chemical supplementation.

Aquascaping is discussed when special substrate or decorative needs are known for a particular animal.

Feeding is a consideration for all fishes and many invertebrates. Advice here includes appropriate food as well as feeding frequency.

Compatibility covers a range of important issues, including aggressiveness of the species toward its own kind and toward other animals. "Keep singly" is a rule that applies to many reef fishes that will compete aggressively with members of their own species, especially in smaller systems. Predatory habits are noted where applicable. Animals that are considered "reef safe" are generally known to exist peaceably with other typical inhabitants of a reef aquarium.

Hazards are highlighted for any animal that poses a danger to humans.

Conservation notes those animals that survive poorly in captivity and are generally best left in the wild.

CODE COLOR KEY

A SIMPLE SYSTEM OF COLORED BOXES denotes special concerns or degree of difficulty in a particular area:

■ **Requirements easily met** with good, basic aquarium husbandry and typical conditions.

■ **Caution:** requires special attention. May demand conditions and care beyond the ability of a new hobbyist.

■ **Warning:** requirements or facts requiring special attention by the aquarist. Husbandry demands are appropriate only for advanced aquarists.

Easy to keep soft coral (*Efflatounaria* sp.) contains symbiotic zooxanthellae that provide it with nourishment in well-lit conditions. Compare to the similar species below.

Difficult to maintain soft coral (*Nephthyigorgia* sp.) lacks zooxanthellae and demands frequent feedings of small plankton.

Elephant Ear Anemone (*Amplexidiscus fenestrafer*) is a fascinating animal but can close up like a purse and capture fishes.

Porifera; Demospongiae, Dictyoceratida
Ear Sponge   *Collospongia auris*
Grows indefinitely   Indo-Pacific

■ **Lighting** Contains symbiotic algae and needs bright lighting.
■ **Compatibility** Expands rapidly in good conditions and may become a nuisance, overgrowing sessile invertebrates, including corals, and requiring trimming by hand.

An attractive bluish gray sponge found on shallow coral reefs in brightly lit situations. Encrusting or forming horizontal plates with upright lobes resembling tiny ears, hence the popular name.

Porifera; Demospongiae; Haplosclerida; Chalinidae
Soft blue sponge   *Haliclona* sp.
Grows slowly to medium-sized colonies   Indo-Pacific

■ **Circulation** Needs medium to strong water currents.
■ **Feeding** Difficult to keep nourished. Requires dissolved or very fine suspended organic particles and minute plankton.

Forms bright blue branching colonies. The tissue is soft in comparison to *Xestospongia* (below). Difficult to keep in well-skimmed, nutrient-poor reef systems. Best broken into smaller fragments and planted in different spots in the aquarium.

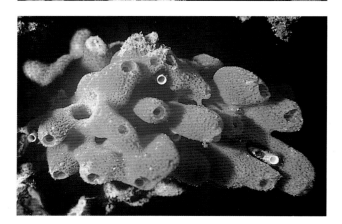

Porifera; Demospongiae; Haplosclerida; Petrosiidae
Hard blue sponge   *Xestospongia* sp.
Grows slowly to medium-sized colonies   Indo-Pacific

■ **Circulation** Needs medium to strong water currents.
■ **Feeding** Difficult to keep well fed. Sponges are filter feeders that needs fine suspended organic particles and minute plankton.
■ **Compatibility** Dead or dying colonies may release toxins that can kill corals and other invertebrates.

A beautiful blue sponge with dense, hard tissue. Unfortunately, very difficult to keep and often dead upon arrival. Best broken into smaller fragments and planted in different spots in the aquarium.

Porifera; Demospongiae, Halichondrida, Axinellidae
Cork Sponge   *Stylissa carteri*
Grows slowly to medium-sized colonies   Indo-Pacific

■ **Lighting** Needs medium to low light intensities.
■ **Circulation** Needs medium to strong alternating water motion.
■ **Feeding** Filter feeder that needs fine suspended organic particles and minute plankton.

This orange or yellow-orange sponge forms irregular colonies and is fairly easy to keep. The outward parts of the colonies are thin, laminar and irregular in shape. *Stylissa flabelliformis* is a similar-looking species.

Porifera; Demospongiae; Spirophorida; Suberitidae
Yellow Encrusting Sponge   *Pseudosuberites andrewsi*
Grows slowly to medium-sized colonies   Indo-Pacific

■ **Lighting** Needs medium to low light intensities.
■ **Circulation** Needs medium to strong alternating water motion.
■ **Feeding** Filter feeder that needs dissolved or very fine suspended organic particles and minute plankton.

This is a hardy and easy to keep sponge with a bright or light yellow color. Frequently arrives on live rock. Colony may be encrusting or lumpy and irregular.

Porifera; Demospongiae; Halichondrida, Axinellidae
Strawberry sponge   *Pseudaxinella* sp.
Grows slowly to medium-sized colonies   Caribbean Sea

■ **Lighting** Needs medium to low light intensities.
■ **Circulation** Needs medium to strong alternating water motion.
■ **Feeding** Filter feeder that needs dissolved or very fine suspended organic particles and minute plankton.

This pretty species is frequently imported but relatively difficult to keep in most well-skimmed reef systems. As with most sponges, this species must never be exposed to open air, which can become trapped in the animal and lead to tissue decay.

Porifera; Demospongiae; Halichondrida, Desmoxyidae
Red branching sponge   *Higginsia* sp.
Grows slowly to medium-sized colonies   Circumtropical

■ **Lighting** Needs medium to low light intensities.
■ **Circulation** Needs medium to strong alternating water motion.
■ **Feeding** Somewhat demanding filter feeder that needs dissolved or very fine suspended organic particles and minute plankton.

This frequently imported genus includes red branching species from the Caribbean and several yellow or orange species from the Indo-Pacific. They are all eye-catching but rather to difficult to keep over time without special feeding.

Porifera; Demospongiae; Halichondrida, Axinellidae
Yellow finger sponges   *Auletta* spp.
Grow slowly to medium-sized colonies   Indo-Pacific

■ **Lighting** Need medium to low light intensities.
■ **Circulation** Need medium to strong alternating water motion.
■ **Feeding** Demanding filter feeders that need dissolved or very fine suspended organic particles and minute plankton.

Several similar species form colorful fingerlike and/or tubular branches rising from a single stalk. Difficult to keep; must be provided with sufficient food and adequate water motion.

Cnidaria; Hydrozoa, Milleporidae
Fire Coral   *Millepora alcicornis*

Encrusting, can form large colonies   Caribbean Sea

■ **Lighting** Photosynthetic species that needs strong light.
■ **Compatibility** Aggressively competes for space with other corals; must not be placed close to other sessile invertebrates.
■ **Hazards** Has a powerful sting that will burn humans as well as neighboring corals.

Grows as an encrusting coral with upright branches. Yellow or yellow-orange color. Hairy-like polyps scattered over the entire surface. Occasionally offered for sale.

Cnidaria; Scyphozoa; Rhizostoma, Cassiopeidae
Upside-down jellyfishes   *Cassiopea* spp.

10-15 cm (3.9-5.9 in.) in diameter   Indo-Pacific; Caribbean Sea

■ **Lighting** Photosynthetic species that need strong light.
■ **Aquascaping** Requires a special aquarium with sandy, open areas, weak water motion, and protection from pump and filter intakes.

Like most jellyfishes, this group alternates between a sexual freeliving medusa generation and a sessile asexual polyp generation. The medusa stage commonly lives upside-down on the bottom, but can also swim in the water column and may have beautiful colors. Not recommended for most reef or "community" aquariums.

Cnidaria; Anthozoa; Ceriantharia; Cerianthidae
Tube anemone   *Cerianthus* sp.

20-40 cm (7.8-15.6 in.) high   Circumtropical

■ **Aquascaping** Needs thick bottom layer in which the animal can bury its leathery tube and plenty of room to expand its tentacles.
■ **Feeding** Needs small live or frozen plankton suspended in the water column for capture by its long, sticky tentacles.
■ **Compatibility** Some species have a powerful sting delivered by long tentacles; can easily damage other animals and catch fishes.

A number of genera and species are collected, some very colorful, but most are best kept in their own specialized aquarium.

Cnidaria; Anthozoa; Alcyonacea; Stolonifera, Tubiporidae
Organ-pipe Coral   *Tubipora musica*

Medium to large   Indo-Pacific

■ **Lighting** Photosynthetic species that needs very strong light.
■ **Water Quality** Demands nutrient-poor water and conditions that prevent the colony from being overgrown by hair algae.

Not a true stony coral, but with a distinctive dark red brittle skeleton composed of calcite tubes. Polyps may be light brown, green, or white, and are highly variable in shape, suggesting that several different species may exist. Can be rather difficult to keep, compared with other members of the Order Stolonifera.

Cnidaria; Anthozoa; Alcyonacea; Stolonifera, Clavulariidae
Clove polyp *"Clavularia* sp."
Medium-sized Central Pacific

■ **Lighting** Photosynthetic species needs very strong light.
■ **Feeding** This and other related soft corals may absorb dissolved nutrients, but otherwise need no intentional feeding.

Although nearly impossible to identify, this is one of several similar species that are common and easy to keep. Has long calyces (tubes) into which the polyps can retract completely.

Cnidaria; Anthozoa; Alcyonacea; Alcyoaniina; Xeniidae
"Sansibia," Brown star polyp *Sansibia* sp.
Spreads indefinitely Central Pacific

■ **Lighting** Photosynthetic species that requires very strong light.
■ **Feeding** This and other related soft corals may absorb dissolved nutrients, but otherwise need no intentional feeding.

Although brown, this genus makes an attractive addition to the reef tank, with iridescent green or blue highlights, predominantly in the tentacles. Easy to keep and can spread throughout the aquarium.

Cnidaria; Anthozoa; Alcyonacea; Alcyoaniina; Xeniidae
Waving hand polyps *Anthelia* spp.
Medium-sized Indo-Pacific

■ **Lighting** Photosynthetic species need very strong light. Probably feed exclusively from symbiotic algae products.
■ **Water Quality** Can be very sensitive to changes in water quality or lighting, for example if activated carbon filtration is suddenly added or increased.

Often imported and hardy. Can grow fast and colonize large areas. Easy to confuse with Stolonifera (see above), but polyps do not retract. The *Xenia*-like polyps arise from a mat, rather than a stalk.

Cnidaria; Anthozoa; Alcyonacea; Alcyoaniina; Xeniidae
"Blue Xenia" *Cespitularia* sp.
Small to medium-sized Indo-Pacific

■ **Lighting** Photosynthetic species that requires very strong light.
■ **Water Quality** Can be very sensitive to changes in water quality or lighting, for example if activated carbon filtration is suddenly added or increased.

A highly prized soft coral with bright fluorescent colors and polyps that will "pulse" (open and close rhythmically) in certain conditions. This coral is sensitive to transportation and more challenging to keep than other Xeniidae.

Cnidaria; Anthozoa; Alcyonacea; Alcyoaniina; Xeniidae
Pulse corals, "Xenia"   *Xenia* spp.
Small to medium-sized (10 cm [3.9 in.])   Indo-Pacific

■ **Lighting** Photosynthetic species that need strong light. Supplemental feeding not required.
■ **Water Quality** Can be very sensitive to changes in water quality or lighting, for example if carbon filtration is suddenly added or increased. Sometimes thrive in systems with minimal skimming.

The "pulsing" polyps of this genus can captivate reef observers. Some species are hardy and easy to keep, while others are more demanding. Colors range from white and pale yellow to light brown and brown.

Cnidaria; Anthozoa; Alcyonacea; Alcyoaniina; Nephtheidae
Broccoli corals   *Nephthea* spp.
Medium-sized to large colonies   Indo-Pacific

■ **Lighting** Photosynthetic species that need strong light.
■ **Feeding** Derive most of their nutrition from photosynthetic products produced by their symbiotic algae, but may also utilize minute plankton.

Excellent "beginner's corals" that are easily kept and fast growing. Simple to propagate by cuttings. Color is usually light brown, with nonretractable polyps. Related to a complex group of large, branching soft corals, including the genera *Neospongodes* and *Litophyton*.

Cnidaria; Anthozoa; Alcyonacea; Alcyoaniina; Nephtheidae
Broccoli coral   *Neospongodes* sp.
Medium-sized to large colonies   Indo-Pacific

■ **Lighting** Most (but far from all) species are photosynthetic and need medium to strong lighting.
■ **Circulation** Requires moderate to relatively strong water motion.
■ **Feeding** Many of these corals demand regular feedings of minute plankton to thrive.

These are very delicate soft corals, with thin tissue, and are difficult to keep without daily feeding and excellent water conditions.

Cnidaria; Anthozoa; Alcyonacea; Alcyoaniina; Nephtheidae
Kenya Tree   *Capnella imbricata*
Medium-sized colonies   Indo-Pacific

■ **Lighting** Photosynthetic species that needs very strong light.
■ **Feeding** Nourished primarily by the photosynthetic products produced by its symbiotic algae; does not require intentional feeding.

A hardy, popular coral that is very easy to keep and propagate by cuttings. Reproduces asexually by releasing daughter colonies from its branches. Color may be brown, yellowish brown, or pale yellow, with polyps located at the ends of small branches. One of the first soft corals to be established in European reef tanks in the late 1970s.

Cnidaria; Anthozoa; Alcyonacea; Alcyoaniina; Nephtheidae

Spaghetti coral   *Lemnalia* sp.

Medium-sized to large colonies   Indo-Pacific

■ **Lighting** Photosynthetic species that needs very strong light.

■ **Feeding** Nourished primarily by the photosynthetic products produced by its symbiotic algae; does not require intentional feeding.

An easily kept soft coral that forms large, branching and fleshy colonies. The branches are stiff and supported by many internal sclerites (tiny bits of calcium). Polyps are found only along the small, outer (third) branchlets. Usually brownish yellow or yellow.

Cnidaria; Anthozoa; Alcyonacea; Alcyoaniina; Nephtheidae

Finger leather   *Paralemnalia* sp.

Medium-sized to large colonies   Indo-Pacific

■ **Lighting** Photosynthetic species that needs very strong light.

■ **Circulation** Benefits from active, alternating water currents.

■ **Feeding** Nourished primarily by the photosynthetic products produced by its symbiotic algae; does not require intentional feeding.

As with many of the soft corals, easy to keep but challenging to identify. Forms medium- to large-sized colonies with distinct branches that arise from an encrusting base. Polyps are often scattered along the branches.

Cnidaria; Anthozoa; Alcyonacea; Alcyoaniina; Nephtheidae

Strawberry corals   *Dendronephthya* spp.

Small to very large colonies   Indo-Pacific

■ **Lighting** Do not contain symbiotic algae and have no protection against UV-radiation. Require dim to moderate lighting.

■ **Circulation** Must have strong back-and-forth water motion.

■ **Feeding** Require almost constant feedings with minute phytoplankton—their primary source of nutrition.

Although brightly colored and very beautiful, these corals are delicate and difficult to keep. Suitable only for expert aquarists who can meet their requirements for food and water movement.

Cnidaria; Anthozoa; Alcyonacea; Alcyoaniina; Nephtheidae

Strawberry coral   *Scleronephthya* sp.

Small to medium-sized colonies   Indo-Pacific

■ **Lighting** Does not contain symbiotic algae and has no protections against UV-radiation. Requires dim to moderate lighting.

■ **Circulation** Must have strong back-and-forth water motion.

■ **Feeding** Requires almost constant feedings with minute zoo- and phytoplankton—its primary source of nutrition.

Resembles *Dendronephthya* but polyps are contractile and lack large, polyp-supporting sclerites. Difficult to keep. Often yellow or orange.

Cnidaria; Anthozoa; Alcyonacea; Alcyoaniina; Nidalidae
"Chironephthya"   *Chironephthya* sp.
Medium-sized colonies   Indo-Pacific

■ **Lighting** Does not contain symbiotic algae and has no protections against UV-radiation. Requires dim to moderate lighting.
■ **Circulation** Must have strong back-and-forth water motion.
■ **Feeding** Requires almost constant feedings with minute plankton and dissolved organic compounds.

A beauty in the wild, but very difficult to keep. Forms tree-shaped colonies often hanging from the roofs of caves in the nature. The colonies can retract and change their size dramatically.

Cnidaria; Anthozoa; Alcyonacea; Alcyoaniina; Nidalidae
Devil's hand   *Nephthyigorgia* sp.
Small colonies   Indo-Pacific

■ **Lighting** Lacks symbiotic algae and should be given moderate to dim lighting and protection from UV-radiation.
■ **Circulation** Needs strong water motion.
■ **Feeding** Must be provided with tiny planktonic foods, such as enriched *Artemia* (brine shrimp), that are fed directly to the polyps.

These small finger-shaped colonies are appealing, but difficult to keep for an extended period of time. Best given a special aquarium, where sufficient food and proper water motion can be provided.

Cnidaria; Anthozoa; Alcyonacea; Alcyoaniina; Alcyoniidae
Encrusting leather coral   *Rhytisma* sp.
Medium-sized colonies   Indo-Pacific

■ **Lighting** Photosynthetic; needs moderate to strong lighting.
■ **Compatibility** Competes with neighboring corals and algae by releasing irritating chemical compounds. Can therefore be a potential threat to other corals.

This encrusting soft coral (formerly known as *Parerythropodium* sp.) is regularly imported and both easy to keep and simple to propagate by cuttings. Usually bright yellow, occasionally brown, with long polyps and a thin encrusting base.

Cnidaria; Anthozoa; Alcyonacea; Alcyoaniina; Alcyoniidae
Mushroom coral, Leather coral   *Sarcophyton* sp.
Medium-sized colonies   Indo-Pacific

■ **Lighting** Contains symbiotic algae; needs high light intensity.
■ **Feeding** Nourished primarily by the photosynthetic products produced by its symbiotic algae; probably does not require feeding.
■ **Water Quality** Often found on oceanic reefs in nutrient-poor water.

This bright yellow species normally grows in very shallow water and has a mushroom colony shape typical of the *Sarcophyton* genus. An excellent candidate for a special biotope aquarium copying a shallow reef with strong light and water flows.

Cnidaria; Anthozoa; Alcyonacea; Alcyoaniina; Alcyoniidae
Mushroom Coral, Leather Coral   *Sarcophyton ehrenbergi*
Medium-sized colonies   Indo-Pacific

■ **Lighting** Contains symbiotic algae and needs strong lighting.
■ **Feeding** Nourished primarily by the photosynthetic products produced by its symbiotic algae; does not require intentional feeding.
■ **Circulation** Needs moderate to strong water motion.

A hardy and desirable coral that can only be distinguished from other *Sarcophyton* spp. by the shape of its internal sclerites. Can be propagated by splitting large colonies into two halves.

Cnidaria; Anthozoa; Alcyonacea; Alcyoaniina; Alcyoniidae
Mushroom Coral   *Sarcophyton tenuispiculatum*
Large colonies   Indo-Pacific

■ **Lighting** Contains symbiotic algae and therefore needs strong lighting.
■ **Circulation** Moderate to strong water motion.
■ **Aquascaping** Grows to form a huge colony that will need ample room to expand.

Very hardy and easy to keep leather coral that can reach more than 50 cm (19.5 in.) in diameter in captivity. Difficult to identify when small, but develops a very thick stalk as it matures.

Cnidaria; Anthozoa; Alcyonacea; Alcyoaniina; Alcyoniidae
Leather Coral   *Sinularia dura*
Small to medium-sized colonies   Indo-Pacific

■ **Lighting** Contains symbiotic algae and needs moderate to high light intensity. May be sensitive to strong UV-light.
■ **Feeding** Does not require intentional feeding.

Very common coral in the wild; both hardy and easy to propagate in the aquarium. Forms leaf- or cuplike colonies, which are normally light brown or yellow, with scattered small polyps. Like all *Sinularia* spp. it has only feeding polyps. (Many other soft corals have freckle-like circulatory polyps.) Other closely related species also occur in the trade.

Cnidaria; Anthozoa; Alcyonacea; Alcyoaniina; Alcyoniidae
Finger Leather   *Sinularia flexibilis*
Large colonies   Indo-Pacific

■ **Lighting** Photosynthetic; needs moderate to high light intensity.
■ **Circulation** Requires moderate to strong water motion.
■ **Aquascaping** Needs plenty of space to expand.

Hardy and easy to keep and propagate from cuttings. In the wild, it forms large groups of colonies with long and slender fingerlike lobes flowing from a long, fleshy stalk. Like all *Sinularia* spp. it has only feeding polyps.

Cnidaria; Anthozoa; Alcyonacea; Alcyoaniina; Alcyoniidae
Finger leather   *Sinularia* sp.
Medium to large colonies   Indo-Pacific

■ **Lighting** Photosynthetic; needs moderate to high light intensity.
■ **Circulation** Requires moderate to strong water motion.
■ **Aquascaping** Grows rather large and needs space to expand.

Mostly yellowish or light brown, these soft corals are hardy and easy to keep and propagate from cuttings. There are more than 100 described species of finger-shaped *Sinularia*, some with pulsing polyps.

Cnidaria; Anthozoa; Alcyonacea; Alcyoaniina; Alcyoniidae
Finger leather corals   *Lobophytum* spp.
Medium-sized to very large colonies   Indo-Pacific

■ **Lighting** Contain symbiotic algae, need moderate to strong light.
■ **Circulation** Require moderate to strong water motion.
■ **Aquascaping** Can form large colonies; need plenty of space.

Hardy, common, and easy to keep and propagate from cuttings. These species typically form large, fleshy brown or yellow colonies, usually forming distinct lobes. In the wild, it is not uncommon to see colonies several meters (yards) across.

Cnidaria; Anthozoa; Alcyonacea; Alcyoaniina; Alcyoniidae
Cauliflower coral   *Cladiella* sp.
Medium-sized to large colonies   Indo-Pacific

■ **Lighting** Contains symbiotic algae and needs intense lighting.
■ **Circulation** Needs moderate to strong water motion.
■ **Water Quality** Needs the best possible water quality; more sensitive than other species when it comes to shifting water quality.

More difficult to keep and propagate than other genera in the family. Usually has white tissue with brown polyps, a coloration that separates the genus from other genera in the family. Colonies are usually slimy to touch and appear bright white with polyps retracted.

Cnidaria; Anthozoa; Alcyonacea; Alcyoaniina; Alcyoniidae
Colt coral   *Klyxum* sp.
Medium-sized colonies   Indo-Pacific

■ **Lighting** Most species contain symbiotic algae and need strong to moderate light intensities.
■ **Circulation** Requires strong to moderate water motion.
■ **Feeding** Does not require intentional feeding.

A favorite among reef aquarists; relatively hardy and easy to keep. Formerly regarded as members of *Alcyonium*, this group has many species in the Indo-Pacific. Most are upright and branching, but some encrusting species do occur. Typically slimy to the touch.

Cnidaria; Anthozoa; Alcyonacea; Alcyoaniina; Paralcyoniidae

Christmas tree coral   *Studeriotes* **sp.**

To 30 cm (11.7 in.) high   Indo-Pacific

■ **Lighting** Does not contain symbiotic algae and should be kept in moderate to dim light intensity.

■ **Circulation** Needs strong and alternating water motion.

■ **Aquascaping** Provide a deep substrate where it can anchor itself.

■ **Feeding** Requires tiny planktonic fare, such as live brine shrimp nauplii.

Difficult to feed and keep for a longer period of time, these distinctive corals tend to collapse with little chance of recovery.

Cnidaria; Anthozoa; Alcyonacea; Scleraxonia, Briareidae

Green star polyp   *Briareum* **sp.**

Spreads indefinitely   Indo-Pacific

■ **Lighting** Photosynthetic species that needs very strong light. Probably feeds exclusively from symbiotic algae products.

■ **Compatibility** Grows rapidly but can easily be trimmed with a razor, peeled up, and transplanted .

Able to form large, bright green patches on rockwork or the walls of the aquarium, this popular star polyp is readily available and easy to keep. The stolon base mat that anchors the polyps is membranous and leathery with a purplish color. The polyps are brown or green.

Cnidaria; Anthozoa; Alcyonacea; Scleraxonia; Briareidae

Green star polyps   *Briareum* **spp.**

Grows indefinitely   Circumtropical

■ **Lighting** Contain symbiotic algae and need strong light intensity.

■ **Compatibility** Some encrusting species grow rapidly and can overgrow neighboring corals if not controlled by hand trimming.

Hardy and easy to keep. The finger-shaped *Briareum asbestinum* from the Caribbean is the best known species, but many poorly known species exist in the tropical seas. Many of the Indo-Pacific encrusting species strongly resemble star polyps.

Cnidaria; Anthozoa; Alcyonacea; Scleraxonia; Anthothelidae

Colorful Sea Rod   *Diodogorgia nodulifera*

10-30 cm (3.9-11.7 in.)   Caribbean

■ **Lighting** Does not contain symbiotic algae and does best in moderate to dim light.

■ **Circulation** Requires strong, alternating water motion.

■ **Feeding** Needs daily feedings of minute planktonic food; small live *Cyclops* or enriched *Artemia* are best.

Unfortunately impossible to keep if not given proper water motion and planktonic food. Two color forms are frequently imported, one bright red with white polyps, the other yellow with red calyces (right).

Cnidaria; Anthozoa; Alcyonacea; Scleraxonia; Anthothelidae
Encrusting Gorgonian   *Erythropodium caribaeorum*
Grows indefinitely   Caribbean

▓ **Lighting** Contains symbiotic algae; needs strong light intensity.
▓ **Compatibility** Fast-growing and can smother and kill neighboring corals if not controlled by hand trimming.

This is a hardy and easy to propagate coral that will grow very fast if given favorable conditions. It will encrust rock or aquarium glass and has long thin tentacles resembling very fine hair. Usually brown or purple encrusting base and tan tentacles. (Unusual blue morph shown.)

Cnidaria; Anthozoa; Alcyonacea; Holaxonia; Plexauridae
Sea rods   *Plexaura* spp.
To 1.5 m (4.9 ft.)   Caribbean

▓ **Lighting** Contain symbiotic algae and need moderate to strong light intensities.
▓ **Circulation** Need alternating medium to strong water currents.
▓ **Aquascaping** Grow large and requires plenty of space.

Hardy and relatively easy to keep. Two species are common: *P. homomalla* (black sea rod, shown at left) with dark brown branches and light brown polyps; and *P. flexuosa* (bent sea rod), with varying colors but often purple with white polyps. Good choice for Caribbean biotopes.

Cnidaria; Anthozoa; Alcyonacea; Holaxonia; Plexauridae
Porous sea rods   *Pseudoplexaura* spp.
To 2 m (6.6 ft.) tall   Caribbean

▓ **Lighting** Contain symbiotic algae and need moderate to strong light intensities.
▓ **Circulation** Need alternating medium to strong water currents.
▓ **Aquascaping** Grow large and require plenty of space.

Robust gorgonians suited to large reef aquariums and Caribbean exhibits. Branches are long and rather thick, with large polyps that are fully retractable. Colors usually grayish with brown polyps. At least four species are known.

Cnidaria; Anthozoa; Alcyonacea; Holaxonia; Plexauridae
Knobby sea rods   *Eunicea* spp.
To 60 cm (23 in.) tall   Caribbean

▓ **Lighting** Contain symbiotic algae and need moderate to strong light intensities.
▓ **Circulation** Need alternating medium to strong water currents.
▓ **Aquascaping** Grow large and require plenty of space.

This is a hardy and relatively easy to keep genus with several species that are quite eye-catching when their polyps are fully expanded. The polyp openings (calyces) of some species protrude above the branch surface, giving the colony a knobby appearance.

Cnidaria; Anthozoa; Alcyonacea; Holaxonia; Plexauridae

Spiny sea fans *Muricea* **spp.**

To 45 cm (17.6 in.) tall Caribbean

■ **Lighting** Contain symbiotic algae and need moderate to strong light intensities.
■ **Circulation** Need alternating medium to strong water currents.
■ **Aquascaping** Grow large and require plenty of space.

Hardy and relatively easy to keep. Easily confused with knobby sea rods (*Eunicea* spp.). Several species have protruding polyp openings (calyces) and sharp terminal spikes that make the colonies prickly to the touch.

Cnidaria; Anthozoa; Alcyonacea; Holaxonia; Plexauridae

Red Polyp Octocoral *Swiftia exserta*

15-45 cm (5.9-17.6 in.) tall Caribbean

■ **Lighting** Does not contain symbiotic algae and should be kept in dimly lit conditions.
■ **Circulation** Needs vigorous, alternating water motion.
■ **Feeding** Must be fed small plankton daily, including enriched brine shrimp (*Artemia*), *Cyclops*, and the like.

A dramatic coral with thin orange branches with large dark red polyps, but one for the advanced aquarist only. Collected in deep reef areas, and difficult to keep without specialized care and equipment.

Cnidaria; Anthozoa; Alcyonacea; Holaxonia; Gorgoniidae

Sea fans *Gorgonia* **spp.**

30-200 cm (11.7-78 in.)tall Caribbean

■ **Lighting** Contain symbiotic algae and need moderate to strong light intensities.
■ **Circulation** Need alternating medium to strong water motion
■ **Conservation** Collection of this genus is prohibited in Florida and many locations in the Caribbean. Buy legal specimens only.

Small colonies have proven to be hardy if given sufficient light and water motion directed perpendicular to the fan. This genus has three species, with *Gorgonia ventalina* (Common Sea Fan) shown at right.

Cnidaria; Anthozoa; Alcyonacea; Holaxonia; Gorgoniidae

Slimy Sea Plume *Pseudopterogorgia americana*

To 2 m (6.6 ft.) tall Caribbean

■ **Lighting** Contains symbiotic algae and needs moderate to strong light intensities.
■ **Circulation** Needs alternating medium to strong water currents.
■ **Aquascaping** Grows large and requires plenty of space.

These bushy or feathery gorgonians are attractive and relatively easy to maintain. *Pseudopterogorgia americana* is one of 15 species in this genus. It produces copious amounts of mucus that is especially slippery to the touch.

Cnidaria; Anthozoa; Alcyonacea; Holaxonia; Gorgoniidae
Sea Plume   *Pseudopterogorgia bipinnata*
To 2 m (6.6 ft.) high   Caribbean

■ **Lighting** Contains symbiotic algae and needs moderate to strong light intensities.
■ **Circulation** Needs alternating medium to strong water currents.
■ **Aquascaping** Grows large and requires plenty of space.

A good beginner's gorgonian; hardy and quite attractive with violet or yellow branches. *Pseudopterogorgia bipinnata* develops feathery branches that are arranged in one plane.

Cnidaria; Anthozoa; Alcyonacea; Holaxonia; Gorgoniidae
Sea whips   *Pterogorgia* spp.
30-60 cm (11.7-23 in.) tall   Caribbean

■ **Lighting** Photosynthetic; need moderate to strong lighting.
■ **Circulation** Need alternating medium to strong water motion.
■ **Aquascaping** Grow large and take up plenty of space. Best kept in a sand-zone aquarium where sea whips are allowed to dominate.

Relatively hardy, but more demanding than other photosynthetic species of Caribbean gorgonians. Bushy with well developed, often flattened branches. There are three species, with colors that range from olive to green, bright yellow, or violet, with contrasting polyps.

Cnidaria; Anthozoa; Alcyonacea; Holaxonia; Gorgoniidae
Sea rod   *Rumphella* sp.
Medium to large colonies   Indo-Pacific

■ **Lighting** Contains symbiotic algae and needs moderate to strong light intensities.
■ **Circulation** Needs alternating medium to strong water motion.
■ **Aquascaping** Can grow to form huge colonies and may need a large aquarium.

A very hardy coral and one of only a few photosynthetic gorgonians found in the Indo-Pacific. The common *R. aggregata* forms bushy colonies, usually with a gray or light brown color.

Cnidaria; Anthozoa; Alcyonacea; Holaxonia; Ellisellidae
Sea whips   **Ellisellidae**
Small to very large colonies   Circumtropical

■ **Lighting** Do not contain symbiotic algae and should be kept in moderate to dim lighting.
■ **Circulation** Must be given strong alternating water motion.
■ **Feeding** Require frequent or continuous feeding of suspended plankton, such as live brine shrimp (*Artemia*).

All members of this family are demanding and very difficult to keep. Thin, colorful branches typically sport gray, yellow, or white polyps. The photo at left shows *Ctenocella pectinata*.

Cnidaria; Anthozoa; Helioporacea; Helioporidae

Blue Coral *Heliopora coerulea*

Medium-sized to large colonies Central Pacific

■ **Lighting** Contains symbiotic algae and needs moderate to high light intensity.

■ **Circulation** Often found on exposed reefs and should be given moderate to strong water motion.

This unique species has a blue skeleton and resembles a stony coral, but is in fact a very special octocoral. It is hardy, easy to keep and can be propagated by taking fragments. Common in the trade, often growing from live rock.

Cnidaria; Anthozoa; Pennatulacea; Veretillidae

Sea pen *Cavernularia* sp. (?)

10-30 cm (3.9-11.7 in.) Indo-Pacific

■ **Lighting** Nocturnal; keep in very dim light so that it will expand during the day.

■ **Circulation** Needs strong alternating water motion

■ **Aquascaping** Needs a thick bottom layer of sandy substrate.

■ **Feeding** Must be fed regularly with mixed live and frozen plankton.

Interesting animal, but difficult to sustain because of its feeding habits. Has a buried "foot" (peduncle) and an upright part (rachis) containing the feeding and water-pumping polyps.

Cnidaria; Anthozoa; Pennatulacea; Pteroeididae

Sea pen *Pteroeides* sp.

10-30 cm (3.9-11.7 in.) Indo-West-Pacific, Eastern Atlantic, Mediterranean

■ **Lighting** Nocturnal; keep in very dim light so that it will expand during the day.

■ **Circulation** Needs strong alternating water motion

■ **Aquascaping** Needs a thick bottom layer of sandy substrate.

■ **Feeding** Must be fed regularly with mixed live and frozen plankton.

A real curiosity, but difficult to keep in the aquarium. Big polyp leaves contain the polyps as well as large supporting sclerites.

Cnidaria; Anthozoa; Actiniaria; Actiniidae

Bubble Tip Sea Anemone *Entacmaea quadricolor*

To 40 cm (15.6 in.) across Indo-Pacific

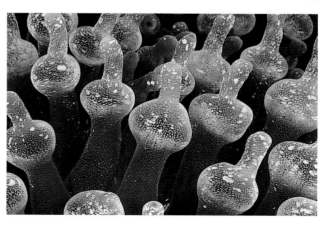

■ **Lighting** Contains symbiotic algae and needs strong lighting.

■ **Circulation** Requires moderate but steady water motion.

■ **Compatibility** Has a strong sting and will severely burn neighboring sessile animals. Best kept in a special aquarium as a host anemone for clownfishes.

Among the more hardy of the sea anemones. Usually brown or greenish brown. Long tentacles, often—but not always—with a bubblelike swelling near the tips. Usually anchored among coral branches

Cnidaria; Anthozoa; Actiniaria; Actiniidae
Caribbean Giant Anemone   *Condylactis gigantea*
To 30 cm (11.7 in.) across   Caribbean

■ **Lighting** Photosynthetic; needs strong light intensity.
■ **Circulation** Needs moderate but steady water motion.
■ **Compatibility** Has a strong sting and will severely burn neighboring sessile animals. Best suited for a special aquarium with sand, algae, and crustaceans naturally associated with this anemone.

Relatively hardy, with tentacles that can be purple, pink, green, or whitish, often tipped with color. Commensal shrimps are often associated with this anemone.

Cnidaria; Anthozoa; Actiniaria; Actiniidae
Corkscrew Anemone   *Macrodactyla doreensis*
To 50 cm (19.5 in.) across   Central Pacific

■ **Lighting** Photosynthetic; needs strong light intensity.
■ **Circulation** Needs moderate but steady water motion.
■ **Aquascaping** Needs a deep sand bed in which to bury its column.
■ **Compatibility** Has a strong sting and will severely burn neighboring sessile animals.

A commonly available and relatively hardy anemone. The lower column is orange to brilliant red, and the disc is purplish gray to brown, sometimes with radial lines. Has tentacles of equal length.

Cnidaria; Anthozoa; Actiniaria; Stichodactylidae
Magnificent Sea Anemone   *Heteractis magnifica*
To 100 cm (39 in.) across   Indo-Pacific

■ **Lighting** Photosynthetic; needs strong light intensity.
■ **Circulation** Needs moderate but steady water motion.
■ **Compatibility** Has a strong sting and will severely burn neighboring sessile animals.
■ **Feeding** Carnivore that needs meaty marine foods.

A large anemone with a poor record of survival in the aquarium. Very sensitive to physical damage to its tissue. The column is brilliant purple or bright orange; the tentacles are greenish.

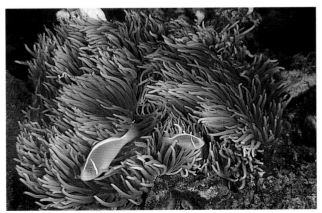

Cnidaria; Anthozoa; Actiniaria; Stichodactylidae
Leathery Sea Anemone   *Heteractis crispa*
25-50 cm (9.8-19.5 in.) across   Indo-Pacific

■ **Lighting** Photosynthetic; needs strong light intensity.
■ **Circulation** Requires moderate to strong water motion.
■ **Compatibility** Has a strong sting and can harm sessile animals.
■ **Feeding** Carnivore that needs meaty marine foods, such as pieces of shrimp or squid and live adult brine shrimp.

Has a mixed reputation for aquarium survival, and is very sensitive to physical damage to its tissue. The column feels thick and leathery, and the tapering tentacles are the same colors as the disc.

Cnidaria; Anthozoa; Actiniaria; Stichodactylidae

Beaded Sea Anemone   *Heteractis aurora*

5-25 cm (2-9.8 in.) across   Indo-Pacific

▦ **Lighting** Contains symbiotic algae; needs strong light intensity.
▦ **Circulation** Needs moderate to strong water motion.
▦ **Water Quality** Needs long acclimation and perfect water quality.
■ **Compatibility** Has a strong sting and will severely burn neighboring sessile animals.

With its beaded tentacles (see photo), this is an interesting and relatively hardy anemone if provided with the proper conditions. Upper stem and disc are gray, brownish, or green.

Cnidaria; Anthozoa; Actiniaria; Stichodactylidae

Sun Anemone   *Stichodactyla helianthus*

To 12 cm (4.7 in.) across   Caribbean

▦ **Lighting** Contains symbiotic algae and needs intense lighting.
▦ **Water Quality** Needs long acclimation and perfect water quality.
■ **Compatibility** Strong sting; will severely burn neighboring sessile animals.

There are no anemonefishes in the Caribbean, but commensal crustaceans, such as *Thor amboinensis* shrimp and *Mitrax* crabs, do find protection with these small carpet-type anemones. Relatively hardy.

Cnidaria; Anthozoa; Actiniaria; Stichodactylidae

Saddle Anemone   *Stichodactyla haddoni*

30-50 cm (11.7-19.5 in.) across   Indo-Pacific

▦ **Lighting** Contains symbiotic algae and need bright lighting.
▦ **Water Quality** Needs long acclimation and perfect water quality.
■ **Compatibility** Has a strong sting and can harm sessile animals.
▦ **Feeding** Carnivore that needs regular meals of high-quality meaty foods.

A large, beautiful anemone, but not for beginners. More sensitive to water quality than other host sea anemones. Color morphs may be gray, light green, striped, bright green, or reddish orange.

Cnidaria; Anthozoa; Actiniaria; Stichodactylidae

Giant Carpet Anemone   *Stichodactyla gigantea*

15-50 cm (5.9-19.5 in.)   Indo-Pacific

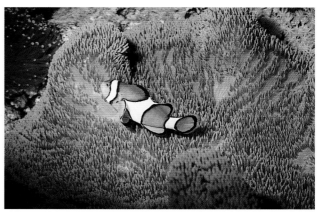

▦ **Lighting** Contains symbiotic algae and requires strong lighting.
▦ **Circulation** Should be given moderate to strong water motion.
■ **Compatibility** Has a strong sting and will severely burn neighboring sessile animals.
▦ **Feeding** Needs regular meals of high-quality meaty foods.

Hardy under the right conditions, but needs special care during acclimation. Variable colors: from yellow to brown and green to purple. Best kept in a species tank with *Amphiprion* spp. clownfishes.

Cnidaria; Anthozoa; Actiniaria; Phymanthidae
Sand Anemone *Phymanthus* sp.
10-15 cm (3.9-5.9 in.) across Indo-Pacific

■ **Lighting** Contains symbiotic algae and needs high light intensity.
■ **Aquascaping** Prefers sandy habitats; this genus is well-suited to small tanks and sand-zone aquariums.
■ **Compatibility** A perfect anemone to combine with corals, commensal shrimps, and other sessile animals in a community tank.

Small, easy to keep, and an excellent host for symbiotic crabs and shrimps. Disc is usually greenish or brownish. Tentacles are long with many treelike outgrowths situated only along the periphery of the disc.

Cnidaria; Anthozoa; Actiniaria; Thalassianthidae
Pizza Anemone *Cryptodendrum adhaesivum*
To 30 cm (11.7 in.) across Indo-Pacific

■ **Lighting** Contains symbiotic algae and needs intense lighting.
■ **Feeding** Carnivore that needs plankton and meaty marine foods, such as pieces of shrimp or squid and live adult brine shrimp.
■ **Compatibility** Extremely "sticky" and a deadly threat to sessile animals it touches. Can kill fishes and corals.
■ **Hazards** Sting is painful to most humans. Handle with gloves.

Hardy and handsome, this anemone is a potent hazard in most aquariums and is best kept in its own display system.

Cnidaria; Anthozoa; Actiniaria; Aiptasidae
Curleycue Anemone *Bartholomea annulata*
To 30 cm (11.7 in.) across Caribbean

■ **Lighting** Contains symbiotic algae and needs high light intensity.
■ **Compatibility** Has strong stinging cells and will burn neighboring sessile animals severely.

A common and hardy anemone with knobby, nearly transparent tentacles. It is a good candidate for a small biotope aquarium where the animal can serve as host for its many natural symbiotic shrimps and crabs.

Cnidaria; Anthozoa; Actiniaria; Aiptasidae
Glassrose, "Aiptasia" *Aiptasia* sp.
To 6 cm (2.3 in.) tall Tropical and subtropical seas

■ **Compatibility** Multiplies asexually very quickly, building huge populations in aquariums. Has a nasty stinging ability and the potential to overgrow an aquarium completely, killing many other sessile inhabitants.

This is one of several similar-looking species of small, nuisance anemones. Must be regarded as a pest and should be avoided—or removed promptly if it invades a reef aquarium. Grows under many different conditions and very difficult to control.

Cnidaria; Anthozoa; Actiniaria; Actiniidae

"Anemonia"   *Anemonia* cf. *majano*

To 3 cm (1.2 in.) in diameter   Indo-Pacific

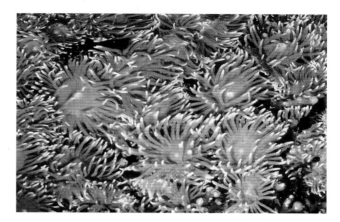

■ **Lighting** Has symbiotic algae and thrives in strong light intensity.

■ **Compatibility** Appealing when it first appears on live rock, this tiny anemone can reproduce wildly and overgrow the aquarium completely, crowding out desirable corals and sessile invertebrates.

These pests can be introduced into the reef aquarium with live rock. They are hard—if not impossible—to control and remove once they are established. Some aquarists have used butterflyfishes as a biological control, with limited success.

Cnidaria; Anthozoa; Zoanthidea; Zoanthidae

Button polyps   *Protopalythoa* spp.

Small to medium-sized colonies   Tropical seas

■ **Lighting** Contain symbiotic algae and need medium to strong light intensity.

■ **Feeding** Do not require intentional feeding.

Many different species occur in the trade, and most are hardy and a nice addition to the reef aquarium. Many colors, green and brown being the most common. Hardy and easy to keep. They are often fast growing and bud off new individuals asexually, spreading the colony.

Cnidaria; Anthozoa; Zoanthidea; Zoanthidae

Sea mats, button polyps   *Zoanthus* spp.

Medium-sized colonies   Tropical seas

■ **Lighting** Usually found in shallow water and require high light intensity.

■ **Feeding** Do not require feeding. Some species, however, will respond to occasional meaty offerings, such as live brine shrimp.

Although difficult to identify, the various zoanthids are generally hardy and easy to keep. They reproduce asexually in the aquarium, expanding over the hard substrate to form lovely mats.

Cnidaria; Anthozoa; Zoanthidea

Yellow zoanthid   **Not yet described**

Small to medium-sized colonies   Indo-Pacific

■ **Lighting** Contains symbiotic algae and should be given moderate to strong light intensity.

■ **Compatibility** Has a moderately damaging sting and the potential to multiply and overtake large areas of an aquarium.

Its beautiful bright yellow color and rapid growth makes this colonial polyp a perfect animal for the reef aquarium. Hardy and easy to keep. Has been sold since the early 1970s as "*Parazoanthus gracilis.*" This name is definitely wrong and its identity remains unknown.

Cnidaria; Anthozoa; Zoanthidea; Zoanthidae
Worm tube zoanthid   *Acrozoanthus* sp.

Small to medium-sized colonies   Indo-Pacific

■ **Compatibility** Part of a unique symbiotic relationship. Probably both partners are necessary for successful keeping.
■ **Conservation** Should not be imported until more is known about its husbandry.

These polyps live with tube-dwelling bristleworms from the genus *Eunice* by attaching themselves to the upper part of the worm tubes, which are normally cut off during collection. The polyps seem unable to live on any other substrate and are hard if not impossible to keep.

Cnidaria; Anthozoa; Zoanthidea; Zoanthidae
Sea mats   *Palythoa* spp.

Medium-sized to large colonies   Tropical seas

■ **Lighting** Photosynthetic; need moderate to high light intensity.
■ **Hazards** Symbiotic bacteria living with *Palythoa* spp. produce palytoxin, a potent toxin in the mucus. Handle with care—gloves are recommended.

These easily kept polyps are connected by fleshy tissue that encrusts the substrate. They often form large colonies in shallow water. Colors are usually yellowish or brownish.

Cnidaria; Anthozoa; Zoanthidea; Zoanthidae
Snake polyps   *Isaurus* sp.

Medium-sized colonies   Indo-Pacific

■ **Lighting** Probably needs moderate light intensity.
■ **Feeding** Should be given minute plankton during the night when the polyps are open.

These nocturnal polyps usually refuse to open during the day and are difficult to feed and keep. Little is known about their requirements in the aquarium. The stems of their long polyps are usually covered with large tubercles.

Cnidaria; Anthozoa; Corallimorpharia; Ricordeidae
Florida False Coral   *Ricordea florida*

To 8 cm (3.1 in.) across   Caribbean

■ **Lighting** Contains symbiotic algae but does best in medium light intensity.
■ **Feeding** Carnivorous and should be fed from time to time, which will increase its budding potential.

Relatively easy to keep and perfect for a Caribbean aquarium or Gulf of Mexico biotope. Usually found in dense colonies as a result of asexual reproduction. Usually greenish, but sometimes orange or pink.

Cnidaria; Anthozoa; Corallimorpharia; Discosomatidae
Large Elephant Ear *Amplexidiscus fenestrafer*
20-45 cm (7.8-17.6 in.) across Indo-Pacific

■ **Lighting** Contains symbiotic algae, but like most mushroom anemones, seems to do best with moderate light intensities.
■ **Aquascaping** Needs plenty of space.
■ **Feeding** Carnivorous and should regularly be fed meaty foods.
■ **Compatibility** Has the potential to capture crustaceans and small fishes by ensnaring them in a balloonlike trap.

This mushroom anemone grows large and is not difficult to keep, but is responsible for catching and eating many prized aquarium fishes.

Cnidaria; Anthozoa; Corallimorpharia; Discosomatidae
Mushroom anemone *Discosoma* sp. A
To 6 cm (2.3 in.) across Indo-Pacific

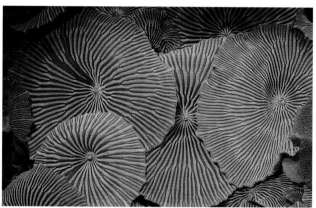

■ **Lighting** Contains symbiotic algae, but most mushroom anemones seem to do best with moderate light intensities.
■ **Compatibility** These mushroom anemones can bud rapidly and have the potential to form large, dominant colonies.

These beautiful solitary polyps are hardy and easily recommended to beginning reef aquarists. The blue, green, striped, or red colors may reflect different species, but are probably color morphs of one or a few species. Bright light may cause them to lose color.

Cnidaria; Anthozoa; Corallimorpharia; Discosomatidae
Mushroom anemone *Discosoma* sp. B
To 10 cm (3.9 in.) across Indo-Pacific

■ **Lighting** Contains symbiotic algae, but most mushroom anemones seem to do best with moderate light intensities.
■ **Compatibility** These mushroom anemones can bud rapidly and have the potential to form large, dominant colonies.

Easy to keep but even experts find them difficult to identify. Discs have many rudimentary tentacles, and the colors are usually brownish or greenish. Good for lower regions of a reef tank.

Cnidaria; Anthozoa; Corallimorpharia; Discosomatidae
Hairy Mushroom Anemone *Rhodactis indosinensis*
To 11 cm (4.3 in.) across Indo-Pacific

■ **Lighting** Does contain symbiotic algae and seems to thrive in bright light intensities, although moderate lighting will suffice.
■ **Compatibility** These mushroom anemones can bud rapidly and have the potential to overgrow large portions of the aquascape.

There are many similar species in this easy to keep genus. Disc is brown and covered with prominent branched tentacles.

Cnidaria; Anthozoa; Scleractinia; Pocilloporidae
Birdsnest Coral   *Pocillopora damicornis*
Medium-sized colonies   Indo-Pacific

▪ **Lighting** Photosynthetic; needs high-intensity lighting.
▪ **Water Quality** Demands excellent water quality, including calcium supplementation for skeletal growth.

Grows fast in the reef aquarium and is easy to keep and propagate, making it a favorite of hobbyists and researchers alike. Highly variable branch and colony shape, depending on the habitat. Can form large stands in captivity.

Cnidaria; Anthozoa; Scleractinia; Pocilloporidae
Warty Bush Coral   *Pocillopora verrucosa*
Medium-sized colonies   Indo-Pacific

▪ **Lighting** Contains symbiotic algae and needs high-intensity lighting.
▪ **Circulation** Requires strong water movement.
▪ **Water Quality** Demands excellent water quality, including calcium supplementation for skeletal growth.

Not as easy to keep as *P. damicornis* (above), but generally a hardy species that grows well and can be propagated asexually by cuttings. Usually brownish, but sometimes pink or red.

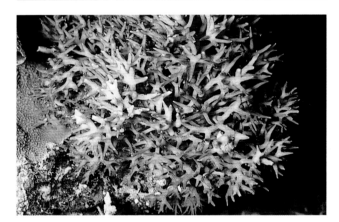

Cnidaria; Anthozoa; Scleractinia; Pocilloporidae
Thorny Bush Coral   *Seriatopora hystrix*
Small to medium-sized colonies   Indo-Pacific

▪ **Lighting** Contains symbiotic algae and needs high-intensity lighting.
▪ **Circulation** Requires strong water movement.
▪ **Water Quality** Demands excellent water quality, including calcium supplementation for skeletal growth.

With its needle-sharp branches, this is a distinctive coral but delicate and sensitive to being overgrown by algae. The branches break easily. Usually pale brownish, occasionally pink.

Cnidaria; Anthozoa; Scleractinia; Pocilloporidae
Cat's Paw, Club Finger Coral   *Stylophora pistillata*
Medium-sized colonies   Indo-Pacific

▪ **Lighting** Contains symbiotic algae and needs high-intensity lighting.
▪ **Circulation** Requires strong water movement.
▪ **Water Quality** Demands excellent water quality, including calcium supplementation for skeletal growth.

Hardy and relatively easy to keep and propagate by cuttings. Forms a variety of colony shapes, depending on lighting and current conditions. Usually yellow or green, occasionally pink.

Cnidaria; Anthozoa; Scleractinia; Acroporidae

Cabbage corals, velvet corals *Montipora* **spp.**

Small to very large colonies   Indo-Pacific

■ **Lighting** Contain symbiotic algae and need high-intensity lighting.

■ **Circulation** Require strong water movement.

■ **Water Quality** Demand excellent water quality, including calcium supplementation for skeletal growth.

This hardy genus has many encrusting species, but can also form branches, plates, and whorling vase shapes. The polyps are small and live in "open" corallites. Occasionally arrives on live rock.

Cnidaria; Anthozoa; Scleractinia; Acroporidae

Pearled Staghorn Coral *Acropora gemmifera*

Medium-sized colonies   Indo-Pacific

■ **Lighting** Photosynthetic; needs high-intensity lighting.

■ **Circulation** Requires strong, surging water movement.

■ **Water Quality** Demands excellent water quality, including calcium supplementation for skeletal growth.

Among the more demanding species in the genus to sustain in captivity and recommended for experts only. The colonies form heavy, clustering (corymbose) plates with thick, tapering branches. A variety of colors from pale yellow and whitish to bright pink.

Cnidaria; Anthozoa; Scleractinia; Acroporidae

Staghorn Coral *Acropora formosa*

Medium-sized to very large colonies   Indo-Pacific

■ **Lighting** Photosynthetic; needs high-intensity lighting.

■ **Circulation** Requires strong water movement.

■ **Water Quality** Demands excellent water quality, including calcium supplementation for skeletal growth.

The classic "beginner's *Acropora*"—fast growing and easy to keep. This species is referred to as *A muricata* by some. Usually brownish with colorful branch tips.

Cnidaria; Anthozoa; Scleractinia; Acroporidae

Table corals *Acropora* **spp.**

Form large colonies   Indo-Pacific

■ **Lighting** Photosynthetic; need high-intensity lighting.

■ **Circulation** Require strong water movement.

■ **Water Quality** Demand excellent water quality, including calcium supplementation for skeletal growth.

■ **Aquascaping** Need plenty of space; should be affixed to form coral tiers in the water column. Will expand to shade other corals.

With good conditions, many of the table-shaped *Acropora* grow extraordinarily fast and are relatively easy to keep and propagate.

Cnidaria; Anthozoa; Scleractinia; Acroporidae
Bushy Acropora   *Acropora elseyi*
Medium-sized to very large colonies   Indo-Pacific

■ **Lighting** Contains symbiotic algae and needs high-intensity lighting.
■ **Circulation** Requires strong water movement.
■ **Water Quality** Demands excellent water quality, including calcium supplementation for skeletal growth.

This species can form huge stands in protected habitats in the wild. Relatively easy to keep and to propagate by cuttings. Usually brown with interesting, subdividing branches covered with branchlets.

Cnidaria; Anthozoa; Scleractinia; Poritidae
Jewel stone corals   *Porites* spp.
Small to very large colonies   Tropical seas

■ **Lighting** Photosynthetic; need high-intensity lighting.
■ **Circulation** Requires strong water movement.
■ **Water Quality** Demand excellent water quality, including calcium supplementation for skeletal growth.

This genus has many forms—encrusting, mounding, plating, and branching—that typically grow slowly but are hardy in the aquarium. Similar to *Montipora* spp., but corallites are filled with spines and septa.

Cnidaria; Anthozoa; Scleractinia; Poritidae
Daisy coral   *Goniopora* sp.
Medium-sized colonies   Indo-Pacific

■ **Lighting** Contains symbiotic algae and needs medium to strong light intensity.
■ **Water Quality** Demands excellent water quality, including calcium supplementation for skeletal growth.
■ **Feeding** Difficult to feed. Dissolved organic nutrients are likely important for these corals, but their needs are still poorly understood.

Long-term survival is unusual. Often declines gradually, with polyps refusing to open completely and tissue slowly receding.

Cnidaria; Anthozoa; Scleractinia; Agariciidae
Lettuce Coral   *Pavona cactus*
Medium-sized colonies   Indo-Pacific

■ **Lighting** Contains symbiotic algae and needs high-intensity lighting.
■ **Circulation** Requires strong water movement.
■ **Water Quality** Demands excellent water quality, including calcium supplementation for skeletal growth.

The foliaceous, twisted, and thin branches are fragile but give the species a distinct appearance. Easy to keep and propagate by taking cuttings. Color is often pale brown or yellowish.

Cnidaria; Anthozoa; Scleractinia; Fungiidae
Anemone Mushroom Coral   *Heliofungia actiniformis*
Huge solitary polyp   Central Pacific

■ **Lighting** Photosynthetic—needs medium to strong lighting.
■ **Water Quality** Demands excellent water quality, including calcium supplementation for skeletal growth.
■ **Aquascaping** Should be on a quiet sandy bottom where it can expand freely. Keep away from strong currents.

Resembles an anemone, but is a solitary (single polyp) stony coral. Often damaged in collection or shipping, but is hardy once established. Needs very careful acclimation.

Cnidaria; Anthozoa; Scleractinia; Fungiidae
Plate corals, mushroom corals   *Fungia* spp.
14-30 cm (5.5-11.7 in.) across   Indo-Pacific

■ **Lighting** Photosynthetic—need medium to strong lighting.
■ **Aquascaping** Should be kept on a flat bottom with sand or rubble.
■ **Water Quality** Demand excellent water quality, including calcium supplementation for skeletal growth.

Showy specimens that are typically hardy and long-lived. Often greenish, but other colors are seen. This genus has separate sexes, and spawning in captivity is not uncommon.

Cnidaria; Anthozoa; Scleractinia; Fungiidae
Slipper Coral   *Polyphyllia talpina*
Small, elongated colonies   Indo-Pacific

■ **Lighting** Photosynthetic—needs medium to strong lighting.
■ **Aquascaping** Should be kept on a flat bottom with sand or rubble.
■ **Water Quality** Demands excellent water quality, including calcium supplementation for skeletal growth.

Easy to keep and grow and can live for many years in captivity. Elongated colony with a distinct axial furrow and long, pointed tentacles.

Cnidaria; Anthozoa; Scleractinia; Fungiidae
Tongue Coral   *Herpolitha limax*
To 50 cm (19.5 in.)   Indo-Pacific

■ **Lighting** Photosynthetic—needs medium to strong lighting.
■ **Aquascaping** Should be kept on a flat bottom with sand or rubble.
■ **Water Quality** Demands excellent water quality, including calcium supplementation for skeletal growth.

Hardy and easy to keep. Grows well and can live for many years in captivity. Each specimen has several mouth openings and long, pointed tentacles. Colors are normally green or light brown to yellow.

Cnidaria; Anthozoa; Scleractinia; Oculinidae
Crystal Coral *Galaxea fascicularis*
Medium-sized to large colonies Indo-Pacific

▨ **Lighting** Photosynthetic but accepts moderate light intensities.
▨ **Circulation** Requires strong water movement.
▨ **Water Quality** Demands excellent water quality, including calcium supplementation for skeletal growth.
■ **Compatibility** Can expose long sweeper tentacles with a powerful sting and needs sufficient distance from neighboring corals.

In favorable conditions, a hardy, fast growing, and easy to keep stony coral. Better suited to larger aquariums with space for it to expand.

Cnidaria; Anthozoa; Scleractinia; Pectiniidae
Palm Lettuce Coral *Pectinia paeonia*
Medium-sized colonies Indo-Pacific

▨ **Lighting** Contains symbiotic algae and needs high-intensity lighting.
▨ **Water Quality** Demands excellent water quality, including calcium supplementation for skeletal growth.

This unusual coral is not difficult to keep and has thin, irregular, upward projecting plates and spires. Colors are subtle but appealing in brown, green, or gray.

Cnidaria; Anthozoa; Scleractinia; Mussidae
Button Coral *Cynarina lacrymalis*
5-30 cm (2-11.7 in.) across Indo-Pacific

▨ **Lighting** Contains symbiotic algae, but does best in moderate and even dim lighting.
▨ **Water Quality** Demands excellent water quality, including calcium supplementation for skeletal growth.
▨ **Aquascaping** Best kept flat on the bottom of the aquarium, away from the bright light at the surface.

A beautiful curiosity, generally hardy and easy to keep. Becomes huge when fully inflated and needs plenty of space.

Cnidaria; Anthozoa; Scleractinia; Mussidae
Pineapple Coral *Blastomussa wellsi*
Medium-sized colonies Indo-Pacific

▨ **Lighting** Contains symbiotic algae but does best in subdued or indirect lighting.
▨ **Circulation** Prefers locations with quiet water conditions.
▨ **Water Quality** Demands excellent water quality, including calcium supplementation for skeletal growth.

Somewhat uncommon, this is a beautiful, hardy coral with large, robust corallites. Normally bright red in color, sometimes with fluorescent green highlights.

Cnidaria; Anthozoa; Scleractinia; Mussidae

Meat Coral   *Lobophyllia hemprichii*

Medium-sized colonies   Indo-Pacific

■ **Lighting** Contains symbiotic algae and needs high-intensity lighting.

■ **Water Quality** Demands excellent water quality, including calcium supplementation for skeletal growth.

■ **Feeding** Needs meaty foods 1-2 times weekly to thrive.

This is an impressive, heavy-bodied coral with large polyps, but not difficult to keep. Colors vary widely, often greenish or brownish. Seems to prefer calm water conditions.

Cnidaria; Anthozoa; Scleractinia; Merulinidae

Horn Coral   *Hydnophora exesa*

Medium-sized to large colonies   Indo-Pacific

■ **Lighting** Contains symbiotic algae and needs high-intensity lighting.

■ **Circulation** Requires moderately strong water movement.

■ **Water Quality** Demands excellent water quality, including calcium supplementation for skeletal growth.

Fluorescent green colonies are very eye-catching, but this is not among the easiest stony corals to keep. Growth form may be branching, massive, or encrusting. Some aquarium keepers offer meaty foods.

Cnidaria; Anthozoa; Scleractinia; Faviidae

Trumpet Coral   *Caulastrea furcata*

Medium-sized to large colonies   Indo-Pacific

■ **Lighting** Contains symbiotic algae but does best with moderate light intensity.

■ **Aquascaping** Common in calm areas with clear water, especially on sand, and therefore excellent in a sandy lagoon aquarium.

■ **Water Quality** Like all stony corals it needs excellent water quality, including calcium for building the calcareous skeleton.

Spectacular colonies are easy to keep. Grows quickly by polyp division. New colonies can be created by taking fragments or cuttings.

Cnidaria; Anthozoa; Scleractinia; Faviidae

Moon corals   *Favia* spp.

Small to large colonies   Indo-Pacific

■ **Lighting** Contain symbiotic algae and need medium- to high-intensity lighting.

■ **Circulation** Require moderate water movement.

■ **Water Quality** Demand excellent water quality, including calcium supplementation for skeletal growth.

These massive, flat or dome-shaped corals are not difficult to keep, although they grow slowly. They may respond well to occasional feeding at night, when the feeding tentacles are extended.

Cnidaria; Anthozoa; Scleractinia; Faviidae
Moon corals *Favites* spp.
Medium-sized to large colonies Indo-Pacific

■ **Lighting** Contain symbiotic algae and need medium- to high-intensity lighting.
■ **Circulation** Require moderate water movement.
■ **Water Quality** Demand excellent water quality, including calcium supplementation for skeletal growth.

Most species are hardy and easy to keep. Similar to *Favia* spp., except that adjoining polyps share a common wall, which gives many *Favites* species a honeycomb appearance.

Cnidaria; Anthozoa; Scleractinia; Faviidae
Honeycomb corals *Goniastrea* spp.
Small to large colonies Indo-Pacific

■ **Lighting** Photosynthetic; need high-intensity lighting.
■ **Circulation** Require moderate water movement.
■ **Water Quality** Demand excellent water quality, including calcium supplementation for skeletal growth.

These rugged corals are normally found on inshore reefs and reef flats, often exposed to open air during low tide and therefore excellent in a tidal aquarium. Very hardy and easy to keep. Massive colonies are usually cream or pale brown, sometimes greenish.

Cnidaria; Anthozoa; Scleractinia; Faviidae
Boulder corals, moon corals *Montastraea* spp.
Small to large colonies Circumtropical

■ **Lighting** Photosynthetic; need high-intensity lighting.
■ **Circulation** Require moderate water movement.
■ **Water Quality** Demand excellent water quality, including calcium supplementation for skeletal growth.

Hardy corals that form massive colonies, flat or dome-shaped. Some species create large boulders in the wild. Polyps open to feed during the night when sweeper tentacles may be observed.

Cnidaria; Anthozoa; Scleractinia; Trachyphylliidae
Open Brain Coral *Trachyphyllia geoffroyi*
To 20 cm (7.8 in.) across Indo-Pacific

■ **Lighting** Contains symbiotic algae and needs moderate- to high-intensity lighting.
■ **Water Quality** Demands excellent water quality, including calcium supplementation for skeletal growth.
■ **Feeding** Responds well to occasional meals of meaty foods.

With large, fleshy polyps, this is one of the most distinctive and oldest species of stony corals in the aquarium hobby. Generally hardy, but sensitive to green algae invading the skeleton.

Cnidaria; Anthozoa; Scleractinia; Caryophylliidae
Anchor Coral   *Euphyllia ancora*
Medium to large   Indo-Pacific

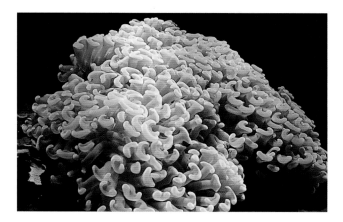

■ **Lighting** Photosynthetic—needs medium- to high-intensity light.
■ **Circulation** Requires moderate water movement.
■ **Water Quality** Demands excellent water quality, including calcium supplementation for skeletal growth.
■ **Hazards** Has a powerful sting; aquarists have experienced allergic reactions to this coral, and it will harm nearby corals in the reef.

Attractive and interesting species that is moderately easy to keep. Sensitive to green algae invading the skeleton. Needs plenty of space.

Cnidaria; Anthozoa; Scleractinia; Caryophylliidae
Frogspawn Coral   *Euphyllia divisa*
Medium-sized to large colonies   Indo-Pacific

■ **Lighting** Photosynthetic—needs medium- to high-intensity light.
■ **Circulation** Requires moderate water movement.
■ **Water Quality** Demands excellent water quality, including calcium supplementation for skeletal growth.
■ **Compatibility** As with other *Euphyllia* species,it has sweeper tentacles and can attack and harm other corals within its reach.

A hardy coral that grows fast and is generally easy to keep. The sexes are separate. Needs plenty of space to expand and grow.

Cnidaria; Anthozoa; Scleractinia; Caryophylliidae
Torch Coral   *Euphyllia glabrescens*
Medium-sized colonies   Indo-Pacific

■ **Lighting** Photosynthetic—needs medium- to high-intensity light.
■ **Circulation** Requires moderate water movement.
■ **Water Quality** Demands excellent water quality, including calcium supplementation for skeletal growth.

More demanding than the other *Euphyllia* spp. and subject to shipping damage and "brown jelly" infections. Individual branches may die, while others survive. Typical of this genus, the coral will not extend its polyps fully unless aquarium conditions are right.

Cnidaria; Anthozoa; Scleractinia; Caryophylliidae
Elegance Coral   *Catalaphyllia jardinei*
To 50 cm (19.5 in.) across   Indo-Pacific

■ **Lighting** Photosynthetic; needs medium to strong light intensity.
■ **Water Quality** Like all stony corals it needs excellent water quality, including calcium for building the calcareous skeleton.
■ **Aquascaping** Occurs in turbid water, often on muddy or sandy bottoms or among seagrass, and is best kept in similar habitats—placed in soft substrate and not wedged among live rocks.

Often a centerpiece coral, growing large and beautiful. Usually easy to keep, but sometimes prone to unexplained demise.

Cnidaria; Anthozoa; Scleractinia; Caryophylliidae
Bubble Coral   *Plerogyra sinuosa*
To 1 m (3.3 ft.) across   Indo-Pacific

■ **Lighting** Photosynthetic, needs medium to strong light intensity.
■ **Water Quality** Demands excellent water quality, including calcium supplementation for skeletal growth.
■ **Feeding** Responds well to occasional meals of meaty foods offered at night when its feeding tentacles are extended.
■ **Compatibility** Will sting other corals within its reach.

A favorite coral that is long-lived in many reef aquariums. Easy to keep, but the skeleton is sensitive to becoming invaded by green algae.

Cnidaria; Anthozoa; Scleractinia; Caryophylliidae
Fox Coral   *Nemenzophyllia turbida*
Small to medium-sized colonies   Central Pacific

■ **Lighting** Photosynthetic— does best under moderate lighting.
■ **Aquascaping** Occurs in turbid water, often on muddy or sandy bottoms or among seagrass, and its best kept in similar habitats.
■ **Water Quality** Like all stony corals it needs excellent water quality, including calcium for building the calcareous skeleton.

Some aquarists consider this a challenging coral, while others believe it is hardy and not difficult to keep. May do best in a seagrass biotope aquarium or a system without aggressive skimming.

Cnidaria; Anthozoa; Scleractinia; Dendrophylliidae
Orange cup corals   *Tubastraea* spp.
Usually less than 20 cm (7.8 in.) across   Tropical Seas

■ **Lighting** Do not contain symbiotic algae—do best in low light intensity locations, even under overhangs or in caves.
■ **Circulation** Need strong alternating water motion.
■ **Feeding** Must be fed regularly with frozen and living foods such as enriched *Artemia, Mysis* shrimp, and the like.

Exceptionally beautiful but very demanding to feed and keep alive. Easier to keep in a small, dedicated tank where they can be hand fed easily. For experienced and advanced aquarists only.

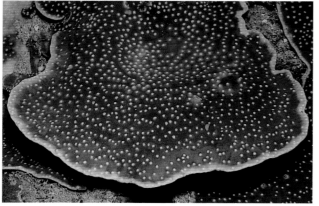

Cnidaria; Anthozoa; Scleractinia; Dendrophylliidae
Scroll Coral   *Turbinaria reniformis*
Medium-sized to very large colonies   Indo-Pacific

■ **Lighting** Photosynthetic—needs medium to strong light intensity.
■ **Circulation** Requires moderate to strong water movement.
■ **Water Quality** Like all stony corals it needs excellent water quality, including calcium for building the calcareous skeleton.

Hardy and easy to keep, but needs a lot of space to grow. May require a regular blast of water current to flush out detritus that may tend to accumulate in the cup or scrolls of the colony.

Cnidaria; Anthozoa; Scleractinia; Dendrophylliidae
Scroll Coral, Turban Coral   *Turbinaria peltata*
Medium-sized colonies   Indo-Pacific

■ **Lighting** Photosynthetic; needs medium to strong light intensity.
■ **Circulation** Requires moderate to strong water movement.
■ **Water Quality** Like all stony corals it needs excellent water quality, including calcium for building the calcareous skeleton.

Forming either flat plates, cups, or upright columns, this is a variable but hardy and interesting coral. May require a regular blast of water current to flush out detritus that may tend to accumulate in the cup of the colony.

Mollusca; Polyplacophora; Neoloricata; Chitonidae
Chitons   *Acanthopleura* spp.
To 10 cm (3.9 in.)   Tropical seas

■ **Aquascaping** These chitons live in tidal zones, such as on beach rocks, and are highly appropriate for a marine aqua-terrarium biotope. They attach themselves very firmly to rocky substrates and can tolerate strong wave action.
■ **Feeding** No intentional feeding necessary. Graze on algal films.
■ **Compatibility** Usually reef safe.

A well-armored mollusk that may arrive on live rock. Long-lived if conditions and food are right.

Mollusca; Gastropoda; Prosobranchia; Neritimorpha; Neritidae
Nerite Snail   *Nerita albicilla*
2.5 cm (1 in.)   Indo-Pacific

■ **Feeding** Grazes on algal films and microalgae only.
■ **Compatibility** Reef safe.

One of a genus of pretty, rounded little snails that are familiar to beachcombers worldwide. Very common and usually found in the tidal zone, periodically living above the sea level. Good as algae grazers, although it may take many snails to perform effectively. Excellent for a tidal aquarium. Natural lifespan may be no more than a year.

Mollusca; Gastropoda; Prosobranchia; Archaeogastropoda; Fissurellidae
Shield Limpet   *Scutus unguis*
To 7 cm (2.7 in.)   Indo-Pacific

■ **Feeding** Usually grazes on algal films and microalgae.
■ **Compatibility** Usually reef safe. Sometimes reported to feed on colonial tunicates and some corals, but survives easily in the reef aquarium and probably feeds on a variety of food and food remains. (The Caribbean keyhole limpets will aggressively graze on corals.)

Usually found beneath rocks in shallow reef zones. Occasionally arrives on live rock. Nocturnal and hardy.

Mollusca; Gastropoda; Prosobranchia; Archaeogastropoda; Turbinidae
Green Turban Snail *Turbo brunneus*
To 5 cm (2 in.) high   Indo-Pacific

■ **Feeding** No intentional feeding necessary. Grazes on algal films, filamentous algae, diatoms, and cyanobacteria.
■ **Compatibility** Reef safe.

Usually found on shallow reefs among coral rubble and rocks where it can find sufficient microscopic algae. Often introduced to the aquarium on live rock. Short-lived; may starve if insufficient algae is present.

Mollusca; Gastropoda; Prosobranchia; Archaeogastropoda; Turbinidae
American Star Shell *Astraea tecta*
To 5 cm (2 in.) high   Caribbean

■ **Feeding** No intentional feeding necessary. Grazes on algal films, filamentous algae, diatoms, and cyanobacteria.
■ **Compatibility** Reef safe.

Some aquarists introduce one of these snails per gallon to control algae in a new reef aquarium. Relatively easy to keep, but generally short-lived—about a year in the aquarium.

Mollusca; Gastropoda; Prosobranchia; Neotaenioglossa; Strombidae
Queen Conch *Strombus gigas*
To 30 cm (11.7 in.)   Caribbean

■ **Aquascaping** A big snail best suited for a shallow-water biotope aquarium with room to graze.
■ **Feeding** Herbivorous, grazes on algae and seagrasses. Will need intentional feeding as it grows to larger sizes.

Overharvested for its meat and shells, this species is now being captive-bred, with small specimens available to aquarists. Not a good prospect for the reef tank, where it will get wedged in the rockwork.

Mollusca; Gastropoda; Prosobranchia; Neotaenioglossa; Strombidae
Spider conchs *Lambis* spp.
To 35 cm (13.7 in.)   Indo-Pacific

■ **Aquascaping** These large snails are best suited for shallow-water biotope aquariums with room to graze. The spined shell is likely to become stuck in rock formations, and an open soft bottom is an appropriate habitat.
■ **Feeding** Herbivorous; feed on microscopic algae.

Strikingly beautiful shelled animals, but not among the easiest gastropods to keep. For advanced aquarists or specialized systems.

Mollusca; Gastropoda; Prosobranchia; Neotaenioglossa; Vermetidae

Small worm snails   *Petaloconchus* spp.

To 20 cm (7.8 in.)   Indo-Pacific

■ **Feeding** No intentional feeding necessary. Capture organic particles suspended in the water column, sometimes by secreting strings of mucus to snare nutrient-rich materials.

■ **Compatibility** Reef safe. May arrive on live rock; can develop large clusters of long calcareous tubes in aquariums without predators.

Known as vermetid gastropods, these snails secret calcareous tubes and have caplike opercula for protection. Hardy and long-lived.

Mollusca; Gastropoda; Prosobranchia; Neotaenioglossa; Vermetidae

Big worm snails   *Serpulorbis* spp.

To 2 cm (0.8 in.) across   Tropical seas

■ **Feeding** Lives as a filter-feeder, screening organic particles from the water column. Needs a lot of particulate food.

■ **Compatibility** Reef safe. May arrive on live rock or embedded in stony corals.

Another genus of vermetid snails that sometime appear in reef aquariums. They are harmless, and a number of species are known. May be successfully kept in nutrient-rich aquariums.

Mollusca; Gastropoda; Prosobranchia; Neotaenioglossa; Cypraeidae

Tiger Cowrie   *Cypraea tigris*

To 13 cm (5.1 in.)   Indo-Pacific

■ **Feeding** Omnivorous. Feeds on a variety of foods, including algae and meaty foods.

■ **Compatibility** Not reef safe. May attack other mollusks, corals, and fishes and will dislodge rocks and corals in its grazing activities.

Glisteningly beautiful when its shell is not covered by the mantle, this common cowrie is hardy but predatory.

Mollusca; Gastropoda; Prosobranchia; Neotaenioglossa; Cypraeidae

Money Cowrie   *Cypraea moneta*

To 3 cm (1.2 in.)   Indo-Pacific

■ **Feeding** Herbivore. Can be used as an algae grazer in the aquarium, especially if stocked in high numbers.

■ **Compatibility** Reef safe. One of the few species in this genus of cowries that feeds on algae only.

Often imported, hardy, and easily kept. The lustrous shells of cowries once served as a medium of exchange for business transactions in tropical coastal societies, hence the common name.

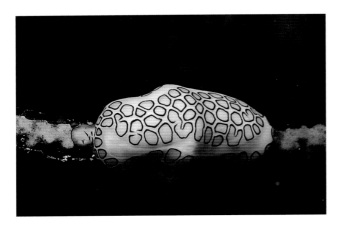

Mollusca; Gastropoda; Prosobranchia; Neotaenioglossa; Ovulidae

Flamingo Tongue *Cyphoma gibbosum*

To 2.5 cm (1 in.) Caribbean

■ **Feeding** Feeds exclusively on the polyps of photosynthetic gorgonians, which it will decimate in a typical home aquarium.
■ **Compatibility** Not reef safe.
■ **Conservation** Cannot be kept unless provided with live gorgonian polyps as food and should neither be collected nor purchased.

One of a genus of extraordinarily beautiful snails that are specialized feeders on live gorgonians.

Mollusca; Gastropoda; Prosobranchia; Neogastropoda; Conidae

Cone shells *Conus* spp.

Normally less than 10 cm (3.9 in.) long Indo-Pacific

■ **Compatibility** Most species eat bristleworms; some will kill and eat fishes. Need a specialized system of their own and expert care.
■ **Hazards** Some cone shells, e.g., *C. geographus* and *C. textile*, are extremely poisonous and their sting can even be fatal to humans.

Cone shells—some 300 species in total— are living works of art that deserve utmost respect. *Conus geographus* is the best-known species and has caused at least 12 fatalities among humans.

Mollusca; Gastropoda; Ophisthobranchia; Cephalaspidea; Aglajidae

Blue-striped Tailed Sea Slug *Chelidonura varians*

To 5 cm (2 in.) Indo-Pacific

■ **Feeding** Very difficult to feed. In nature, it preys on small acoel flatworms like those in the genus *Convoluta*.
■ **Conservation** Will starve in most aquariums. Appropriate only for expert aquarists able to provide proper care and diet.

A strikingly colored sea slug that is virtually impossible to feed and keep. Would require a special aquarium with a soft bottom for grazing and a ready supply of the tiny flatworms that are its primary prey.

Mollusca; Gastropoda; Ophisthobranchia; Sacoglossa; Elysiidae

Ornate Sea Slug *Elysia ornata*

To 5 cm (2 in.) in length Pantropical

■ **Lighting** Photosynthetic; requires brightly lit conditions.
■ **Feeding** Herbivore. Feeds on cell fluids from green algae of the genus *Bryopsis* only. Needs a peaceful aquarium with enough light and nutrients to support lush algal growth.
■ **Conservation** Doomed in most reef tanks because of its special way of feeding.

This attractive slug lives in shallow water and incorporates photosynthesizing chloroplasts from the algae it consumes into its own tissue.

Mollusca; Gastropoda; Ophisthobranchia; Sacoglossa; Elysiidae

Lettuce Sea Slug   *Elysia crispata*

To 10 cm (3.9 in) long   Caribbean

▪ **Lighting** Photosynthetic; requires brightly lit conditions.

▪ **Feeding** Feeds on green algae in the genera *Caulerpa* and *Halimeda* as well as on brown *Sargassum* spp.

▪ **Compatibility** Reef safe, but will eat ornamental macroalgae.

A pretty species with highly variable colors that depend on the food eaten. Easier to keep than most other sea slugs but requires a special aquarium that supports lush algae growth. Has been bred in captivity. Formerly known as *Tridachia crispata*.

Mollusca; Gastropoda; Ophisthobranchia; Nudibranchia; Diodorididae

Blue Sponge Nudibranch   *Jorunna funebris*

To 10 cm (3.9 in.) in length   Indo-Pacific

▪ **Feeding** Lives in association with the bright blue sponge *Haliclona* sp. and not known to take any other food.

▪ **Conservation** Will starve in most aquariums. Suitable only for expert aquarists able to provide proper care and diet.

Like so many nudibranchs, this species is very distinctive in appearance but impossible to keep and should not be imported.

Mollusca; Gastropoda; Ophisthobranchia; Nudibranchia; Phyllididae

Warty Nudibranch   *Phyllida varicosa*

To 11 cm (4.3 in.) in length   Indo-Pacific

▪ **Feeding** Carnivorous. Feeds exclusively on sponges and will not accept other foods in captivity.

▪ **Conservation** Will starve in most aquariums. Do not purchase.

▪ **Compatibility** Carries a deadly toxin that can wipe out a reef tank.

The most common of the about 70 spp. in the genus, this species is similar to the others in being nearly impossible to feed. It is also highly toxic and a threat to both fishes and invertebrates.

Mollusca; Gastropoda; Ophisthobranchia; Nudibranchia; Chromodoridae

Chromodorid nudibranchs   *Chromodoris* spp.

To about 5 cm (2 in.) in length   Distribution

▪ **Feeding** Prey only on certain species of sponges and will ignore all other foods in captivity.

▪ **Conservation** Will starve in most aquariums. Should neither be collected nor purchased.

This is one of a group of small and very colorful nudibranchs that are best viewed in the wild. They are may live for some months in captivity, but will eventually perish for lack of appropriate food.

Mollusca; Gastropoda; Ophisthobranchia; Nudibranchia; Hexabranchidae

Spanish Dancer   *Hexabranchus sanguineus*

To 60 cm (23 in.) in length   Indo-Pacific

■ **Feeding** Cannot be sustained in a home aquarium. Feeds mainly on sponges, but also on tiny invertebrates like sea squirts, mollusks, and echinoderms.

■ **Conservation** Will starve in most aquariums. Do not purchase.

A stunning animal, often seen swimming with graceful movements that give it its common name. Will die shortly after being purchased and should not be caught, imported, or kept.

Mollusca; Gastropoda; Ophisthobranchia; Nudibranchia; Aeolidinia

Aiptasia-eating Nudibranch   *Berghia verrucicornis*

Normally around 2 cm (5 in.) long   Caribbean

■ **Feeding** Feeds exclusively on glass anemones from the genus *Aiptasia*. Can be used as a predator in a tank infested with an un-controlled population of *Aiptasia*.

■ **Compatibility** Reef safe. Will die if its food supply is eradicated.

A small, rather delicate nudibranch that is being tank-raised and sold as a biocontrol agent for nuisance *Aiptasia*. Short-lived. Careful acclimation needed.

Mollusca; Bivalvia; Mytiloida; Mytilidae

Green Mussel   *Mytilus smaragdinus*

To 6.5 cm (2.5 in.) long   Western Pacific

■ **Water Quality** Lives in shallow, brackish coastal waters where the salinity is 20-30% and the temperature 20-28°C (68-82°F).

■ **Feeding** Filter feeder that extracts small organic particles and plankton from the water column. May need intentional feeding.

This brilliant bluish green mussel is an important source of food in Southeast Asia and sometimes appears in the aquarium trade. Difficult to keep in normal reef tanks where the salinity is too high for its long-term survival.

Mollusca; Bivalvia; Pteroidea; Pectiniidae

Caribbean Scallop   *Lyropecten nodosus*

To 15 cm (5.9 in.) across   Caribbean; northern South America

■ **Feeding** Filter feeder that extracts small organic particles and plankton from the water column. Difficult to feed.

■ **Compatibility** Reef safe, but will do poorly in nutrient-poor, efficiently skimmed systems.

An interesting animal with long tentacles along its rim and numerous small, blue compound eyes. Difficult to keep. Needs a special aquarium where planktonic food can be provided on a regular basis.

Mollusca; Bivalvia; Pteroidea; Spondylidae
Variable Thorny Oyster *Spondylus varius*
To 30 cm (11.7 in.) across Indo-Pacific

▪ **Lighting** Should be placed in moderate to dim lighting.
▪ **Feeding** A typical filter feeder that requires intentional feeding of suspended organic particles and microplankton.
▪ **Compatibility** Reef safe, but will do poorly in nutrient-poor, efficiently skimmed systems.

With its showy mantle and blue compound eyes, this is an attractive bivalve. Unfortunately, it is difficult to keep well fed in a typical reef aquarium. Try a cave aquarium with strong currents.

Mollusca; Bivalvia; Pteroidea; Limidae
Rough Fileclam, Flame Scallop *Lima scabra*
To 8 cm (3.1 in.) across Caribbean

▪ **Aquascaping** Needs protected crevices where it can hide. Tends to be reclusive to avoid having fishes nibble at its tentacles.
▪ **Feeding** A typical filter feeder that usually requires intentional feeding of suspended organic particles and microplankton.
▪ **Compatibility** Reef safe, but will do poorly in nutrient-poor, efficiently skimmed systems. Best kept in a small system where it can be studied and fed properly.

Very appealing bivalve, but delicate and prone to staying hidden.

Mollusca; Bivalvia; Pteroidea; Limidae
File Shell *Limaria orientalis*
To 5 cm (2 in.) across Indo-Pacific

▪ **Aquascaping** Lives under rocks on sandy bottoms and requires a similar habitat in the aquarium.
▪ **Feeding** A typical filter feeder that usually requires intentional feeding of suspended organic particles and microplankton.
▪ **Compatibility** Reef safe, but will do poorly in nutrient-poor, efficiently skimmed systems.

An animal with flashy coloration, but very fragile and demanding of careful handling. Easily kept, but must be given a special aquarium.

Mollusca; Bivalvia; Veneroida; Tridacnidae
Smooth Giant Clam *Tridacna derasa*
To 50 cm (19.5 in.) long Central Indo-Pacific

▪ **Lighting** Contains symbiotic algae and needs strong light intensity.
▪ **Water Quality** Like all giant clams, it needs excellent water quality, including calcium for building its calcareous shell.
▪ **Feeding** Photosynthetic; no intentional feeding necessary.

Generally regarded as the hardiest of the giant clams. Distinguished by its smooth shell. Found in exposed waters. Aquacultured specimens are readily available.

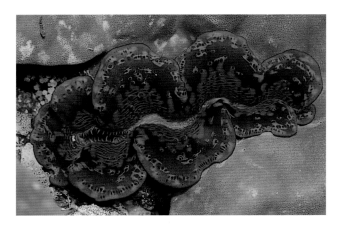

Mollusca; Bivalvia; Veneroida; Tridacnidae
Rugose Clam, Maxima Clam   *Tridacna maxima*
To 35 cm (13.7 in.) long   Indo-Pacific; Red Sea

■ **Lighting** Contains symbiotic algae and needs strong light intensity.
■ **Water Quality** Like all giant clams, it needs excellent water quality, including calcium for building its calcareous shell.
■ **Feeding** Photosynthetic; no intentional feeding necessary.

Arguably the most colorful and spectacular of the *Tridacna* clams, this species also bores into the substrate, like *T. crocea* (bottom of page). Has prominent, widely spaced scutes (flutes) on its shell.

Mollusca; Bivalvia; Veneroida; Tridacnidae
Fluted Clam   *Tridacna squamosa*
To 40 cm (15.6 in.) long   Indo-Pacific and Red Sea

■ **Lighting** Contains symbiotic algae; needs strong light intensity.
■ **Water Quality** Like all giant clams, it needs excellent water quality, including calcium for building its calcareous shell.
■ **Feeding** Photosynthetic; no intentional feeding necessary.

A favorite of many clam keepers, this species is not difficult to keep and is often beautifully pigmented. It has prominent, widely spaced scalelike flutes on its shells, hence the name "squamosa," meaning scales.

Mollusca; Bivalvia; Veneroida; Tridacnidae
Giant Clam   *Tridacna gigas*
To 137 cm (53 in.) long   Central Indo-Pacific

■ **Lighting** Photosynthetic—needs strong light intensity.
■ **Water Quality** Like all giant clams, it needs excellent water quality, including calcium for building its calcareous shell.
■ **Feeding** Photosynthetic; no intentional feeding necessary.

This is the largest bivalve known and is easy to keep. The mantle may be rather plain, or brightly colored. Commercially raised specimens readily are available. Grows fast and needs plenty of space on a bed of sand or coral rubble.

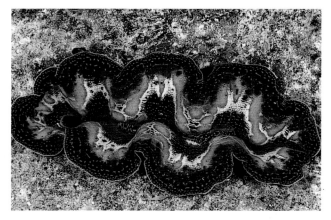

Mollusca; Bivalvia; Veneroida; Tridacnidae
Boring Clam   *Tridacna crocea*
To 19 cm (7.4 in.) long   Central Indo-Pacific

■ **Lighting** Photosynthetic—needs strong light intensity.
■ **Water Quality** Like all giant clams, it needs excellent water quality, including calcium for building its calcareous shell.
■ **Feeding** Photosynthetic; no intentional feeding necessary.

The smallest of the giant clams and one of the most vivid. Needs careful acclimation and very bright light. In the wild, it normally lives completely buried in coral or wedged into crevices between coral rocks.

Mollusca; Cephalopoda; Octopoda; Octopodidae

Eight-armed octopuses *Octopus* spp.

Up to 1 m (3.3 ft.) or more All seas

■ **Aquascaping** Need a large aquarium with many hiding places.

■ **Feeding** Carnivorous; require high-protein meaty foods.

■ **Compatibility** These highly predatory animals feed on other invertebrates and fishes; best kept in their own aquarium. May secrete blue ink that can poison the aquarium

Many octopus species are known, and they make fascinating, relatively hardy aquarium animals. They need special housing, with a secure cover to prevent escape attempts. **For advanced aquarists.**

Mollusca; Cephalopoda; Octopoda; Octopodidae

Blue-ringed Octopus *Hapalochlaena lunulata*

To 10 cm (3.9 in.) long Indo-Pacific

■ **Hazards** This species is extremely poisonous and its bite can be fatal or debilitating to humans.

■ **Compatibility** Very aggressive and will attack almost everything—including its keeper. It is a predator and will decimate any population of crustaceans and fishes.

A deadly animal in a small package decorated with flashing blue markings. This species has taken its toll on Asian fishermen, and it ought not to be collected or sold to amateur aquarists.

Platyhelminthes; "Acoela"

Commensal flatworms *Convoluta* and *Waminoa* spp.

To 1 cm (0.4 in.) Circumtropical

■ **Lighting** May possess symbiotic algae and use light energy.

■ **Feeding** Graze on tiny plants, animals, and detritus trapped in the mucus of corals.

■ **Compatibility** Reef safe, but may blossom into huge populations.

These small commensal flatworms are often introduced to the aquarium with corals. Contrary to some fears, they are not parasitic. Nonetheless, they can reach plague numbers and are regarded as pests in the coral reef aquarium.

Annelida; Polychaeta; Amphinomidae

Blue-striped Fireworm *Eurythoe* sp.

To about 10 cm long Indo-Pacific

■ **Substrate** Usually found in holes in live rock or in calcareous tubes leftover from other animals.

■ **Hazards** Bristles are sharp and contain poison secreted from a gland at their bases. Stings are painful and can lead to inflammation.

■ **Compatibility** Reef safe. Feeds from detritus and food remains.

Introduced to the aquarium on live rock. This species is an example of a useful worm that removes detritus, thrives well, and can establish large populations.

Annelida; Polychaeta; Amphinomida; Amphinomidae
Bearded Fireworm *Hermodice carunculata*
To 30 cm (11.7 in.) Caribbean

■ **Hazards** This worm's bristles are sharp and contain a toxin that causes painful, burning stings and can lead to inflammations.
■ **Compatibility** Not reef safe. An active predator that feeds on corals, anemones, and other sessile invertebrates.

May appear mysteriously in the reef aquarium, usually having arriving with live rock. Bristleworms that become pests can be caught and removed with tube traps available from aquarium suppliers.

Annelida; Polychaeta; Sabellidae
Indo-Pacific Tube Worm *Sabellastarte spectabilis*
To 20 cm (7.8 in.) long Indo-Pacific

■ **Compatibility** Completely harmless and a natural companion for stony corals. Excellent choice for small tanks and sand-bottom biotopes.
■ **Feeding** Feeds on tiny plankton and organic particles collected by the crown. Does well in systems with ample organic matter and detritus, but may need intentional feeding in the reef aquarium.

A good invertebrate for beginning aquarists. Hardy if fed well with microplankton or liquid organic foods for filter feeders.

Annelida; Polychaeta; Sabellidae
Feather duster worm *Megalomma* sp.
To 20 cm (7.8 in.) long Indo-Pacific; Mediterranean

■ **Aquascaping** Best kept on reasonably deep sandy substrate where the worm can bury its tube.
■ **Feeding** Collects tiny plankton and organic particles with its feathery crown. Needs plenty of food in the reef aquarium.

One of many ornamental worms that are peaceful and attractive additions to the marine aquarium. Hardy if well fed. Note sand grains covering the worm's protective tube.

Annelida; Polychaeta; Sabellidae
Social Feather Duster *Bispira brunnea*
Colony 20-30 cm (7.8-11.7 in.) across Caribbean

■ **Aquascaping** Needs peaceful conditions and harmless tankmates; best kept in a small, quiet reef system.
■ **Feeding** Feeds on tiny plankton and organic particles collected by the crown. Needs plenty of food in the reef aquarium.
■ **Compatibility** Reef safe. May fall victim to large brittlestars.

This small feather duster forms dense colonies of clones and varies in color from region to region. These pretty worms are as delicate as they appear, and are among the more difficult feather dusters to keep.

Annelida; Polychaeta; Sabellidae
Feather Duster Worm _Bispira tricyclia_
To 16 cm (6.2 in.) long Indo-Pacific

■ **Aquascaping** Best kept on reasonably deep sandy substrate where the worm can bury its tube.
■ **Feeding** Collects tiny plankton and organic particles with its feathery crown. Needs plenty of food in the reef aquarium.

This species is especially handsome, with a white crown and small, red, compound eyes. Tends to be hardy if fed well. The tube is soft and without attached particles.

Annelida; Polychaeta; Serpulidae
Christmas Tree Worm _Spirobranchus corniculatus_
To 8 cm (3.1 in.) Indo-Pacific

■ **Lighting** Its host coral requires intense lighting to thrive.
■ **Water Quality** Demands excellent water quality, including calcium supplementation for construction of its tubes and for its host.
■ **Feeding** Feeds on tiny plankton and organic particles collected by the crown. Will benefit from regular rations for filter feeders.

Lives in association with stony corals in the genus _Porites_ and must be collected and maintained in a living coral. If the coral dies, the worms will not survive. For advanced aquarists only.

Annelida; Polychaeta; Serpulidae
Magnificent Calcareous Tubeworm _Protula bispiralis_
To 30 cm (11.7 in.) Western Indo-Pacific

■ **Circulation** Requires moderate to strong water movement.
■ **Water Quality** Needs calcium supplementation for skeletal growth.
■ **Feeding** Catches tiny plankton and organic particles with its feathery crown. Will do best in a system where filter feeders are intentionally nurtured.

An impressive worm with a thick, stony tube, this species is not easy to keep, and many specimens probably waste away for lack of food.

Annelida; Polychaeta; Serpulidae
Feather Duster Worm _Filogranella elatensis_
About 1 cm (0.4 in.) long Indo-Pacific and Red Sea

■ **Water Quality** Needs calcium supplementation for skeletal growth.
■ **Feeding** Catches tiny plankton and organic particles with its feathery crown. Will do best in a system where filter feeders are carefully observed and intentionally nurtured.

Distinguished by hard, white, calcareous tubes and bright red crowns, but a difficult species to feed and maintain. Forms dense aggregations, probably as a result of cloning.

Arthropoda; Chelicerata; Merostomata; Limulidae
Horseshoe Crab   *Limulus polyphemus*
To 90 cm (35 in.)   Caribbean

- **Aquascaping** Needs a habitat with a large open sandy area.
- **Water Quality** Needs cooler temperatures, 21-24°C (70-75°F).
- **Feeding** Carnivorous; will eat mussels and shrimps.
- **Compatibility** Potentially destructive and not reef safe.

This a living fossil that occasionally becomes available to aquarists. Hardy, but must have a special aquarium. Beneath the formidable shell are chelicerae (claws) and five pairs of walking legs.

Crustacea; Stomatopoda; Gonodactylidae
Mantis shrimps   *Lysiosquillina* spp.
To 10 cm (3.9 in.) long   Circumtropical

- **Feeding** Carnivorous; will greedily accept all meaty foods.
- **Compatibility** Not reef safe. These aggressive predators will feed on small fishes and other motile invertebrates. Can decimate populations of other crustaceans, such as small shrimps.

A number of species make their way into the reef aquarium, usually arriving with live rock. They are easy to keep, but hard to catch if they start attacking tankmates . The first five pairs of appendages are modified into dangerous clublike claws used for smashing prey.

Crustacea; Stomatopoda; Odontodactylidae
Harlequin Mantis Shrimp   *Odontodactylus scyllarus*
To 15 cm (5.9 in.) long   Indo-Pacific

- **Aquascaping** Best kept in its own aquarium with deep sand, where it can dig burrows up to 40 cm (15.6 in.) long.
- **Feeding** Carnivore; an aggressive predator that will feed on small fishes and other motile invertebrates.
- **Compatibility** Not reef safe. Very aggressive toward other specimens of its species.

A large, vibrantly colored, and very predatory shrimp. Often imported and hardy, but must have its own isolated aquarium.

Crustacea; Decapoda; Alpheidae
Pistol shrimps   *Alpheus* spp.
1-6 cm (0.4-2.3 in.) long   Tropical seas

- **Aquascaping** Need a deep sand bed for their burrowing activities.
- **Feeding** Normal diet is small invertebrates, but will take substitute meaty foods in captivity.
- **Compatibility** Reef safe. Many species live in association with "shrimp gobies" in shared burrows. Best kept in a quiet setting.

Many colorful species are collected. They can be hardy, but need careful acclimation to captivity. By snapping a peg on the right claw the pistol shrimps generate a sharp "POP," hence the common name.

Crustacea; Decapoda; Alpheidae
Red Snapping Shrimp   *Alpheus armatus*
To 5 cm (2 in.) long   Caribbean

■ **Aquascaping** Needs a deep sand bed for its burrowing activities.
■ **Feeding** Normal diet is small invertebrates, but will take substitute meaty foods in captivity.
■ **Compatibility** Reef safe. This species lives in association with the Corkscrew Anemone (page 112) and is best kept in a small, special aquarium where this symbiotic relationship can be displayed.

This is a hardy shrimp seen in colors of red or orange, sometimes brown, with banded red and white antennae.

Crustacea; Decapoda; Hippolytidae
White-banded Cleaner Shrimp   *Lysmata amboinensis*
To 15 cm (5.9 in.) long   Indo-Pacific

■ **Feeding** In nature, this species feeds by picking parasites from fishes. In the aquarium, it will also readily accept to other meaty foods, such as adult brine shrimp, mysis shrimp, and even flakes.
■ **Compatibility** Reef safe. Best kept in small groups.

A graceful addition to any reef tank with its long white antennae—used on the reef to advertise its parasite-cleaning services. Easy to keep, but allow long and careful acclimation to new water conditions (sudden changes of pH, temperature, or salinity can be fatal).

Crustacea; Decapoda; Hippolytidae
Cardinal Cleaner Shrimp   *Lysmata debelius*
To 4 cm (1.6 in.) long   Indo-Pacific

■ **Aquascaping** Collected in deep water; requires an aquarium with shady caves and shelters.
■ **Feeding** In nature, this species feeds by picking parasites from fishes. In the aquarium, it will also readily accept other meaty foods, such as adult brine shrimp, *Mysis* shrimp, and even flakes.
■ **Compatibility** Reef safe. Best kept in small groups.

A brilliant little animal, shy but hardy. Needs slow acclimation to new water—sudden changes of pH, temperature, or salinity can be fatal.

Crustacea; Decapoda; Hippolytidae
Peppermint Shrimp   *Lysmata wurdemanni*
To 5 cm (2 in.) long   Caribbean, Eastern Atlantic

■ **Feeding** In nature, this species feeds by picking parasites from fishes. In the aquarium, it will also readily accept other meaty foods, such as adult brine shrimp, *Mysis* shrimp, and even flakes.
■ **Compatibility** Reef safe. Best kept in small groups.

A small shrimp often associated with sponges of the genus *Aplysina*. Easily kept and has been commercially bred in captivity. Used by some aquarists to control *Aiptasia* anemones, although not all hobbyists report the same degree of success.

Crustacea; Decapoda; Hippolytidae

Red Rock Shrimp   *Lysmata californica*

To 7 cm (2.7 in.) long   Gulf of California to Galapagos

■ **Aquascaping** Needs a rocky habitat where it can hide in small crevices and under rocks.

■ **Feeding** In nature, the species feeds by removing parasites from fishes. It will readily adapt to substitute foods.

■ **Compatibility** Reef safe. Best kept in groups.

Occasionally appears in the aquarium trade and is hardy, but easily confused with *L. wurdemanni* (above). Large numbers of this shrimp are sometimes found in association with the California Moray.

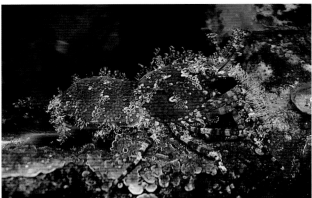

Crustacea; Decapoda; Hippolytidae

Common Marble Shrimp   *Saron marmoratus*

Body to 4 cm (1.6 in.) long   Indo-Pacific

■ **Feeding** Carnivore; a greedy eater that will accept meaty foods.

■ **Compatibility** Not reef safe. May pick on corals and other invertebrates.

Although too potentially destructive for most reef tanks, this is a handsome and hardy shrimp. Ideal for smaller biotope settings, with a small group of males and females. (Males develop long claws, these are lacking in subadult males and females.)

Crustacea; Decapoda; Hippolytidae

Pinecone Marble Shrimp   *Saron inermis*

To 3 cm (1.2 in.) long   Indo-Pacific

■ **Aquascaping** A very shy, nocturnal species that needs shadowy hiding caves and crevices.

■ **Feeding** Natural diet includes tiny invertebrates and small-polyped corals, but it will accept most meaty foods.

■ **Compatibility** Not reef safe. May feed on corals and other invertebrates.

Only moderately hardy and rather reclusive. A candidate for a special system with other nocturnal species.

Crustacea; Decapoda; Hippolytidae

Violet-legged marble shrimp   *Saron* sp.

To 12 cm (4.7 in.)   Indo-Pacific

■ **Aquascaping** Provide protective hiding caves and crevices.

■ **Feeding** Carnivorous; will accept various meaty foods.

■ **Compatibility** Not reef safe. May feed on corals and other invertebrates.

This is a new, undescribed species that is exceptionally beautiful, but about which little is known. Occasionally collected in Indonesia and the Philippines. Care requirements are likely similar to other *Saron* spp.

Crustacea; Decapoda; Hippolytidae
Sexy Shrimp   *Thor amboinensis*
To 2 cm (0.8 in.) long   Circumtropical

■ **Aquascaping** This shrimp lives commensally with corals and anemones and should be kept with a living host. Sand anemones and the Pizza Anemone (page 114) are a perfect match.
■ **Compatibility** Reef safe. Can be preyed upon by fishes.

A very tiny but elegantly beautiful commensal shrimp found living with many species of anemones and corals in the wild. Hardy if given an anemone and a peaceful aquarium. Has an interesting habit of raising and wiggling its abdomen. Best kept in pairs or groups.

Crustacea; Decapoda; Rhynchocinetidae
Common Dancing Shrimp   *Rhynchocinetes durbanensis*
To 4 cm (1.6 in.) long   Indo-Pacific

■ **Aquascaping** Appropriate habitat is a cave or overhanging rocks.
■ **Compatibility** Not perfectly reef safe; may eat some coral polyps. Best kept in groups of males and females (males have bigger claws).
■ **Feeding** Carnivorous; offer meaty foods, such as adult brine shrimp, *Mysis* shrimp, chopped crustaceans, or fish flesh.

If fed properly, this is a hardy little shrimp. Needs slow acclimation to new water conditions—sudden changes of pH, temperature, or salinity can be fatal. Often misidentified as "*R. uritai.*"

Crustacea; Decapoda; Gnathophyllidae
Harlequin Shrimp   *Hymenocera picta*
To about 5 cm (2 in.) long   Indo-Pacific; Red Sea

■ **Aquascaping** Most appropriate for a small reef aquarium where the beauty of this species can be appreciated and its interesting biology studied. Best kept in pairs or a small group.
■ **Feeding** Carnivorous. Lives exclusively by attacking and eating sea stars (in particular *Naroda* and *Linckia* species). Must be given "feeder" sea stars in order to survive.

A glorious small shrimp that is hardy and long-lived—if fed with live sea stars—and has been bred in captivity.

Crustacea; Decapoda; Palaemonidae
White-patched
Anemone Shrimp   *Periclimenes brevicarpalis*
To 3 cm (1.2 in.) long   Indo-Pacific

■ **Lighting** Needs a brightly lit aquarium with good circulation for its anemone host.
■ **Compatibility** Reef safe. Lives in association with anemones, most often with the Pizza Anemone (*Cryptodendrum adhaesivum*, page 114). Must be provided with an anemone host in the aquarium.

This is a delicate, beautiful commensal shrimp. It is only moderately hardy and must be carefully acclimated to new water conditions.

Crustacea; Decapoda; Palaemonidae
Emperor Anemone Shrimp   *Periclimenes imperator*
To 2 cm (0.8 in.) long   Indo-Pacific; Red Sea

■ **Feeding** Difficult to keep properly nourished. In nature, it feeds on mucus secreted from its host.
■ **Compatibility** Lives commensally with many animals, often with the Spanish Dancer (*Hexabranchus sanguineus*, page 132), but also with many sea cucumbers. Needs a suitable host in the aquarium, and arranging this is easier said than done.

This is a most-demanding species that ideally should be purchased with its host. For expert aquarists only.

Crustacea; Decapoda; Palaemonidae
Pederson's Commensal Shrimp   *Periclimenes pedersoni*
To 2 cm (0.8 in.) long   Caribbean, Tropical Western Atlantic

■ **Lighting** Requires intense lighting for its host sea anemone.
■ **Compatibility** Reef safe. Lives individually, in pairs, or in larger groups associated with sea anemones. Needs a healthy host sea anemone (for example, *Condylactis gigantea*) to survive in captivity.

A lovely little commensal shrimp that is easy to keep in a quiet dedicated aquarium, but which will often disappear in a reef community tank. Must have slow, careful acclimation to new water conditions. Other *Periclimenes* species need similar care and consideration.

Crustacea; Decapoda; Stenopodidae
White-banded Coral Shrimp   *Stenopus hispidus*
To 9 cm (3.5 in.) long   Circumtropical and partly subtropical

■ **Aquascaping** Appreciates having rocky overhangs or caves.
■ **Feeding** In nature, this species feeds by removing parasites from fishes. It will readily adapt to substitute foods in captivity.
■ **Compatibility** Reef safe. Very aggressive toward other specimens of the same species. Should be kept singly or in male-female pairs.

A hardy, showy shrimp that can be kept for years in a well-maintained coral reef aquarium. Mated pairs will produce eggs and fry regularly and these are relished by fishes and corals.

Crustacea; Decapoda; Stenopodidae
Golden Coral Shrimp   *Stenopus scutellatus*
To 3 cm (1.2 in.) long   Caribbean

■ **Feeding** In nature, this species feeds by removing parasites from fishes. It will readily adapt to substitute foods in captivity.
■ **Compatibility** Reef safe. Very aggressive toward other specimens of the same species. Should be kept singly or in male-female pairs.

This is a delicate species that may not fare well in a large, competitive reef tank. Relatively hardy if carefully acclimated and given a peaceful aquarium.

Crustacea; Decapoda; Nephropidae
Debelius' Reef Lobster   *Enoplometopus debelius*
To 10 cm (3.9 in.) long   Central Indo-Pacific

▪ **Aquascaping** Often disappears into the rockscape of a community aquarium. A smaller reef with limited hiding places will be a better choice to view and study this beautiful lobster.
▪ **Feeding** Carnivorous; readily accepts all meaty foods.
▪ **Compatibility** Generally reef safe, but is a possible threat to small fishes. May be kept singly or in pairs.

This miniature lobster is both beautiful and hardy. It tends to be reclusive, but can be kept for years.

Crustacea; Decapoda; Nephropidae
Hairy Reef Lobster   *Enoplometopus occidentalis*
To 12 cm (4.7 in.) long   Indo-Pacific, Red Sea

▪ **Aquascaping** Often disappears into the rockscape of a community aquarium. A smaller reef with limited hiding places will be a better choice to view and study this small lobster.
▪ **Feeding** Carnivorous; readily accepts all meaty foods.
▪ **Compatibility** Generally reef safe, but is a possible threat to small fishes. May be kept singly or in pairs.

With a red body covered in white, hairlike cirri, this little lobster is interesting and easy to keep.

Crustacea; Decapoda; Synaxidae
Australian
Miniature Spiny Lobster   *Palinurellus wieneckii*
To 15 cm (5.9 in.) long   Central Indo-Pacific

▪ **Aquascaping** This lobster is nocturnal and is best kept in a small aquarium where it can be observed. A sandy aquarium with a few live rocks is ideal—perhaps with some corals that open at night to feed.
▪ **Feeding** As a scavenger that feeds on food remains, this and other lobsters will accept a variety of meaty aquarium foods.

With its long antennae and poorly developed claws, this species resembles its larger, edible relatives. Very hardy and easy to keep.

Crustacea; Decapoda; Palinuridae
Painted Spiny Lobster   *Panulirus versicolor*
Body to 40 cm (15.6 in.) long   Indo-Pacific

▪ **Aquascaping** Should be given overhangs and small caves in which it can hide.
▪ **Feeding** A scavenger that feeds on food remains; will accept a variety of meaty foods, including frozen and dried rations.
▪ **Compatibility** Not completely reef safe. May prey on fishes and invertebrates. May become destructive to the reefscape as it grows.

One of the few spiny lobsters that is suited for a robust community tank with very stable rockwork. Hardy, but allow slow, careful acclimation.

Crustacea; Decapoda, Diogenidae
Caribbean Big Claw Hermit Crab *Calcinus tibicen*
2-3 cm (0.8-1.2 in.) Caribbean

■ **Feeding** Grazes on algae and food remains. May need intentional feeding of dried *Spirulina* or nori (sushi seaweed) if algae supplies are limited.
■ **Compatibility** Reef safe. Needs to be stocked in high numbers to be efficient as an algae control.

One of a group of small, hardy hermit crabs that can help control algae growth in the aquarium. Legs and body are reddish brown, eyestalks are orange, and the left claw is bigger than the right.

Crustacea; Decapoda, Diogenidae
Blue-knuckle Hermit Crab *Calcinus elegans*
2-6 cm (0.8-2.3 in.) Australia

■ **Feeding** Grazes on algae and food remains. May need intentional feeding of dried *Spirulina* or nori (sushi seaweed) if algae supplies are limited.
■ **Compatibility** Reef safe. Needs to be stocked in high numbers to be efficient as an algae control.

An eye-catching species with distinctive jet black legs and bright blue transverse bands, blue eyes and eyestalks, and bright orange antennae. Rarely seen in the trade, but hardy.

Crustacea; Decapoda, Diogenidae
Blue-eyed Hermit Crab *Calcinus laevimanus*
2-3 cm (0.8-1.2 in.) Indo-Pacific

■ **Feeding** Grazes on algae and food remains. May need intentional feeding of dried *Spirulina* or nori (sushi seaweed) if algae supplies are limited.
■ **Compatibility** Reef safe. Needs to be stocked in high numbers to be efficient as an algae control.

Another of the many small, hardy hermit crabs that can help control algae growth in the aquarium. Many color forms exist, but the eyestalks are always orange and blue. Hardy, but lives just 1-2 years.

Crustacea; Decapoda, Diogenidae
Caribbean Equal-handed
Hermit Crab *Clibanarius tricolor*
2-3 cm (0.8-1.2 in.) Caribbean

■ **Feeding** Excellent algae grazer but should be kept in high numbers in order to be effective. Feeds on algae and food remains.

This attractive crab sports blue legs with orange transverse bands as well as blue eyestalks. As the common name implies, both claws are of equal size. The species is hardy but—like many hermits—not long-lived. One of the best of all the algae grazers.

Crustacea; Decapoda, Diogenidae
Green-striped hermit crab   *Clibanarius* sp.
3-4 cm (1.2-1.6 in.)   Indo-Pacific

■ **Feeding** Grazes on algae and food remains. May need intentional feeding of dried *Spirulina* or nori (sushi seaweed) if algae supplies are limited.
■ **Compatibility** Reef safe.

An excellent algae grazer, but needs to be kept in high numbers to serve an effective algae-control function. Hardy and easily kept, it often can be found resting during the day but is more active at night.

Crustacea; Decapoda, Diogenidae
Red Hermit Crab   *Dardanus megistos*
To 30 cm (11.7 in.)   Indo-Pacific

■ **Feeding** Carnivorous; greedily eats all meaty foods.
■ **Compatibility** Not reef safe. Very aggressive and predatory. Can be useful in a system with larger fishes where it scavenges food remains.

A handsome crab, but one that can wreak havoc in a reef aquarium. Common in the trade and often imported as juveniles. Hardy, highly predatory, and only appropriate for a species tank or a fish-only reef.

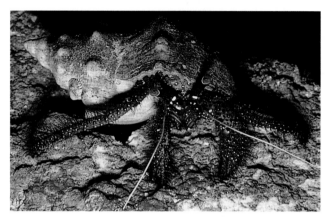

Crustacea; Decapoda, Diogenidae
Anemone Hermit Crab   *Dardanus pedunculatus*
To 10 cm (3.9 in.)   Indo-Pacific

■ **Feeding** Omnivorous; grazes on small invertebrates, dead organisms, and food remains, as well as algae.
■ **Compatibility** Generally reef safe. Lives in association with the *Calliactis polypus* anemones, which attach to the crab's shell. Best kept in a small aquarium where the relationship can be observed.

A fascinating example of mutualism, with two different organisms providing benefit to each other. The anemones provide camouflage, while the hermit crab hunts for food remains.

Crustacea; Decapoda, Diogenidae
Red-legged Hermit Crab   *Paguristes cadenati*
2 cm (0.8 in.)   Caribbean

■ **Feeding** Grazes on algae and food remains. May need intentional feeding of dried *Spirulina* or nori (sushi seaweed) if algae supplies are limited.
■ **Compatibility** Reef safe.

With a bright scarlet body and pale orange eyestalks and antennae, this is a colorful little hermit, both hardy and excellent as an algae grazer. Not long-lived, however.

Crustacea; Decapoda, Diogenidae
American Giant Hermit Crab   *Petrochirus diogenes*
To 25-30 cm (9.8-11.7 in.)   Caribbean; Western Atlantic

■ **Aquascaping** Lives on sandy bottoms and on seagrass beds; perfect for a special aquarium replicating this habitat.
■ **Feeding** A scavenger and carnivore, grazing rather indiscriminately on small invertebrates (e.g., mollusks and worms). Accepts substitute meaty foods in the aquarium.
■ **Compatibility** Not reef safe.

The largest hermit crab from the Caribbean region and a possible choice for a biotope or fish-only reef tank. Hardy and long-lived.

Crustacea; Decapoda, Diogenidae
Polkadot Hermit Crab   *Phimochirus operculatus*
2-3 cm (0.8-1.2 in.)   Caribbean

■ **Feeding** Grazes on algae and food scraps; often steals food from other hermit crabs.
■ **Compatibility** Reef safe.

A common, hardy, and active algae-grazing hermit that is useful in the reef aquarium. It is a bit more aggressive than other such hermits; it may attack snails and members of its own species. Right claw much bigger than left claw.

Crustacea; Decapoda; Porcellanidae
Spotted Porcelain Crab   *Neopetrolisthes ohshimai*
2-3 cm (0.8-1.2 in.)   Indo-Pacific

■ **Lighting** Requires bright lighting for its host sea anemone.
■ **Feeding** A filter feeder that captures suspended organic particles with its specially modified appendages. Will also take bits of meaty foods that come its way.
■ **Compatibility** Reef safe. Lives in pairs commensally with sea anemones. In the aquarium, it must have a host to survive.

Very hardy and can live for years if kept with a host anemone, which the tiny crab never leaves. Larger spots than *P. maculatus* (below).

Crustacea; Decapoda; Porcellanidae
Porcelain Crab   *Neopetrolisthes maculatus*
2-3 cm (0.8-1.2 in.)   Indo-Pacific

■ **Lighting** Requires bright lighting for its host sea anemone.
■ **Feeding** A filter feeder that captures suspended organic particles with its specially modified appendages. Will also take bits of meaty foods that come its way.
■ **Compatibility** Reef safe. Lives in pairs commensally with sea anemones. In the aquarium, it must have a host to survive.

Hardy and long-lived when kept with a healthy host anemone. Has finer spots than the similar *Neopetrolisthes ohshimai* (above).

Crustacea; Decapoda; Dromiidae
Sponge crabs   *Cryptodromia* **spp.**
To about 5 cm (2 in.)   Indo-Pacific; Caribbean

■ **Aquascaping** To keep with its decorative sponge, a small aquarium suited to the needs of the sponge is required.
■ **Feeding** These scavengers will also eat small invertebrates.
■ **Compatibility** Not reef safe. Best kept with aggressive tankmates that can defend themselves.

These primitive, hardy, and predatory crabs carry live sponges or algae on their backs as camouflage and protection. The last pair of legs is modified to hold the sponge. Species are from at least three genera.

Crustacea; Decapoda; Majidae
Decorator Crab   *Camposcia retusa*
To about 10 cm (3.9 in.)across   Indo-Pacific

■ **Aquascaping** To keep with its decorative camouflage made up of various filter-feeding organisms, a special aquarium suited to the needs of the "decorations" will be required.
■ **Feeding** Carnivorous; feeds on all sorts of living and dead food.
■ **Compatibility** Not reef safe. Will attack and eat corals.

This unusual crab decorates its body with all sorts of living organisms (sponges, tunicates, macroalgae) which give the crab a perfect camouflage and a most colorful look. Hardy, but aggressively predatory.

Crustacea; Decapoda; Majidae
Arrow Crab, Spider Crab   *Stenorhynchus seticornis*
5-10 (2-3.9 in.)cm   Caribbean

■ **Aquascaping** Appreciates having rocky ledges and caves.
■ **Feeding** Feeds on small invertebrates and may eat bristleworms.
■ **Compatibility** Not reef safe. May pick on corals and sessile invertebrates and has even been observed to pierce fishes with its sharp rostrum.

With its long, thin walking legs, this crab has a spidery appearance and a not-very-trustworthy nature in the reef aquarium. Hardy and very appropriate for more robust biotope systems.

Crustacea; Decapod; Xanthidae
Boxer Crab   *Lybia tessellata*
2-3 cm (0.8-1.2 in.)   Indo-Pacific; Red Sea

■ **Feeding** Feeds on detritus collected off the substrate by the anemones in its claws. Can be fed finely minced meaty foods.
■ **Compatibility** Reef safe, but should be given a small special aquarium without aggressive tankmates where it can be nurtured and observed.

This crab and its anemone partners are a fantastic example of mutualistic symbiosis.The crab carries a small anemone in each claw for defense and feeding.

Crustacea; Decapoda; Trapeziidae
Coral Crab   *Trapezia ferruginea*
2 cm (0.8 in.)   Indo-Pacific

■ **Feeding** A self-sufficient little crab that lodges within the branches of a stony coral and scrapes the surface of the coral with modified appendages to collect mucus and food particles. Must be kept with a healthy colony of coral in the aquarium.
■ **Compatibility** Reef safe. Does not harm its coral host, usually lives with *Pocillopora* spp. or *Stylophora* spp.

Often hitchhikes into the aquarium with stony corals and should not be removed. Hardy if given a host.

Crustacea; Decapoda; Trapeziidae
Spotted Coral Crab   *Trapezia wardi*
3 cm (1.2 in.)   Indo-Pacific

■ **Feeding** A self-sufficient little crab that lodges within the branches of a stony coral and scrapes the surface of the coral with modified appendages to collect mucus and food particles.
■ **Compatibility** Reef safe. Lives between stony coral branches of *Pocillopora* spp. and must be given such shelter in the aquarium.

A single colony of corals often contains many specimens of this crab and there is absolutely no need to remove the harmless crabs from the host. Hardy if kept with a healthy coral.

Crustacea; Decapoda; Grapsidae
Sally Lightfoot (Urchin) Crab   *Percnon gibbesi*
To 6 cm (2.3 in.)   Caribbean, Atlantic, Eastern Pacific

■ **Aquascaping** Occurs in the tidal zones of rocky shores and coral reefs. Very appropriate for a biotope with a tidal zone or land zone.
■ **Feeding** Omnivorous; feeds primarily by scraping algae off rocks.
■ **Compatibility** Reef safe. Usually harmless, but may catch small fishes. Often associated with the sea urchin *Diadema* spp. (page 153) under which it hides.

A flattened, fast-moving crab that eats algae and will make itself at home on and among live rock aquascapes. Moderately hardy.

Echinodermata; Crinoidea; Comatulida; Himerometridae
Feather star   *Himerometra* sp.
To 20 cm (7.8 in.)   Indo-Pacific

■ **Circulation** Needs vigorous alternating water movement.
■ **Feeding** Lives on tiny plankton only, such as foraminifers, tiny crustaceans, and phytoplankton. Extremely difficult to feed.
■ **Conservation** All crinoids are extremely difficult if not impossible to keep. In general, they should not be collected or purchased.

Beautiful, rather strange animals seen in a rainbow of colors and having featherlike arms and powerful cirri (feet) that allow the animal to walk across the substrate. For expert aquarists only.

Echinodermata; Asteroidea; Valvatida; Oreasteridae
Chocolate Chip Starfish   *Protoreaster nodosus*
To 15 cm (5.9 in.)   Western and Central Pacific

■ **Feeding** Carnivorous. Will scavenge food scraps or pieces of fish or crustacean flesh.
■ **Compatibility** Not reef safe. It is a predatory species that feeds on invertebrates like sponges, worms, and mollusks, and should not be trusted with coral specimens.

This is a hardy, attractive starfish that is not reef safe but can be kept in fish-only reefs or in biotope tanks with a sandy bottom that replicates the seagrass zone where this species is most common.

Echinodermata; Asteroidea; Valvatida; Oreasteridae
Doughboy Starfish   *Choriaster granulatus*
To 40 cm (15.6 in.)   Indo-Pacific, Red Sea

■ **Feeding** This is an active scavenger that feeds mainly on food remains and detritus but will prey on various invertebrates in its path.
■ **Compatibility** Not reef safe. Will eat tiny invertebrates and prey on corals in the aquarium. Too large for many aquariums.

This is a very large species with impressively stout arms. Hardy, but allow slow, careful acclimation to new water conditions. Best kept in a fish-only tank or in a special aquarium where its predatory feeding habits won't be a problem.

Echinodermata; Asteroidea; Valvatida; Oreasteridae
Cushion Star   *Culcita novaeguineae*
To 30 cm (11.7 in.)   Indo-Pacific

■ **Feeding** In the wild it preys on corals, but will accept other foods in the aquarium, including flake food, mussel flesh, and fish flesh.
■ **Compatibility** Not reef safe. Feeds on the polyps of stony corals. Best kept in a fish-only tank or in a special aquarium where its instinctive feeding habits won't prove to be a problem.

Looking much like a pincushion, this is one of three similar species that range in color from green and yellow to brown, orange, and red. Hardy, but allow slow, careful acclimation to new water conditions.

Echinodermata; Asteroidea; Valvatida; Oreasteridae
Knobby Sea Star   *Pentaceraster mammillatus*
To 40 cm (15.6 in.)   Indian Ocean, Red Sea

■ **Feeding** Omnivorous; an active scavenger that also feeds on mollusks and other invertebrates.
■ **Compatibility** Not reef safe. Likely to eat corals in the aquarium. Best kept in a fish-only tank or in a special system due to its feeding habits.

A large, common species with prominent knobs or conical spines on its dorsal surface. Hardy, but allow slow, careful acclimation to new water conditions. (*Protoreaster lincki* shown at rear in photo.)

Echinodermata; Asteroidea; Valvatida; Oreasteridae
Cushion Star, Bahama Star   *Oreaster reticulatus*
To 50 cm (19.5 in.)   Caribbean, Tropical Atlantic

■ **Feeding** Omnivorous, feeds on a variety of food sources, including detritus, algae, sponges, and other echinoderms. Feeds on live mollusks, such as clams and oysters, everting its stomach and digesting them in their own shells.
■ **Compatibility** Not reef safe. Needs a large system with an open sandy bottom. Found in typical seagrass habitats.

Also known as the Reticulated Sea Star, this large, common species needs a roomy aquarium. Hardy, but must be acclimated slowly.

Echinodermata; Asteroidea; Valvatida; Oreasteridae
African Sea Star   *Protoreaster lincki*
To 30 cm (11.7 in.)   Indian Ocean

■ **Feeding** Omnivorous; feeds greedily on a variety of food sources, including sponges, detritus, algae, and other invertebrates.
■ **Compatibility** Not reef safe. Will attack corals and other sessile invertebrates. Needs a large system with an open sandy bottom. Found in seagrass beds.

With brilliant red spines, this is a showy and distinctive species for a large tank and tankmates that are not on its usual list of prey. Hardy, but requires slow, careful acclimation to new water conditions.

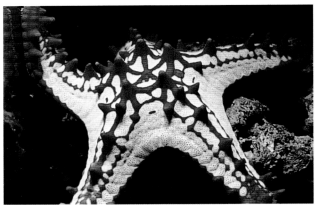

Echinodermata; Asteroidea; Valvatida; Ophidiasteridae
Elegant Sea Star   *Fromia indica*
To 9 cm (3.5 in.)   Indo-Pacific

■ **Feeding** Omnivorous; grazes over rock, eating algae, tiny invertebrates, and microorganisms living with the algae. Difficult to provide with sufficient food in a typical reef system.
■ **Compatibility** Reef safe. Members of this genus are usually trustworthy in a community tank and will not harm sessile invertebrates.

This is one of about a dozen very attractive genus members that are reef safe but difficult to feed and keep the aquarium. Allow slow, careful acclimation to new water conditions.

Echinodermata; Asteroidea; Valvatida; Ophidiasteridae
Elegant Sea Star   *Fromia milleporella*
To 7 cm (2.7 in.)   Indo-Pacific, Red Sea

■ **Feeding** Omnivorous; grazes over rock, eating algae, tiny invertebrates, and microorganisms living with the algae. Difficult to provide with sufficient food in a typical reef system.
■ **Compatibility** Reef safe. members of this genus are usually trustworthy in a community tank and will not harm sessile invertebrates.

Part of a genus that is difficult to keep and probably suffers from lack of food in a nutrient-poor reef aquarium. Must be carefully acclimated. (Blue-spotted form is from Red Sea.)

Echinodermata; Asteroidea; Valvatida; Ophidiasteridae

Elegant Sea Star   *Fromia nodosa*

To 8 cm (3.1 in.)   Western Indian Ocean

■ **Feeding** Omnivorous; grazes over rock, eating algae, tiny invertebrates, and microorganisms living with the algae. Difficult to provide with sufficient food in a typical reef system.

■ **Compatibility** Reef safe. members of this genus are usually trustworthy in a community tank and will not harm sessile invertebrates.

A beautiful and often photographed sea star that is, unfortunately, difficult to feed and keep for long periods in the reef aquarium. Needs slow acclimation to the water of a new system.

Echinodermata; Asteroidea; Valvatida; Ophidiasteridae

Tamarisk Sea Star   *Tamaria stria*

To 20 cm (7.8 in.)   Eastern Pacific

■ **Feeding** Omnivorous; grazes over rock, eating algae, tiny invertebrates, and microorganisms living with the algae. Difficult to provide with sufficient food in a typical reef system.

■ **Compatibility** Generally reef safe, but may attack certain sessile invertebrates.

A richly pigmented sea star that is very sensitive to changing water conditions and thus difficult to ship without damaging stress. Difficult to feed and keep. Must have slow, careful acclimation upon arrival.

Echinodermata; Asteroidea; Valvatida; Ophidiasteridae

Blue Sea Star   *Linckia laevigata*

To 40 cm (15.6 in.)   Indo-Pacific

■ **Feeding** Will graze over live rock, eating detritus, algae, and associated microorganisms, but will accept meaty foods (bits of clam or shrimp) placed in its path.

■ **Compatibility** Reef safe; excellent for a community tank.

A favorite of many aquarists for its startling blue color and general hardiness once settled into the aquarium. Difficult to acclimate; great care should be taken when introducing this species to your tank. Once accustomed to its new conditions, it is easy to keep and long-lived.

Echinodermata; Asteroidea; Valvatida; Ophidiasteridae

Spotted Linckia   *Linckia multifora*

To 15 cm (5.9 in.)   Indo-Pacific and the Red Sea

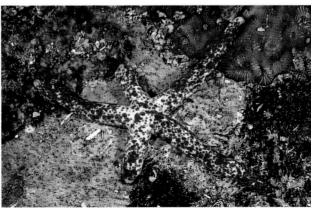

■ **Feeding** Will graze over live rock, eating detritus, algae, and associated microorganisms, but will accept meaty foods (bits of clam or shrimp) placed in its path.

■ **Compatibility** Reef safe. Excellent for a community tank.

A curious starfish whose species name means "many pores" and whose coloration varies greatly, from grayish pink to orange-brown. After very slow and careful acclimation, it is often very hardy and can live for many years.

Echinodermata; Asteroidea; Valvatida; Echinasteridae
Spiny Sea Star *Echinaster echinophorus*
To 7 cm (2.7 in.) Caribbean, south to Brazil

■ **Feeding** Feeds on detritus, microorganisms, and possibly algae. Difficult to feed on substitute food in the aquarium. Must be kept in with live rock and plenty of detritus and nutrients. Without this it does not survive for long.
■ **Compatibility** Reef safe with corals, but may eat some sessile invertebrates.

An intense orange-red species that is often imported but not among the easiest sea stars to keep. Allow careful acclimation.

Echinodermata; Ophiuroidea; Ophiurida; Ophiuridae
Serpent Star *Ophiolepis superba*
To 25 cm (9.8 in.) Indo-Pacific, Red Sea

■ **Feeding** Self-sufficient scavenger, feeds on detritus, feces, and food remains.
■ **Compatibility** Reef safe. Excellent for a reef aquarium. Does not hurt other organisms, except perhaps tiny tubeworms.

Serpent Stars are excellent scavengers, living under live rock and keeping detritus under control. Very hardy and can live for many years. Every reef tank should have several such "cleaners" in the system.

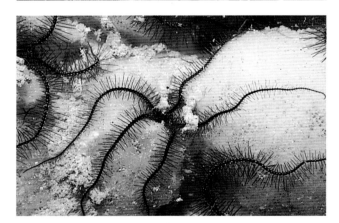

Echinodermata; Ophiuroidea; Ophiurida; Ophiocomidae
Sponge brittle stars *Ophiothrix* **spp.**
To 32 cm (12.5 in.) Circumtropical

■ **Feeding** Self-sufficient scavengers; feed on detritus, feces, food remains, and particles in the water surface film.
■ **Compatibility** Reef safe. Excellent for reef aquariums. Will not hurt other organisms, except perhaps tiny tubeworms.

Very common in the wild and seen in a number of different color variations. Hide under rocks with only their spiny arms stretching out. Sensitive to shipping stresses and changes in water conditions but often hardy and useful scavengers.

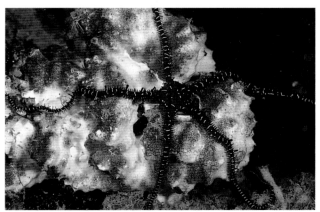

Echinodermata; Ophiuroidea; Ophiurida; Ophiocomidae
Black Brittle Star *Ophiomastix variabilis*
To 25 cm (9.8 in.) Indo-Pacific

■ **Feeding** Self-sufficient scavenger, feeds on detritus, feces, and food remains.
■ **Compatibility** Reef safe. Excellent for a reef aquarium. Does not hurt other organisms, except perhaps tiny tubeworms.

A colorful brittle star and an excellent scavenger, although it will spend most of its time living under live rock and keeping detritus under control. Very hardy and can live for many years. Every reef tank should have several such "cleaners" in the system.

Echinodermata; Ophiuroidea; Ophiurida; Ophiodermatidae
Green Brittle Star   *Ophiarachna incrassata*
To 55 cm (21.6 in.)   Indo-Pacific

■ **Feeding** An opportunistic, self-sufficient omnivore that feeds on a variety of food, including detritus and food remains. It may occasionally hunt and devour small fishes.
■ **Compatibility** Reef safe. A very good scavenger for a community tank, but with a habit of trapping and eating small fishes at night.

A large, robust brittle star, this species is very hardy and a great scavenger. Has been reported to spawn and be raised in captivity

Echinodermata; Ophiuroidea; Ophiurida; Ophiodermatidae
Red Serpent Star   *Ophioderma squamosissimus*
To 44 cm (17.3 in.)   Caribbean

■ **Feeding** Self-sufficient scavenger, feeds on detritus, feces, and food remains.
■ **Compatibility** Reef safe. Excellent for a reef aquarium. Does not hurt other organisms, except perhaps tiny tubeworms.

This beautiful orange-red species has smooth legs (unlike the spiny brittle stars), lives under live rock and keeps detritus under control. Very hardy and can live for many years. Every reef tank should have several such "cleaners" in the system.

Echinodermata; Echinoidea; Diadematoida; Diadematidae
Long-spined sea urchins   *Diadema* **spp.**
To 40 cm (15.6 in.)   Circumtropical

■ **Feeding** Grazes on algae, including red calcareous algae, but also on sessile invertebrates such as bryozoans, sponges, and corals. Will accept dried seaweed in the aquarium.
■ **Compatibility** Not reef safe.
■ **Hazards** The spines are sharp and contain poison; can cause painful stings to humans.

With spines up to 30 cm (11.7 in.) long, these are big urchins. Hardy and easily kept, for fish-keeping systems without corals. Nocturnal.

Echinodermata; Echinoidea; Temnopleuroida; Temnopleuridae
Globe Urchin   *Mespilia globulus*
To 7.5 cm (2.9 in.)   Central Pacific

■ **Feeding** Feeds on algae, including red calcareous algae and filamentous algae, but may also graze on sessile invertebrates.
■ **Compatibility** Reef safe, with caution. One of the few sea urchins that can be kept in a reef aquarium, but it must be watched to ensure that its feeding habits don't turn destructive.

This is an exceptionally attractive urchin and one that may be safe to keep in many reef tanks. Hardy and easily kept. Often carries bits of coral rubble on its bands of short spines.

Echinodermata; Echinoidea; Temnopleuroida; Temnopleuridae
Jewel Urchin *Salmacis bicolor*
To 13 cm (5.1 in.) Indo-Pacific and Red Sea

■ **Feeding** Feeds on algae including red calcareous algae and filamentous algae, but may also graze on sessile invertebrates.
▨ **Compatibility** Reef safe, with caution. One of the few sea urchins that can be kept in a reef aquarium, but it must be watched to ensure that its feeding habits don't turn destructive.

Part of a large group of short-spined, hard-to-identify urchins that generally prove to be hardy and easily kept.

Echinodermata; Echinoidea; Temnopleuroida; Toxopneustidae
Sea Egg *Tripneustes gratilla*
To 15 cm (5.9 in.) Indo-Pacific, Red Sea

■ **Hazards** The pedicellariae contain poison and can cause great pain. Handle with care.
■ **Feeding** Mostly herbivorous, grazing on algae.
▨ **Compatibility** Reef safe, with caution. Must be watched to ensure that it doesn't attack corals or other sessile invertebrates.

Very common in the wild and highly variable in coloration. The body is often camouflaged by seagrass and rubble attached to the spines. Hardy. The very similar Caribbean Sea Egg is *T. ventricosus*.

Echinodermata; Echinoidea; Echinoida; Echinometridae
Rock-boring Urchin *Echinometra mathaei*
To 10 cm (3.9 in.) Indo-Pacific

▨ **Feeding** Herbivorous; eats algae, including red calcareous algae.
▨ **Compatibility** Reef safe, with caution. Will usually ignore corals and other sessile invertebrates, but will graze on calcareous algae and drill holes in live rock. May occasionally develop a taste for corals.

The various species of boring urchins are very common on shallow reef flats where they can be found by the thousands. Very hardy.

Echinodermata; Holothuroidea; Dendrochirotida; Cucumariidae
Sea Apple *Pseudocolochirus axiologus*
To 20 cm (7.8 in.) Indo-Pacific

▨ **Circulation** Needs heavy water motion.
▨ **Feeding** A filter feeder that catches suspended plankton and organic particles with its bushy tentacles. Needs regular feeding.
▨ **Compatibility** Reef safe. All sea cucumbers can evert their internal organs and dispense the poison holothurin, which will kill fishes and affect the aquarium severely but is not poisonous to humans.

Glorious colors, but often slowly starves in the aquarium if not intentionally fed on a regular schedule. Needs slow, careful acclimation.

Echinodermata; Holothuroidea; Dendrochirotida; Cucumariidae
Small Spiny Sea Cucumber　　　　　*Pentacta anceps*
To 8 cm (3.1 in.)　　　　　　　　　　　　　Indo-Pacific

■ **Circulation** Needs heavy water motion.
■ **Feeding** A filter feeder that catches suspended plankton and organic particles with its bushy tentacles. Needs regular feeding.
■ **Compatibility** Reef safe. All sea cucumbers can evert their internal organs and dispense the poison holothurin, which will kill fishes and affect the aquarium severely but is not poisonous to humans.

This small plankton-feeding sea cucumber is perfectly suited for the community tank. Hardy if well fed. Needs careful acclimation.

Echinodermata; Holothuroidea; Dendrochirotida; Cucumariidae
Yellow Sea Apple　　　　　　　*Colochirus robustus*
To 6 cm (2.3 in.)　　　　　　　Indo-Australian Archipelago

■ **Circulation** Needs heavy water motion.
■ **Feeding** A filter feeder that catches suspended plankton and organic particles with its bushy tentacles. Needs regular feeding.
■ **Compatibility** Reef safe. All sea cucumbers can evert their internal organs and dispense the poison holothurin, which will kill fishes and affect the aquarium severely but is not poisonous to humans.

Beautiful, bright yellow little sea cucumbers that are excellent for a community tank. Hardy if fed.

Echinodermata; Holothuroidea; Aspidochirotida; Holothuriidae
Donkey Dung　　　　　　　　　*Holothuria atra*
To 60 cm (23 in.)　　　　　　Indo-Pacific and Red Sea

■ **Aquascaping** Needs a sandy substrate where it can feed.
■ **Feeding** Feeds on detritus and microorganisms found in the substrate. Excellent scavenger in the reef aquarium.
■ **Compatibility** Reef safe. All sea cucumbers can evert their internal organs and dispense the poison holothurin, which will kill fishes and affect the aquarium severely but is not poisonous to humans.

One of a number of large, burrowing sea cucumbers that will keep a sand bed "worked" and clean. Hardy, but allow careful acclimation.

Echinodermata; Holothuria; Aspidochirotida; Holothuriidae
Edible Sea Cucumber　　　　　　*Holothuria edulis*
To 30 cm (11.7 in.)　　　　　　Indo-Pacific and Red Sea

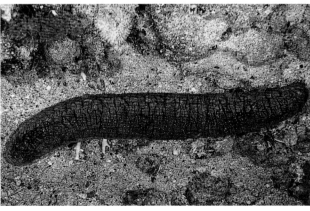

■ **Aquascaping** Needs a sandy substrate where it can feed.
■ **Feeding** Feeds on detritus and microorganisms found in the substrate. Excellent scavenger in the reef aquarium.
■ **Compatibility** Reef safe. All sea cucumbers can evert their internal organs and dispense the poison holothurin, which will kill fishes and affect the aquarium severely but is not poisonous to humans.

A favorite ingredient in certain Asian cuisines, this species has a pinkish red underside. Hardy, but allow careful acclimation.

Echinodermata; Holothuria; Aspidochirotida; Holothuriidae
Slender Sea Cucumber   *Holothuria impatiens*
To 25 cm (9.8 in.)   Circumtropical

■ **Feeding** Feeds on detritus and microorganisms found in the substrate. Excellent scavenger in the reef aquarium.
▩ **Compatibility** Reef safe. Will clean crevices in live rock. Like all sea cucumbers, this species contains the poison holothurin that can kill fishes but is not poisonous to humans.

Not a classic beauty, but with an elongate body mottled in beige and brown and covered with short spines. Hardy, but allow careful acclimation.

Echinodermata; Holothuroidea, Apodida, Synaptidae
Medusa Worm   *Synapta maculata*
To 250 cm (98 in.)   Indo-Pacific, Red Sea

▩ **Feeding** Detritivore; collects detritus and uneaten food off rock and bottom surfaces with its mouth tentacles.
▩ **Compatibility** Reef safe. Will clean crevices in live rock. Like all sea cucumbers, this species contains the poison holothurin that can kill fishes but is not poisonous to humans.

One of a number of species with feeding tentacles and bodies that can be greatly stretched and retracted. Not among the hardiest sea cucumbers; probably suffers from lack of food in most reef tanks.

Chordata; Tunicata; Enterogona; Clavelinidae
Sea Squirts   *Clavelina robusta*
To 4 cm (1.6 in.)   Indo-Pacific

▩ **Lighting** Need shade or moderate illumination.
■ **Feeding** These are filter feeders that screen minute organic particles as they pump water through their hollow body cavities. They are not easy to feed in the aquarium and normally suffer from lack of nutrients in a typical reef system.

These curious animals are often very colorful and sometimes arrive on live rock. Unfortunately, most are very difficult to keep. They will do best in unskimmed systems managed for filter-feeding organisms.

Chordata; Tunicata; Enterogona; Didemnidae
Sea Squirts   *Didemnum molle*
Colony to 4 cm (1.6 in.)   Indo-Pacific

▩ **Lighting** Contain blue green commensal algae (*Prochloron* sp.) and needs strong light intensity.
▩ **Feeding** Filter tiny organic particles from the water. May benefit from intentional feeding week dissolved and suspended organic foods.

These easily recognized sea squirts are common on the reef, but rarely survive collection and introduction to the aquarium. Probably difficult to keep in most nutrient-poor systems.

Chordata; Tunicata; Pleurogona; Styelidae

Sea Squirts *Polycarpa aurata*

To 10 cm (3.9 in.) Indo-Pacific

■ **Lighting** Should be kept in shade or moderately lit areas.
■ **Feeding** Filters tiny organic particles from the water. Will benefit from regular feeding water dissolved and suspended organic foods.

These impressive zooids are big and variable in color, but often yellowish and white with purple stripes. Common on the reef, but rarely imported. Challenging to keep.

Chordata; Tunicata; Pleurogona; Styelidae

Colonial Tunicates *Botrylloides leachi*

Moderate to large colonies All seas

■ **Lighting** Should be kept in shadow or under dim lighting.
■ **Feeding** Filter tiny organic particles from the water. Will benefit from regular feeding with dissolved and suspended organic foods.

These are very common colonial tunicates in most seas, even outside the Tropics. The zooids are highly variable in color and form encrusting colonies on live rock or at the base of corals. If enough nutrients are available, this species can thrive and grow well in the reef aquarium.

Chordata; Tunicata; Pleurogona; Pyuridae

Solitary Tunicate *Herdmania momus*

To 20 cm (7.8 in.) Circumtropical

■ **Lighting** Should be kept in dim to moderately lit conditions.
■ **Circulation** Needs plenty of water motion.
■ **Feeding** Filters tiny organic particles from the water. Will benefit from regular feeding with dissolved and suspended organic foods.

This widespread solitary tunicate is relatively hardy, highly variable in color, and often overgrown with algae or invertebrates. Often found on live rock. Must be well fed in order to grow and thrive.

Vertebrata; Elasmobranchii; Orectolobiformes; Hemiscylliidae

Whitespotted Bamboo Shark *Chiloscyllium plagiosum*

100 cm (39 in.) Indo-West Pacific

■ **Aquascaping** Needs an open sand flat, rocky ledges and caves.
■ **Feeding** Heavy feeder that eats meaty foods, such as pieces of marine fish, shrimp, or other seafood.
■ **Compatibility** Reef safe in certain circumstances. May be safely combined with corals, if good water quality can be maintained. Will eat crustaceans and small fishes.

An attractive small bottom-dwelling shark that forages at night. Hardy and long lived in large tanks—minimum 1,000 L (260 gal.).

Vertebrata; Elasmobranchii; Rajiformes; Dasyatidae
Bluespotted Ribbontail Ray *Taeniura lymma*
70 cm (27 in.) total length Indo-Pacific, Red Sea

■ **Aquascaping** Needs a very large open sand flat overhung by rocky cave formations in a large aquarium.
■ **Feeding** Carnivorous; often difficult to feed. May accept fresh seafood items. Try live shrimp and worms.
■ **Compatibility** Reef safe with corals. Will eat other invertebrates.

One of the most beautiful rays, but the majority of imported specimens die from starvation or other, unknown causes. For experts only.

Vertebrata; Actinopterygii; Anguilliformes; Muraenidae
Snowflake Moray *Echidna nebulosa*
90 cm (35 in.) Indo-Pacific, Red Sea

■ **Aquascaping** Must have caves or other suitable hiding places.
■ **Feeding** Primarily feeds on crustaceans in the wild. Will take a variety of meaty seafoods offered on a feeding stick.
■ **Compatibility** Reef safe, but may eat crustaceans, mollusks, and small fishes.

Among the more peaceful moray eels; very hardy and long-lived. Safe with corals and most fishes. A large eel may put strains on water quality in a captive reef.

Vertebrata; Actinopterygii; Anguilliformes; Muraenidae
Zebra Moray *Gymnomuraena zebra*
130 cm (51 in.) long; 25 cm (9.8 in.) diameter Indo-Pacific

■ **Aquascaping** Must have caves or other suitable hiding places.
■ **Feeding** Primarily feeds on crustaceans in the wild. Often reluctant to feed at first, usually will take a variety of meaty seafoods offered on a feeding stick.
■ **Compatibility** Reef safe, but may eat ornamental crustaceans and mollusks. Usually will not chase fishes.

A strikingly handsome eel, and among the more peaceful morays. Suitable for larger fish tanks. Hardy and long lived.

Vertebrata; Actinopterygii; Anguilliformes; Muraenidae
Gray Moray *Siderea grisea*
65 cm (25 in.) Red Sea, Western Indian Ocean

■ **Aquascaping** Must have caves or other suitable hiding places.
■ **Feeding** Readily accepts meaty foods in the aquarium.
■ **Compatibility** Reef safe and relatively peaceful, but is a threat to most free-living invertebrates, particularly crustaceans. May eat small fishes, under 20 cm (7.8 in.).

An elegant moray that is becoming more common in shipments from the Red Sea. Safe to keep with corals, if its nutrient-generating abilities do not lower the water quality.

Vertebrata; Actinopterygii; Anguilliformes; Muraenidae
Ribbon Eel   *Rhinomuraena quaesita*
120 cm (47 in.)   Indo-west-Pacific

■ **Aquascaping** Needs caves or other suitable hiding places. Easily escapes from tanks that are not tightly covered.
■ **Feeding** Difficult to feed. Usually needs live feeder fish when first acquired. May accept mussel meat and shrimp. Slow feeder; may have difficulty competing with aggressive species.
■ **Compatibility** Reef safe, but a threat to small fishes.

Beautiful hermaphroditic species (juveniles black, males blue, females yellow). Poor survival in captivity. Only for experienced aquarists.

Vertebrata; Actinopterygii; Anguilliformes; Congridae
Spotted Garden Eel   *Heteroconger hassi*
35 cm (13.7 in.)   Indo-Pacific, Red Sea

■ **Aquascaping** Requires a thick bed of fine sand for burrowing; minimum 15 cm (5.9 in.) deep. Needs gentle current along the bottom.
■ **Compatibility** Best in colonies of several specimens. Provide minimum area of 30 x 30 cm (12 x 12 in.) per eel.
■ **Feeding** Carnivores; pluck passing food from the current. Will accept brine shrimp, mysid shrimp, baby mollies, chopped seafood.

Fascinating but very shy fish that retreats into its burrow at the slightest sign of danger. Many similar, related species.

Vertebrata; Actinopterygii; Siluriformes; Plotosidae
Coral Catfish   *Plotosus lineatus*
40 cm (15.6 in.)   Indo-Pacific

■ **Feeding** Omnivorous; readily accepts most foods.
■ **Compatibility** Reef safe, but will eat smaller fishes as it grows. Do not combine with any fish small enough to be swallowed whole.
■ **Hazards** Fin spines equipped with venom glands, can inflict painful stings on humans.

A very appealing and active fish when kept as a juvenile in schools. As it matures, it becomes more solitary and assumes a much less attractive, grayish brown overall coloration. Very hardy.

Vertebrata; Actinopterygii; Lophiiformes; Antennariidae
Warty Frogfish   *Antennarius maculatus*
10 cm (3.9 in.)   Indo-Pacific; Mauritius to Solomon Islands

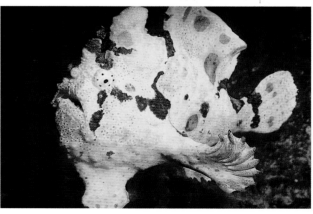

■ **Feeding** Highly voracious fish predator. May ingest slender fishes longer than itself. Live fish may be needed to initiate feeding. Once settled, usually accepts nonliving, meaty foods from a feeding stick.
■ **Compatibility** Reef safe, but will eat smaller fishes or crustaceans. Tends to be aggressive toward members of its own species and will eat conspecifics that are smaller than itself.

A fascinating species with many different color morphs. May change colors to blend with the surroundings. Good choice for species tank.

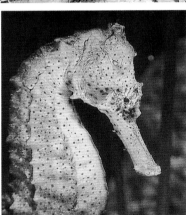

Vertebrata; Actinopterygii; Syngnathiformes; Centriscidae
Coral Shrimpfish   *Aeoliscus strigatus*
15 cm (5.9 in.)   Indo-Pacific

■ **Aquascaping** Does best with established live rock or dense sea-grass to provide a varied, rich supply of live, tiny food organisms.
■ **Feeding** Requires frequent feedings of small benthic and/or planktonic crustaceans, like brine shrimp, mysid shrimp, copepods.
■ **Compatibility** Reef safe but shy. Keep in schools of 7 or more, with peaceful fishes—pipefishes, seahorses, gobies, or blennies.

An unusual fish that looks great schooling in a tank of healthy branching corals, such as *Acropora* spp.

Vertebrata; Actinopterygii; Syngnathiformes; Syngnathidae
Banded Pipefish   *Doryrhamphus pessuliferus*

16 cm (6.2 in.)   Western Pacific
■ **Aquascaping** Does best with established live rock or dense sea-grass to provide a varied, rich supply of live, tiny food organisms.
■ **Feeding** Feeds on small benthic and planktonic organisms—brine shrimp, copepods, and amphipods. Often accepts moving food only.
■ **Compatibility** Reef safe. Needs a peaceful aquarium with non-competitive tankmates. Easily burned by stinging corals or anemones.

A pretty, peaceful fish that demands expert feeding and peaceful surroundings. Known to clean other fishes for parasites in nature.

Vertebrata; Actinopterygii; Syngnathiformes; Syngnathidae
Common Seahorse   *Hippocampus kuda*
7 to 17 cm (2.7-6.6 in.)   Indo-Pacific

■ **Feeding** Difficult to feed. Needs frequent feedings of vitamin-enriched live or frozen mysid shrimp. May accept only moving foods.
■ **Compatibility** Not safe in a reef aquarium. Will be harmed by long-tentacled corals or anemones. Needs peaceful tankmates.
■ **Conservation** An endangered species in many areas. Look for captive-propagated specimens.

Very interesting animals, but not especially hardy and very demanding of special feeding and care. A small species tank is recommended.

Vertebrata; Actinopterygii; Scorpaeniformes; Scorpaenidae
Leaf Scorpionfish   *Taenianotus triacanthus*
10 cm (3.9 in.)   Indo-Pacific

■ **Feeding** Carnivorous; takes meaty foods, but will frequently refuse anything but live food.
■ **Compatibility** Reef safe, but may eat any fish or crustacean that is small enough to be swallowed.
■ **Hazards** Fin spines are equipped with venom glands. Can inflict painful stings on humans, occasionally with severe side effects.

This quiet species has many color morphs and is an interesting fish, but avoid housing it with smaller fishes and crustaceans.

Vertebrata; Actinopterygii; Scorpaeniformes; Scorpaenidae
Twinspot Lionfish   *Dendrochirus biocellatus*
12 cm (4.7 in.)   Indo-Pacific; Sri Lanka to the Society Islands.

■ **Aquascaping** Needs caves and crevices for hiding.
■ **Feeding** Meaty foods: crustaceans and fish meat. Perhaps the most difficult lionfish to feed, often refuses anything but live food.
■ **Compatibility** Reef safe, but will eat small fishes and shrimps.
■ **Hazards** Fin spines equipped with venom glands. Can inflict painful stings on humans, occasionally with severe side effects.

A rather shy and secretive species that tends to hide much of the time, particularly when first added to an aquarium. Not a beginner's fish.

Vertebrata; Actinopterygii; Scorpaeniformes; Scorpaenidae
Zebra Lionfish   *Dendrochirus zebra*
25 cm (9.8 in.)   Indo-Pacific; East Africa to Samoa

■ **Aquascaping** Needs rocky caves and crevices for hiding.
■ **Feeding** Meaty foods: crustaceans and fish meat. May need live food to encourage feeding.
■ **Compatibility** Reef safe, but will eat small fishes and shrimps.
■ **Hazards** Fin spines equipped with venom glands. Can inflict painful stings on humans, occasionally with severe side effects.

Excellent aquarium fish to combine with corals in a reef tank, but often secretive. Tends to be aggressive toward other lionfishes.

Vertebrata; Actinopterygii; Scorpaeniformes; Scorpaenidae
Common Lionfish   *Pterois volitans*
30 cm (11.8 in.)   Eastern Indo-Pacific

■ **Feeding** Meaty foods; crustaceans and fish meat. May need live food to initiate feeding.
■ **Compatibility** Reef safe, but large and will eat any fish or crustacean that is small enough to be swallowed.
■ **Hazards** Fin spines equipped with venom glands. Can inflict painful stings on humans, occasionally with severe side effects.

Excellent aquarium fish to keep with corals in a reef tank, and much less secretive than most of its relatives. Very hardy but predatory.

Vertebrata; Actinopterygii; Scorpaeniformes; Scorpaenidae
Spotfin Lionfish   *Pterois antennata*
20 cm (7.8 in.)   Indo-Pacific

■ **Aquascaping** Requires rocky caves and crevices for hiding.
■ **Feeding** Meaty foods; crustaceans and fish meat. May need live food to initiate a feeding response.
■ **Compatibility** Reef safe, but will eat small fishes and shrimps.
■ **Hazards** Fin spines equipped with venom glands. Can inflict painful stings on humans, occasionally with severe side effects.

A flamboyant fish with its fins fully spread and very compatible with live corals. It does tend to be secretive and is difficult to feed at first.

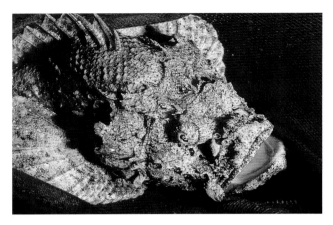

Vertebrata; Actinopterygii; Scorpaeniformes; Scorpaenidae
Stonefish   *Synanceia verrucosa*
35 cm (13.7 in.)   Indo-Pacific; Red Sea to Mangareva

■ **Feeding** Carnivore: meaty foods, crustaceans, and fish meat.
■ **Compatibility** Reef safe, but will eat any fish it can swallow.
■ **Hazards** Fin spines equipped with venom glands and the most powerful toxin produced by any known fish. Can inflict painful wounds, dangerous to humans. Deaths have occurred.

For professional keepers only. Stonefish have no place in a home aquarium because of the severe health risks associated with their handling.

Vertebrata; Actinopterygii; Perciformes; Serranidae
Panther Grouper   *Cromileptes altivelis*
70 cm (27 in.)   Indo-Pacific

■ **Aquascaping** Needs rocky hiding places or caves.
■ **Feeding** Carnivorous; accepts all meaty foods.
■ **Compatibility** Safe with corals, but gets large and is likely to eat any animal small enough to be swallowed whole.

Extremely attractive as a juvenile, this is a hardy, fairly peaceful fish, but one that can get quite large. Should be housed in a large aquarium of at least 1,000 L (260 gal.) with powerful filtration to cope with the heavy load of wastes that it will generate.

Vertebrata; Actinopterygii; Perciformes; Serranidae
Coral Hind, Miniata Grouper   *Cephalopholis miniata*
41 cm (16 in.)   Indo-Pacific

■ **Aquascaping** Needs rocky hiding places or caves.
■ **Feeding** Carnivorous; accepts all meaty foods.
■ **Compatibility** Safe with corals. Grows large and is likely to eat any and all smaller tankmates. Aggressive toward its own species.

A gorgeous fish that is fairly peaceful, often lying in wait for its next meal. Will need a large aquarium of at least 600 L (150 gal.), equipped with powerful filtration.

Vertebrata; Actinopterygii; Perciformes; Serranidae
Blue Hamlet   *Hypoplectrus gemma*
14 cm (5.5 in.)   Caribbean

■ **Aquascaping** Needs rocky caves and good hiding places.
■ **Feeding** Carnivorous; prefers live crustaceans, but accepts many substitute foods.
■ **Compatibility** Reef safe, but will eat crustaceans and small fishes. In smaller systems, keep singly to avoid aggression.

Brilliant blue and well-suited to a tankful of corals, this is a rather shy fish that needs plenty of hiding places to avoid being stressed.

Vertebrata; Actinopterygii; Perciformes; Serranidae

Butter Hamlet   *Hypoplectrus unicolor*

14 cm (5.5 in.)   Caribbean

■ **Aquascaping** Needs rocky caves and good hiding places.

■ **Feeding** Carnivorous; prefers live crustaceans, but accepts many substitute foods.

■ **Compatibility** Reef safe, but will eat crustaceans and small fishes. In smaller systems, keep singly to avoid aggression.

Related to the dwarf seabasses, this is an attractive but rather shy fish that needs plenty of hiding places to avoid being stressed.

Vertebrata; Actinopterygii; Perciformes; Serranidae

Harlequin Bass   *Serranus tigrinus*

10 cm (3.9 in.)   Caribbean

■ **Aquascaping** Needs rocky caves and good hiding places.

■ **Feeding** Carnivorous; prefers live crustaceans, but accepts many substitute foods.

■ **Compatibility** Reef safe, but will eat crustaceans and small fishes and may harass other tankmates. Keep singly or in mated pairs to avoid fierce aggression.

This is a feisty little bass that may terrorize other tankmates, especially in a smaller aquarium. Will not harm corals.

Vertebrata; Actinopterygii; Perciformes; Serranidae

Swissguard Basslet   *Liopropoma rubre*

8.5 cm (3.3 in.)   Caribbean

■ **Aquascaping** Needs plenty of caves and crevices for hiding.

■ **Water Quality** Sensitive to poor or fluctuating water quality.

■ **Feeding** Carnivorous; accepts many meaty foods.

■ **Compatibility** Reef safe, but may eat small fishes or ornamental crustaceans.

This is a prized species for reef tanks—small, colorful, and an excellent tankmate for corals. It cannot be kept with smaller fishes or crustaceans.

Vertebrata; Actinopterygii; Perciformes; Serranidae

Lyretail Anthias   *Pseudanthias squamipinnis*

12 cm (4.7 in.)   Indo-Pacific

■ **Compatibility** Reef safe. Does best in groups consisting of one male and several females.

■ **Feeding** Difficult to feed adequately. Needs zooplankton or substitutes: fresh or frozen mysid and adult brine shrimp. At minimum, must be fed (with automatic feeder) at least several times per day. A varied diet, preferably vitamin enriched, is necessary for good health.

Perhaps the most-photographed fish in the sea. Spectacular in large schools, but rather difficult to keep because of its feeding demands.

Vertebrata; Actinopterygii; Perciformes; Serranidae
Purple Anthias *Pseudanthias tuka*
12 cm (4.7 in.) Indo-west-Pacific

■ **Compatibility** Reef safe. Does best in large groups consisting of one male and several females.
■ **Feeding** Difficult to feed adequately. Needs zooplankton or substitutes: fresh or frozen mysid and adult brine shrimp. At minimum, must be fed (with automatic feeder) at least several times per day. A varied diet, preferably vitamin enriched, is necessary for good health.

A typical anthias: beautiful, difficult to transport, acclimate, feed, and keep. Suitable for experienced aquarists only.

Vertebrata; Actinopterygii; Perciformes; Grammistidae
Sixline Soapfish *Grammistes sexlineatus*
27 cm (10.5 in.) Indo-Pacific

■ **Aquascaping** Needs caves or other good hiding places.
■ **Feeding** Carnivorous; accepts most meaty foods.
■ **Compatibility** Reef safe and not aggressive, but will eat any fish or crustacean small enough to be swallowed whole. When stressed or injured, the soapfishes exude a toxic slime that can severely harm or kill their tankmates.

Juveniles have a dramatic appearance, but become less spectacular with age. Potential toxicity is real a liability a in heavily stocked tank.

Vertebrata; Actinopterygii; Perciformes; Pseudochromidae
Oblique-lined Dottyback *Cypho purpurascens*
7.5 cm (2.9 in.) Western Pacific

■ **Aquascaping** Needs numerous hiding places: caves and crevices.
■ **Feeding** Prefers crustaceans and other small, free-living invertebrates, but accepts many substitute foods.
■ **Compatibility** Very aggressive, particularly toward similar looking fishes. Keep singly or in mated pairs.

Like many dottybacks, colorful but very territorial. Excellent tankmate with corals, but a potential terror for other small fishes. Larger fishes are generally ignored.

Vertebrata; Actinopterygii; Perciformes; Pseudochromidae
Arabian
Bluelined Dottyback *Pseudochromis aldabraensis*
8.5 cm (3.3 in.) Arabian Gulf to Sri Lanka

■ **Aquascaping** Needs numerous hiding places: caves and crevices.
■ **Feeding** Prefers crustaceans and other small, free-living invertebrates, but accepts many substitute foods.
■ **Compatibility** Reef safe, but very aggressive, particularly toward similar looking fishes. Keep singly or in mated pairs.

A beauty with a predisposition to attack. Select tankmates carefully; larger fishes are generally ignored. Often confused with *P. dutoiti*.

Vertebrata; Actinopterygii; Perciformes; Pseudochromidae
Royal Dottyback *Pseudochromis paccagnellae*
7 cm (2.7 in.) Indo-Australian Archipelago

■ **Aquascaping** Needs numerous hiding places: caves and crevices.
■ **Feeding** Carnivorous; accepts most meaty foods.
■ **Compatibility** Reef safe, but extremely aggressive. Should not be kept with docile and shy species, crustaceans, or small free-living invertebrates. Keep singly (only one member of the species).

Excellent in combination with corals, but a territorial fish that can disrupt the social balance of an aquarium with its never-ending aggressiveness. Even much larger fishes are often attacked.

Vertebrata; Actinopterygii; Perciformes; Pseudochromidae
Magenta Dottyback *Pseudochromis porphyreus*
6.5 cm (2.5 in.) Western Pacific

■ **Aquascaping** Needs numerous hiding places: caves and crevices.
■ **Feeding** Carnivorous; accepts most meaty foods.
■ **Compatibility** Reef safe, but fairly aggressive, particularly toward similar-looking fishes. Keep singly, except in large systems, where pairs or groups may be introduced.

A vivid purple fish that fits in nicely with corals. Somewhat less aggressive than most of its relatives, but choose its tankmates carefully.

Vertebrata; Actinopterygii; Perciformes; Grammatidae
Royal Gramma *Gramma loreto*
8 cm (3.1 in.) Caribbean

■ **Aquascaping** Needs numerous hiding places: caves and crevices.
■ **Feeding** Carnivorous; prefers large zooplankton, but accepts many substitute meaty foods.
■ **Compatibility** Reef safe. May show aggression toward specimens of the same species or other similar-looking fishes, particularly if kept in a small tank. May be kept in groups in large reef systems.

A wonderful fish for reef tanks, long a favorite of aquarists, and one that can be combined with most other commonly kept animals.

Vertebrata; Actinopterygii; Perciformes; Grammatidae
Brazilian Gramma *Gramma brasiliensis*
12 cm (4.7 in.) Brazil

■ **Aquascaping** Needs numerous hiding places: caves and crevices.
■ **Feeding** Carnivorous; prefers large zooplankton, but accepts many substitute meaty foods.
■ **Compatibility** Reef safe. May show aggression toward specimens of the same species or other similar-looking fishes, particularly in small tanks. Will often eat shrimps and harass smaller, shy fishes.

Larger and more aggressive than the similar Royal Gramma, which has a smaller mouth and yellow lines on the head.

Vertebrata; Actinopterygii; Perciformes; Grammatidae
Blackcap Basslet   *Gramma melacara*
10 cm (3.9 in.)   Caribbean

■ **Aquascaping** Needs numerous hiding places: caves and crevices.
■ **Feeding** Carnivorous; accepts most meaty foods.
■ **Compatibility** Reef safe, but fairly aggressive, particularly toward similar looking fishes. Should not be kept with docile and shy species, crustaceans, or other small free-living invertebrates.

Highly sought-after fish for reef tanks, and one that can be combined with most other commonly kept animals. May be shy and secretive, particularly for the first few weeks in a new aquarium.

Vertebrata; Actinopterygii; Perciformes; Plesiopidae
Blue Assessor   *Assessor macneilli*
6 cm (2.3 in.)   Great Barrier Reef, New Caledonia

■ **Aquascaping** Needs a big cave or other overhanging cliff formation to simulate its natural habitat. Commonly swims upside down with its belly against the cave roof.
■ **Compatibility** Reef safe. Keep in schools of several specimens.
■ **Feeding** Picks zooplankton out of the water column in the wild, but will accept many substitute foods.

In beauty, size, and disposition, a near-perfect fish for a reef aquarium, especially one with a rocky cave. Rarely imported.

Vertebrata; Actinopterygii; Perciformes; Plesiopidae
Yellow Assessor   *Assessor flavissimus*
5.5 cm (2.1 in.)   Northern Great Barrier Reef

■ **Aquascaping** Needs a big cave or other overhanging cliff formation to simulate its natural habitat. Commonly swims upside down with its belly against the cave roof.
■ **Compatibility** Reef safe. Keep in schools of several specimens.
■ **Feeding** Picks zooplankton out of the water column in the wild, but will accept many substitute foods.

Although rarely available, this is a brightly colored, ideal fish for a reef aquarium, especially one with a rocky cave.

Vertebrata; Actinopterygii; Perciformes; Plesiopidae
Comet   *Calloplesiops altivelis*
20 cm (7.8 in.)   Indo-Pacific

■ **Aquascaping** Shy; needs a cave or rocky crevice for hiding.
■ **Feeding** Carnivorous; accepts most meaty foods.
■ **Compatibility** Reef safe. Will eat small crustaceans and very small fishes; otherwise peaceful.

Sometimes called the "Marine Betta" for its flowing fins, this is an excellent fish for reef a tank, especially with a cave. Quite secretive, but will gradually become less shy once established.

Vertebrata; Actinopterygii; Perciformes; Apogonidae
Flamefish *Apogon maculatus*
11 cm (4.3 in.) Caribbean

■ **Aquascaping** Does best with caves and crevices for hiding.
■ **Feeding** Carnivorous; accepts many substitute foods. Needs a varied and vitamin-enriched diet to keep its brilliant red color.
■ **Compatibility** Reef safe, but likely to eat shrimps and small crustaceans. Often aggressive toward other members of its genus and similar-looking species. Keep in groups in a large aquarium.

A common but interesting Caribbean cardinalfish for a reef tank, especially one with a shadowy cave. Nocturnal.

Vertebrata; Actinopterygii; Perciformes; Apogonidae
Barred Cardinalfish *Apogon binotatus*
13 cm (5.1 in.) Caribbean

■ **Aquascaping** Does best with caves and crevices for hiding.
■ **Feeding** Carnivorous; accepts many substitute foods. Needs a varied diet enriched with color enhancers (carotenoids) and vitamins to keep its red color.
■ **Compatibility** Reef safe, but likely to eat ornamental shrimps. May be successfully kept in groups in a large aquarium.

An interesting red cardinalfish that will hover in the shadows of a cave or under a ledge while the tank is brightly lit. Nocturnal.

Vertebrata; Actinopterygii; Perciformes; Apogonidae
Redstriped Cardinalfish *Apogon margaritophorus*
8 cm (3.1 in.) Indo-Australian Archipelago

■ **Aquascaping** Does best with caves and crevices for hiding.
■ **Feeding** Carnivorous; accepts many substitute foods. Needs a varied diet enriched with color enhancers (carotenoids) and vitamins to keep its bright colors.
■ **Compatibility** Reef safe, but likely to eat shrimps and other small crustaceans. Best kept in groups of several specimens.

One of many cardinalfish species that populate coral reefs, this is a small, fairly peaceful fish. Hardy and easy to keep.

Vertebrata; Actinopterygii; Perciformes; Apogonidae
Pajama Cardinalfish *Sphaeramia nematoptera*
8 cm (3.1 in.) Indo-Pacific; Malaysia to Micronesia

■ **Feeding** Carnivorous; accepts many substitute foods.
■ **Compatibility** Reef safe, but likely to eat shrimps and polychaete worms. Best kept in groups of several specimens or in pairs.

A marine aquarium favorite—exotic color scheme, hardy, and peaceful. Reported to spawn regularly in some reef systems. This mouthbrooder often spawns in captivity.

Vertebrata; Actinopterygii; Perciformes; Apogonidae
Orbiculate Cardinalfish   *Sphaeramia orbicularis*
12 cm (4.7 in.)   Indo-Pacific; East Africa to Micronesia

■ **Feeding** Carnivorous; accepts many substitute foods.
■ **Compatibility** Reef safe, but likely to eat shrimps and polychaete worms. Best kept in groups of several specimens or in pairs.

This is a rather plain cardinalfish, but hardy and peaceful. Looks its best when kept in large schools.

Vertebrata; Actinopterygii; Perciformes; Apogonidae
Banggai Cardinalfish   *Pterapogon kauderni*
7.5 cm (2.9 in.)   Indonesia

■ **Compatibility** Reef safe. Excellent schooling fish for large aquariums. In smaller tanks, keep singly or in mated pairs, as aggression between species members is likely to become a problem.
■ **Feeding** Carnivorous; accepts many substitute foods.
■ **Conservation** A possible candidate for overexploitation, as it is in high demand and collected only in a very small geographical area.

A beautiful species for reef aquariums, and one that can easily be bred in the home aquarium. Ask for captive-bred specimens.

Vertebrata; Actinopterygii; Perciformes; Malacanthidae
Golden Tilefish   *Hoplolatilus luteus*
14 cm (5.5 in.)   Indonesia

■ **Aquascaping** Should have a large, open area of sandy substrate and a covered aquarium to prevent it from jumping out.
■ **Feeding** Needs frequent feedings of zooplankton-type meaty foods. Can be difficult to convert to nonliving foods.
■ **Compatibility** Reef safe, but likely to eat small crustaceans. May chase and harass smaller plankton-feeding fishes.

A streamlined fish that swims fast and jumps with little provocation, this genus is somewhat delicate in captivity. For experienced aquarists.

Vertebrata; Actinopterygii; Perciformes; Malacanthidae
Purple Tilefish   *Hoplolatilus purpureus*
15 cm (5.9 in.)   Indo-west-Pacific

■ **Aquascaping** Should have a large, open area of sandy substrate and a covered aquarium to prevent it from jumping out.
■ **Feeding** Needs frequent feedings of zooplankton-type meaty foods. Can be difficult to convert to nonliving foods.
■ **Compatibility** Reef safe, but likely to eat small crustaceans. May chase and harass smaller plankton-feeding fishes.

A shy fish with great swimming and jumping talents, it is somewhat delicate in captivity. For experienced aquarists only.

Vertebrata; Actinopterygii; Perciformes; Lutjanidae
Emperor Snapper *Lutjanus sebae*
80 cm (31 in.) Indo-Pacific

■ **Aquascaping** Needs plenty of open swimming space as well as some secluded caves or hiding places.
■ **Feeding** Carnivorous; readily accepts most meaty foods.
■ **Compatibility** Not safe with most smaller reef fishes and crustaceans. Its large size will strain water quality in its system.

This is a big, spectacular show fish for a very large (2,000 L [520 gal.] or larger) fish-only reef tank. Juveniles (photo) can be kept in smaller quarters in groups, but adults will fight except in huge systems.

Vertebrata; Actinopterygii; Perciformes; Lutjanidae
Black Snapper *Macolor niger*
65 cm (25 in.) Indo-Pacific

■ **Aquascaping** Needs plenty of open swimming space as well as some secluded caves or hiding places.
■ **Feeding** Carnivorous; readily accepts most meaty foods.
■ **Compatibility** Not safe with most smaller reef fishes and crustaceans. Its large size will strain water quality in its system.

Cute and colorful as a juvenile (photo), but a fish that turns quite dull as it gets older. Best avoided unless you have particular interests in the species.

Vertebrata; Actinopterygii; Perciformes; Haemulidae
Harlequin Sweetlips *Plectorhinchus chaetodonoides*
70 cm (27 in.) Widespread in the Indo-Pacific

■ **Aquascaping** Needs plenty of open swimming space.
■ **Feeding** Carnivorous; accepts fresh or frozen crustaceans and fishes. Live foods may be needed to initiate feeding in juveniles.
■ **Compatibility** Too large and predatory for most reef tanks, although it will ignore corals. Its adult size will strain water quality.

A showstopper with an intriguing, paddlelike swimming motion as a juvenile (photo). Adults are large and not so charming. Difficult to acclimate and feed. Not for beginners.

Vertebrata; Actinopterygii; Perciformes; Haemulidae
Twostriped Sweetlips *Plectorhinchus albovittatus*
30 cm (11.7 in.) Widespread in the Indo-Pacific

■ **Aquascaping** Needs plenty of open swimming space.
■ **Feeding** Carnivorous; accepts fresh or frozen meaty foods, especially crustaceans and fish meat.
■ **Compatibility** Safe with corals, but grows rather large and digs through the substrate in search of worms, crustaceans, mollusks, and echinoderms. May also eat small fishes.

Bright and interesting as a juvenile (photo), but much less spectacular with advancing age.

Vertebrata; Actinopterygii; Perciformes; Haemulidae
Porkfish   *Anisotremus virginicus*
40 cm (15.6 in.)   Western Atlantic

■ **Aquascaping** Needs plenty of open swimming space.
■ **Feeding** Meaty foods, e.g. crustaceans and fish meat; fresh or frozen. Accepts many substitute foods.
■ **Compatibility** Will eat many kinds of worms, crustaceans, mollusks, and echinoderms. May also eat small fishes.

A handsome member of the grunt family, which is a most important group of food fishes from the reef. This is an interesting species for large fish tanks only. Makes distinctive underwater grunting sounds.

Vertebrata; Actinopterygii; Perciformes; Nemipteridae
Twoline Spinecheek   *Scolopsis bilineatus*
23 cm (9 in.)   Indo-west-Pacific

■ **Aquascaping** Requires an area of deep (minimum 5 cm [2 in.]) sandy substrate for digging.
■ **Feeding** Meaty foods, e.g. crustaceans and fish meat; fresh or frozen. Accepts many substitute foods.
■ **Compatibility** Safe with corals, but will eat worms, crustaceans, mollusks, and echinoderms. Actively forages in the substrate.

A reasonably hardy and pretty species, but grows rather large and is a threat to a number of invertebrates.

Vertebrata; Actinopterygii; Perciformes; Sciaenidae
Jackknife Fish   *Equetus lanceolatus*
25 cm (9.8 in.)   Caribbean

■ **Aquascaping** Shy fish that needs many good, shady hiding places. A thick sand bed and live rock will provide live foods.
■ **Feeding** Feeds on crustaceans and polychaete worms in the wild. Expect to use live foods only, at least initially.
■ **Compatibility** Safe with corals, but will eat various invertebrates and small fishes. Grows too large for most reef systems.

Very unusual, beautiful fish, but a delicate and hard-to-keep species. Needs peaceful surroundings.

Vertebrata; Actinopterygii; Perciformes; Sciaenidae
Highhat   *Pareques acuminatus*
23 cm (9 in.)   Caribbean

■ **Aquascaping** Shy fish that needs many good, shady hiding places. A thick sand bed and live rock provide live, natural foods.
■ **Feeding** Feeds on crustaceans and polychaete worms in the wild. Expect to use live foods only, at least initially.
■ **Compatibility** Safe with corals, but will eat various invertebrates and small fishes. Grows too large for most reef systems

An interesting Caribbean species, and not quite as delicate and demanding as the related Jackknife Fish. Needs peaceful surroundings.

Vertebrata; Actinopterygii; Perciformes; Mullidae
Bicolor Goatfish *Parupeneus barberinoides*
25 cm (9.8 in.) Western Pacific

■ **Aquascaping** Needs plenty of thick, soft substrate for digging.
■ **Feeding** Feeds on benthic invertebrates, such as worms and crustaceans. Substitute meaty foods are often accepted, but appropriate nutrition in captivity is often a problem.
■ **Compatibility** Safe with corals. Will eat bottom-dwelling invertebrates, worms, and crustaceans, and occasionally smaller fishes.

An appealing fish that grovels in the sand, but surprisingly difficult to feed and keep. For experienced aquarists only.

Vertebrata; Actinopterygii; Perciformes; Mullidae
Yellowsaddle Goatfish *Parupeneus cyclostomus*
50 cm (19.5 in.) Indo-Pacific, Red Sea

■ **Aquascaping** Needs ample swimming space. (1,000 L [260 gal.])
■ **Feeding** Carnivorous; adapts to a diet of meaty aquarium foods more readily than most of its goatfish relatives.
■ **Compatibility** Will eat smaller fishes. Free living invertebrates, e.g., shrimps are also not safe.

Unlike most goatfishes, this species is not a substrate sifter and seems to feed on small fishes in the wild. Easier to keep than other goatfishes, but grows far too large for most tanks.

Vertebrata; Actinopterygii; Perciformes; Mullidae
Blackstriped Goatfish *Upeneus tragula*
28 cm (10.9 in.) Indo-Pacific

■ **Aquascaping** Needs plenty of thick, soft substrate for digging.
■ **Feeding** Feeds on benthic invertebrates, such as worms and crustaceans. Substitute meaty foods are often accepted, but appropriate nutrition in captivity is often a problem.
■ **Compatibility** Safe with corals. Will eat bottom-dwelling invertebrates, worms, and crustaceans, and occasionally smaller fishes.

An industrious forager and interesting to watch, but hard to keep. For experienced aquarists with large systems.

Vertebrata; Actinopterygii; Perciformes; Ephippidae
Orbiculate Batfish *Platax orbicularis*
57 cm (22 in.) Indo-Pacific

■ **Aquascaping** Adults will need plenty of swimming space.
■ **Feeding** Carnivorous; accepts various meaty foods.
■ **Compatibility** Not reef safe. May feed on or damage sponges, corals, other invertebrates, and small fishes.

Fairly peaceful, and reasonably hardy in comparison to other batfishes. Grows very fast and demands a very large aquarium, minimum 1,000 liters (260 gal.).

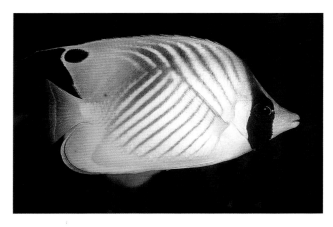

Vertebrata; Actinopterygii; Perciformes; Chaetodontidae
Threadfin Butterflyfish   *Chaetodon auriga*
23 cm (9 in.)   Indo-Pacific, Red Sea

■ **Aquascaping** Well-established live rock provides natural surroundings and a variety of food organisms for butterflyfishes.
■ **Feeding** Carnivorous; accepts most meaty foods.
■ **Compatibility** Not reef safe. Will eat and damage a large number of sessile invertebrates, including corals.

Among the hardiest butterflyfishes, but generally not suitable for invertebrate tanks. (A Red Sea subspecies lacks the black spot on its
dorsal fin.) Good beginner's butterfly.

Vertebrata; Actinopterygii; Perciformes; Chaetodontidae
Collare Butterflyfish   *Chaetodon collare*
16 cm (6.2 in.)   Indo-Pacific

■ **Aquascaping** Well-established live rock provides natural surroundings and a variety of food organisms for butterflyfishes.
■ **Feeding** Feeds on stony coral polyps and small invertebrates in
the wild. May accept fresh or frozen crustaceans (shrimps) and fish
meat. Often difficult to feed.
■ **Compatibility** Not reef safe. Will eat stony coral polyps, although
soft corals appear to be safe under most circumstances.

A classic butterflyfish—exceptionally handsome but hard to feed.

Vertebrata; Actinopterygii; Perciformes; Chaetodontidae
Foureye Butterflyfish   *Chaetodon capistratus*
15 cm (5.9 in.)   Caribbean, Western Tropical Atlantic

■ **Aquascaping** Well-established live rock provides natural surroundings and a variety of food organisms for butterflyfishes.
■ **Feeding** In nature, it feeds on zoanthids, gorgonians, tunicates,
worms, and other invertebrates. Usually refuses substitute foods.
■ **Compatibility** Not reef safe.

A common and familiar Caribbean species that survives poorly in the
aquarium. Only for very experienced aquarists who are able to put
effort into experimental husbandry techniques.

Vertebrata; Actinopterygii; Perciformes; Chaetodontidae
Blackback Butterflyfish   *Chaetodon melannotus*
15 cm (5.9 in.)   Indo-west-Pacific

■ **Aquascaping** Well-established live rock provides natural surroundings and a variety of food organisms for butterflyfishes.
■ **Feeding** Feeds on soft coral polyps in the wild, but substitute
meaty foods are normally accepted. Feed several times daily.
■ **Compatibility** Not reef safe. Will eat and damage soft and stony
corals. Aggressive toward its own species.

Among the hardiest of butterflyfishes, but generally not suitable for
invertebrate tanks.

Vertebrata; Actinopterygii; Perciformes; Chaetodontidae
Klein's Butterflyfish   *Chaetodon kleinii*
13 cm (5.1 in.)   Indo-Pacific

■ **Aquascaping** Well-established live rock provides natural surroundings and a variety of food organisms for butterflyfishes.
■ **Feeding** Appears to have different food preferences, depending
on its geographic origin. Meaty foods are readily accepted.
■ **Compatibility** Some specimens are reef safe. Most will not actively eat corals, but some may pick at soft corals.

Among the more hardy of the butterflyfishes, sometimes introduced to
prey on *Aiptasia* spp. anemones. Needs vigilance in a reef tank.

Vertebrata; Actinopterygii; Perciformes; Chaetodontidae
Orangeface Butterflyfish   *Chaetodon larvatus*
12 cm (4.7 in.)   Red Sea

■ **Feeding** This fish is an obligate corallivore—it feeds primarily on
live coral polyps. Nearly impossible to adapt to substitute foods.
■ **Compatibility** Not reef safe. Will eat and damage corals.
■ **Conservation** Not suitable for aquarium keeping with currently
known husbandry methods. Should not be collected or purchased.

One of the beautiful butterflyfishes that aquarists need to avoid. Very
difficult to keep.

Vertebrata; Actinopterygii; Perciformes; Chaetodontidae
Eightbanded Butterflyfish   *Chaetodon octofasciatus*
12 cm (4.7 in.)   Indo-west-Pacific

■ **Feeding** This fish is an obligate corallivore—it feeds primarily on
live coral polyps. Nearly impossible to adapt to substitute foods.
■ **Compatibility** Not reef safe. Will eat and damage corals.
■ **Conservation** Not suitable for aquarium keeping with currently
known husbandry methods. Should not be collected or purchased.

One of the beautiful butterflyfishes that aquarists need to avoid. Very
difficult to keep.

Vertebrata; Actinopterygii; Perciformes; Chaetodontidae
Indian Ocean Redfin Butterflyfish   *Chaetodon trifasciatus*
15 cm (5.9 in.)   Red Sea and Indian Ocean

■ **Feeding** This fish is an obligate corallivore—it feeds primarily on
live coral polyps. Near impossible to adapt to substitute foods.
■ **Compatibility** Not reef safe. Will eat and damage corals.
■ **Conservation** Not suitable for aquarium keeping with currently
known husbandry methods. Should not be collected or purchased.

Like its sibling, the Pacific Redfin Butterflyfish (*Chaetodon lunulatus*),
this is a very difficult species to keep.

Vertebrata; Actinopterygii; Perciformes; Chaetodontidae
Yellowtail Butterflyfish   *Chaetodon xanthurus*
14 cm (5.5 in.)   Western Pacific

■ **Aquascaping** Well-established live rock provides natural sur-roundings and a variety of food organisms for butterflyfishes.
■ **Feeding** In the wild, eats crustaceans, worms, and other free liv-ing invertebrates. Many substitute meaty foods are readily accepted.
■ **Compatibility** Not perfectly reef safe. Most specimens will not ac-tively eat corals, but are likely to pick at them, causing damage.

One of the reasonably hardy butterflyfishes, attractive and a possible choice for keeping with soft corals of the more noxious species.

Vertebrata; Actinopterygii; Perciformes; Chaetodontidae
Copperband Butterflyfish   *Chelmon rostratus*
20 cm (7.8 in.)   Indo-west-Pacific

■ **Aquascaping** Well-established live rock needed.
■ **Feeding** In nature, eats crustaceans and other benthic inverte-brates. May accept substitute foods, but can be difficult to feed.
■ **Compatibility** Generally reef safe, but may pick at corals, colo-nial anemones, and worms.

One of the unpredictable butterflyfishes, very handsome and hardy in some instances, but often prone to starving for lack of live food. Sometimes introduced as a predator on small nuisance anemones.

Vertebrata; Actinopterygii; Perciformes; Chaetodontidae
Big Longnose Butterflyfish   *Forcipiger longirostris*
22 cm (8.9 in.)   Indo-Pacific

■ **Aquascaping** Well-established live rock provides natural sur-roundings and a variety of food organisms for butterflyfishes.
■ **Feeding** In the wild, feeds on crustaceans, worms, and other benthic invertebrates. Substitute foods may be accepted.
■ **Compatibility** Generally reef safe. Will occasionally pick at corals.

A somewhat delicate species, best for experienced aquarists. Similar to *F. flavissimus,* but with a longer snout, black edged scales on the belly, and a totally black eye.

Vertebrata; Actinopterygii; Perciformes; Chaetodontidae
Yellow Longnose Butterflyfish   *Forcipiger flavissimus*
22 cm (8.9 in.)   Indo-Pacific

■ **Aquascaping** Well-established live rock provides natural sur-roundings and a variety of food organisms for butterflyfishes.
■ **Feeding** The mouth of this species is adapted for feeding on corals and other invertebrates. Accepts many substitute foods.
■ **Compatibility** Not reef safe. Likely to damage corals.

A showy species and one of the more hardy butterflyfishes. Not a good tankmate with most corals, except possibly the noxious soft coral species (*Sinularia, Litophyton*). Compare to *F. longirostris* (above).

Vertebrata; Actinopterygii; Perciformes; Chaetodontidae
Longfin Bannerfish   *Heniochus acuminatus*
20 cm (7.8 in.)   Indo-west-Pacific

■ **Aquascaping** Well-established live rock provides natural surroundings and a variety of food organisms for butterflyfishes.
■ **Feeding** In nature, feeds on zooplankton and benthic invertebrates. Accepts many types of substitute meaty foods.
■ **Compatibility** Not reef safe. Will pick at various sessile invertebrates.

Among the more hardy butterflyfishes, and one that can be kept in schools. The similar Schooling Bannerfish (*H. diphreutes*) is reef safe.

Vertebrata; Actinopterygii; Perciformes; Pomacanthidae
Flagfin Angelfish   *Apolemichthys trimaculatus*
25 cm (9.8 in.)   Indo-west-Pacific

■ **Aquascaping** Live rock provides natural surroundings and a source of live food organisms for all angelfishes.
■ **Feeding** Feeds primarily on sponges and tunicates. Often difficult, but not impossible, to adapt to substitute foods.
■ **Compatibility** Not reef safe. Will usually eat or nip at corals and other sessile invertebrates.

A rather delicate and challenging species. Best reserved for experienced aquarists.

Vertebrata; Actinopterygii; Perciformes; Pomacanthidae
Goldenflake Angelfish   *Apolemichthys xanthopunctatus*
25 cm (9.8 in.)   Central Pacific

■ **Aquascaping** Live rock will provide this fish with natural surroundings and a source of live food organisms.
■ **Feeding** A specialized sponge feeder that is difficult to adapt to substitute foods.
■ **Compatibility** Not reef safe. Will usually eat or nip at corals and other sessile invertebrates.

Sadly, a difficult species to keep. Suitable for advanced aquarists able to invest time and effort in experimental husbandry techniques.

Vertebrata; Actinopterygii; Perciformes; Pomacanthidae
Cherub Angelfish   *Centropyge argi*
8 cm (3.1 in.)   Tropical Western Atlantic

■ **Aquascaping** Live rock will provide this fish with natural surroundings and a source of live food organisms.
■ **Feeding** Grazes on algae and tiny benthic invertebrates. Accepts a variety of substitute meaty and algae-based foods in the aquarium.
■ **Compatibility** Generally reef safe. May occasionally nip at some coral species. Can be very aggressive toward its own species.

One of the best aquarium species among the dwarf angelfishes of the genus *Centropyge*. Will form pairs and spawn in captivity.

Vertebrata; Actinopterygii; Perciformes; Pomacanthidae
Bicolor Angelfish   *Centropyge bicolor*
15 cm (5.9 in.)   Indo-west-Pacific

- ■ **Aquascaping** Live rock will provide this fish with natural surroundings and a source of live food organisms.
- ■ **Feeding** Grazes on algae and tiny benthic invertebrates. Accepts a variety of substitute meaty and algae-based foods.
- ■ **Compatibility** Not reef safe. Will usually eat or nip at corals and other sessile invertebrates, including *Tridacna* spp. clams.

Hardy and beautiful species if properly collected, but it can be a major threat to invertebrates.

Vertebrata; Actinopterygii; Perciformes; Pomacanthidae
Coral Beauty   *Centropyge bispinosus*
10 cm (3.9 in.)   Widely distributed in the Indo-Pacific

- ■ **Aquascaping** Live rock provides natural surroundings and a source of live food organisms.
- ■ **Feeding** Grazes on algae and tiny benthic invertebrates. Accepts a variety of substitute meaty and algae-based foods.
- ■ **Compatibility** Generally reef safe. May nip at sessile invertebrates, but is often kept with corals without any noticeable ill effects.

A fine little angelfish that lives up to its name and is one of the best aquarium species in the genus. Usually safe with corals.

Vertebrata; Actinopterygii; Perciformes; Pomacanthidae
Flame Angelfish   *Centropyge loriculus*
12 cm (4.7 in.)   Pacific

- ■ **Aquascaping** Live rock provides natural surroundings and a source of live food organisms.
- ■ **Feeding** Grazes on algae and tiny benthic invertebrates. Accepts a variety of substitute meaty and algae-based foods.
- ■ **Compatibility** Not always reef safe. Can turn destructive in some reef tanks. Often aggressive toward its own and related species.

A beautiful and fairly hardy species, but it can be a major threat to invertebrates and a bully with more delicate fishes.

Vertebrata; Actinopterygii; Perciformes; Pomacanthidae
Multibarred Angelfish   *Paracentropyge multifasciatus*
10 cm (3.9 in.)   Indo-west-Pacific
- ■ **Aquascaping** This shy species requires caves and crevices for refuge, as well as live rock as a source of live food organisms.
- ■ **Feeding** Natural diet is largely unknown; possibly sponges, algae and tiny benthic invertebrates. Very difficult to feed in the aquarium. Does not readily accept substitute foods.
- ■ **Compatibility** Not fully reef safe, but will ignore most soft corals.

A very pretty fish, but shy, hard to feed, and with poor chances of survival. For experienced aquarists with appropriate systems or new experimental husbandry techniques.

Vertebrata; Actinopterygii; Perciformes; Pomacanthidae
Scribbled Angelfish   *Chaetodontoplus duboulayi*
25 cm (9.8 in.)   NE Australia, Papua New Guinea

◼ **Aquascaping** Live rock provides natural surroundings and a source of live food organisms.
◼ **Feeding** In nature, grazes on sponges and algae. Accepts a variety of substitute foods in the aquarium.
◼ **Compatibility** Not completely reef safe. May eat or nip at corals and other sessile invertebrates.

Fairly hardy species that adapts well to aquarium life. Many aquarists report success with this species in large, coral-filled reef tanks.

Vertebrata; Actinopterygii; Perciformes; Pomacanthidae
Vermiculated Angelfish   *Chaetodontoplus mesoleucus*
17 cm (6.6 in.)   Western Pacific

◼ **Aquascaping** Needs well-established live rock for hiding places and to provide a source of algae and live food organisms.
◼ **Feeding** In nature, eats sponges, other sessile invertebrates, and algae. Usually—but not always—accepts substitute foods.
◼ **Compatibility** Not reef safe. Likely to pick at many coral species, like zoanthids, as well as clams and other sessile invertebrates.

A hardy species for some aquarists, a challenge for others. Many individuals adapt well to aquarium life, others hide and refuse to eat.

Vertebrata; Actinopterygii; Perciformes; Pomacanthidae
Blackspot Angelfish   *Genicanthus melanospilos*
20 cm (7.8 in.)   Indo-Pacific

◼ **Aquascaping** Active fish that needs plenty of swimming space.
◼ **Feeding** Eats large zooplankton in the wild. Often difficult to adapt to substitute foods. Should be fed several times per day.
◼ **Compatibility** Reef safe. Can be very aggressive toward its own species and related species. Keep singly, or, in large systems, in male-female pairs or groups with only one male. (*Female at right.*)

An excellent, unusual angelfish for reef aquariums, but not among the easiest angelfishes to keep. For experienced aquarists.

Vertebrata; Actinopterygii; Perciformes; Pomacanthidae
Watanabe's Angelfish   *Genicanthus watanabei*
18 cm (7 in.)   Western Pacific

◼ **Aquascaping** Active fish that needs plenty of swimming space.
◼ **Feeding** Eats large zooplankton in the wild. Often difficult to adapt to substitute foods. Should be fed several times per day.
◼ **Compatibility** Reef safe. Can be very aggressive toward its own species and related species. Keep singly, or, in large systems, in male-female pairs or groups with only one male. (*Male at right.*)

Like others in this genus, very attractive and absolutely reef safe, but needs the feeding and care of an experienced aquarist.

Vertebrata; Actinopterygii; Perciformes; Pomacanthidae
Regal Angelfish   *Pygoplites diacanthus*
25 cm (9.8 in.)   Indo-Pacific

■ **Aquascaping** Must have a tank with well-established live rock, providing natural hiding places and a source of live food organisms.
■ **Feeding** Typically feeds on sponges, tunicates, and other sessile invertebrates. Some individuals refuse to accept aquarium foods.
■ **Compatibility** Not fully reef safe. May pick at corals, clams, and other sessile invertebrates. Still some aquarists report success with this species in large coral tanks. (*Australian morph at left.*)

A prized species, but demanding of experienced care and feeding.

Vertebrata; Actinopterygii; Perciformes; Pomacanthidae
Queen Angelfish   *Holacanthus ciliaris*
45 cm (17.6 in.)   Caribbean to Central Atlantic

■ **Aquascaping** Live rock provides natural surroundings and a source of live food organisms.
■ **Feeding** A sponge feeder in the wild, but young specimens readily accept a variety of substitute foods in the aquarium.
■ **Compatibility** Not reef safe. Can be very aggressive toward its own species and related or similar looking fishes.

Beautiful and hardy species, but grows far too large for most home tanks. Suitable as a show fish in very large tanks.

Vertebrata; Actinopterygii; Perciformes; Pomacanthidae
Rock Beauty   *Holacanthus tricolor*
20 cm (7.8 in.)   Tropical Western Atlantic

■ **Aquascaping** Live rock provides natural surroundings and a source of live food organisms.
■ **Feeding** Eats sponges in the wild, and very difficult to switch to substitute foods in the aquarium. Offer sponge-based rations.
■ **Compatibility** Not reef safe. Will usually eat or nip at corals and other sessile invertebrates.

A Caribbean beauty, but difficult to feed. For experienced aquarists willing to put effort into experimental husbandry techniques.

Vertebrata; Actinopterygii; Perciformes; Pomacanthidae
Gray Angelfish   *Pomacanthus arcuatus*
50 cm (19.5 in.)   Tropical Western Atlantic

■ **Aquascaping** Live rock provides natural surroundings and a source of live food organisms.
■ **Feeding** In nature it feeds on sponges and other sessile invertebrates. Accepts a variety of substitute foods in the aquarium.
■ **Compatibility** Not reef safe. Will usually eat or nip at corals and other sessile invertebrates.

An elegant, hardy species, but far too large for most aquariums. Suitable as a show fish in very large tanks.

Vertebrata; Actinopterygii; Perciformes; Pomacanthidae
French Angelfish   *Pomacanthus paru*
38 cm (14.8 in.)   Caribbean to West Africa

■ **Aquascaping** Live rock provides natural surroundings and a source of live food organisms.
■ **Feeding** Mostly sponges, but also other sessile invertebrates and algae. Accepts a variety of substitute foods in the aquarium.
■ **Compatibility** Not reef safe. Will usually eat or nip at corals and other sessile invertebrates. Often aggressive toward similar fishes.

A famously hardy and beautiful species suitable for a large tank with live rock, fishes, and rugged invertebrates. (*Subadult shown at right.*)

Vertebrata; Actinopterygii; Perciformes; Pomacanthidae
Blue-ring Angelfish   *Pomacanthus annularis*
30 cm (11.7 in.)   Indo-west-Pacific

■ **Aquascaping** Live rock provides natural surroundings and a source of live food organisms.
■ **Feeding** In nature it eats sponges, tunicates, other sessile invertebrates, and algae. Readily accepts a variety of aquarium foods.
■ **Compatibility** Not reef safe. Will usually eat or nip at corals and other sessile invertebrates. Often aggressive toward similar fishes.

An exotic-looking but hardy species suitable for a large fish tank with other robust species.

Vertebrata; Actinopterygii; Perciformes; Pomacanthidae
Emperor Angelfish   *Pomacanthus imperator*
40 cm (15.6 in.)   Indo-Pacific

■ **Aquascaping** Does best in systems with establish live rock decor.
■ **Feeding** Eats sponges, various invertebrates, and algae in the wild. Needs a varied diet with enriched foods for maintenance of good health and vivid coloration.
■ **Compatibility** Not reef safe, but some aquarists report success with this species in large coral tanks.

A spectacular fish that is quite hardy and suited to large tanks with robust tankmates. May be safe with some corals.

Vertebrata; Actinopterygii; Perciformes; Pomacanthidae
Majestic Angelfish   *Pomacanthus navarchus*
25 cm (9.8 in.)   Indo-Australian Archipelago

■ **Aquascaping** Live rock provides natural surroundings and a source of live food organisms.
■ **Feeding** In nature it eats, sponges, tunicates, other sessile invertebrates, and algae. Can be difficult to feed in the aquarium.
■ **Compatibility** Not reef safe. Will usually eat or nip at corals and other sessile invertebrates. Avoid keeping with aggressive fishes.

This is a rather shy species and not among the easiest angelfishes to keep. Needs a varied diet and experienced care.

Vertebrata; Actinopterygii; Perciformes; Pomacanthidae
Koran Angelfish   *Pomacanthus semicirculatus*
40 cm (15.6 in.)   Indo-Pacific

■ **Aquascaping** Live rock is excellent decor for tanks with angelfishes, providing natural surroundings and a variety of food organisms.
■ **Feeding** In the wild, eats sponges, tunicates, other sessile invertebrates, and algae. Readily accepts a variety of aquarium foods.
■ **Compatibility** Not reef safe. Often aggressive toward other fishes.

This is a hardy, attractive species suitable for a large fish tank with other robust species. (Subadult shown at left.)

Vertebrata; Actinopterygii; Perciformes; Pomacanthidae
Blueface Angelfish   *Pomacanthus xanthometopon*
38 cm (14.8 in.)   Indo-west-Pacific

■ **Aquascaping** Live rock provides excellent natural surroundings and a variety of food organisms for all angelfishes.
■ **Feeding** In the wild, eats sponges, tunicates, other sessile invertebrates, and algae. May be slow to accept substitute foods.
■ **Compatibility** Not reef safe. Not as aggressive as other large angelfishes.

A coveted species, but not among the easiest angelfishes to keep. A fish suited to more experienced aquarists.

Vertebrata; Actinopterygii; Perciformes; Pomacentridae
Maroon Anemonefish   *Premnas biaculeatus*
13 cm (5.1 in.)   Indo-Australian Archipelago and Western Pacific

■ **Aquascaping** Best kept with the Bubble Tip Sea Anemone (page 111), but will thrive without a host anemone.
■ **Feeding** Omnivore; readily accepts a variety of meaty and algae-based foods. Color-enhancing rations help maintain bright colors.
■ **Compatibility** Reef safe. Very aggressive toward anemonefishes and similar species. Keep singly, in pairs, or in groups of one large female and several small males—introduce all simultaneously.

An excellent fish for reef tanks, but may bully shy and delicate fishes.

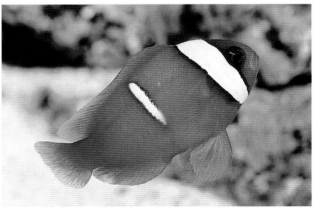

Vertebrata; Actinopterygii; Perciformes; Pomacentridae
Tomato Anemonefish   *Amphiprion frenatus*
11 cm (4.3 in.)   Indo-Australian Archipelago and Western Pacific

■ **Aquascaping** Best kept with the Bubble Tip Sea Anemone (page 111), but will thrive without a host anemone.
■ **Feeding** Omnivore; readily accepts a variety of meaty and algae-based foods. Color-enhancing rations help maintain bright colors.
■ **Compatibility** Reef safe. Very aggressive toward anemonefishes and similar species. Keep singly, in pairs, or in groups of one large female and several small males—introduce all simultaneously.

A bright, very hardy species, ideally suited for reef aquariums.

Vertebrata; Actinopterygii; Perciformes; Pomacentridae
Clark's Anemonefish   *Amphiprion clarkii*
14 cm (5.5 in.)   Widespread in the Indo-Pacific

■ **Aquascaping** Best kept with one of many species of large sea anemones. Will also thrive without an anemone.
■ **Feeding** Omnivore; readily accepts a variety of meaty and algae-based foods. Color-enhancing rations help maintain bright colors.
■ **Compatibility** Reef safe. Very aggressive toward anemonefishes and similar species. Keep singly, in pairs, or in groups of one large female and several small males—introduce all simultaneously.

A great fish for reef tanks, but may bully shy and delicate fishes.

Vertebrata; Actinopterygii; Perciformes; Pomacentridae
Ocellaris Anemonefish   *Amphiprion ocellaris*
8 cm (3.1 in.)   Indo-Pacific

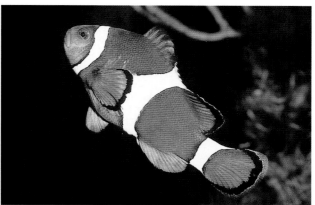

■ **Aquascaping** Display with a large sea anemone, e.g., *Heteractis magnifica, Stichodactyla gigantea, S. mertensii.* Also thrives without.
■ **Feeding** Omnivore; readily accepts a variety of meaty and algae-based foods. Color-enhancing rations help maintain bright colors.
■ **Compatibility** Reef safe and peaceful. May be kept in groups. Introduce all simultaneously.

The perfect reef aquarium fish. Wild-caught specimens tend to be difficult to adapt to captivity. Captive-breds are generally very hardy.

Vertebrata; Actinopterygii; Perciformes; Pomacentridae
Percula Anemonefish   *Amphiprion percula*
7 cm (2.7 in.)   Western Pacific

■ **Aquascaping** Makes a great display with a large sea anemone. Prefers *Heteractis magnifica, Stichodactyla gigantea,* and *S. mertensii.* Will also thrive without a host anemone.
■ **Feeding** Omnivore; readily accepts a variety of meaty and algae-based foods. Color-enhancing rations help maintain bright colors.
■ **Compatibility** Reef safe and very peaceful. May be kept in groups, pairs, or singly. Introduce all simultaneously.

Peaceful and ideal for reef aquariums. Captive-breds are hardy.

Vertebrata; Actinopterygii; Perciformes; Pomacentridae
Pink Skunk Anemonefish   *Amphiprion perideraion*
8 cm (3.1 in.)   Indo-west-Pacific

■ **Aquascaping** Makes a great display with a large sea anemone. Prefers *Heteractis magnifica, H. crispa, Macrodactyla doreensis,* and *Stichodactyla gigantea.* Will also thrive without an anemone.
■ **Feeding** Omnivore; readily accepts a variety of meaty and algae-based foods. Color-enhancing rations help maintain bright colors.
■ **Compatibility** Reef safe and peaceful. Keep singly, in pairs, or in groups consisting of one large female and several small males, introduced simultaneously.

A delicately colored fish that is ideally suited for reef aquariums.

Vertebrata; Actinopterygii; Perciformes; Pomacentridae
Blue Chromis *Chromis cyanea*
10 cm (3.9 in.) Caribbean

■ **Feeding** Omnivore; constantly plucks zooplankton from the water column in the wild. Needs meaty foods, such as fresh or frozen *Mysis* and brine shrimp, or high-protein flakes, at least several times per day.
■ **Compatibility** Reef safe. Should be kept in schools of 7 or more.

Glittering, peaceful fish that looks highly spectacular in large schools. Can be rather difficult to keep because of their feeding demands. Automatic feeders are useful for fishes such as this.

Vertebrata; Actinopterygii; Perciformes; Pomacentridae
Blue Green Chromis *Chromis viridis*
9 cm (3.5 in.) Indo-Pacific

■ **Feeding** Omnivore; constantly seeks plankton in the water column. Needs meaty foods, such as fresh or frozen *Mysis* and brine shrimp, or high-protein flakes, at least several times per day.
■ **Compatibility** Reef safe. Should be kept in schools of 7 or more. Especially appropriate with branching stony corals in which they will seek cover.

Pretty, peaceful fishes that demonstrate interesting schooling behaviors. Automatic feeders are useful for feeding these fish.

Vertebrata; Actinopterygii; Perciformes; Pomacentridae
Humbug Dascyllus *Dascyllus aruanus*
7 cm (2.7 in.) Indo-Pacific

■ **Aquascaping** Juveniles do best with holes, crevices, or branching *Acropora* or *Pocillopora* corals for hiding.
■ **Feeding** Easily fed on a variety of meaty and algae-based foods.
■ **Compatibility** Reef safe, but may eat small shrimps. Can be extremely aggressive toward smaller, delicate fishes. Juveniles do well in groups, but adults become very aggressive toward their own kind. Will need a large tank for full-grown specimens.

Extremely hardy fish that will grow into a bully in community tanks.

Vertebrata; Actinopterygii; Perciformes; Pomacentridae
Reticulate Dascyllus *Dascyllus reticulatus*
7 cm (2.7 in.) Indo-west-Pacific

■ **Aquascaping** Juveniles do best with holes, crevices, or branching *Acropora* or *Pocillopora* corals for hiding.
■ **Feeding** Easily fed on a variety of meaty and algae-based foods.
■ **Compatibility** Reef safe, but can be extremely aggressive toward smaller, delicate fishes. Juveniles do well in groups, but adults become very aggressive toward their own species.

Cute juveniles tend to grow into big, aggressive adults that can terrorize a whole aquarium. Very hardy.

Vertebrata; Actinopterygii; Perciformes; Pomacentridae
Threespot Dascyllus　　　　　*Dascyllus trimaculatus*
11 cm (4.3 in.)　　　　　　　　　　　　　Indo-Pacific

■ **Aquascaping** Juveniles will shelter in *Cryptodendrum adhaesivum* anemones if available.
■ **Feeding** Easily fed a varied diet of meaty and algae-based foods.
■ **Compatibility** Reef safe, but adults are often extremely aggressive toward other fishes. Should be kept singly, or in a mated pair.

Once considered a good, hardy beginner's fish, but its bullying tactics as an adult make it a questionable introduction to a community tank.

Vertebrata; Actinopterygii; Perciformes; Pomacentridae
Blue Devil　　　　　　　　　　　*Chrysiptera cyanea*
6 cm (2.3 in.)　　　　　　　　　　　　Indo-west-Pacific

■ **Aquascaping** Will make good use of rocky hiding places.
■ **Feeding** Easily fed a varied diet of meaty and algae-based foods.
■ **Compatibility** Reef safe. Can be aggressive toward its own species as well as other fishes, especially in small systems. Several can be housed in a large aquarium with a many hiding places.

This stunningly attractive, electric-blue fish is very hardy but can live up to its common name. Has many geographical color morphs, with or without yellow markings on the tail and breast.

Vertebrata; Actinopterygii; Perciformes; Pomacentridae
Yellowtail Blue Damselfish　　　*Chrysiptera parasema*
5 cm (2 in.)　　　　　　　　　　　　　Western Pacific

■ **Feeding** Easily fed a varied diet of meaty and algae-based foods.
■ **Compatibility** Reef safe. A relatively mild-mannered fish that is a much better choice than many other damsels, especially for small-to-average-size systems. Avoid keeping with aggressive fishes, particularly other damselfishes. Several specimens can be kept together without much trouble.

A beautiful and hardy fish that is far more peaceful than the majority of its relatives. Ideal fish for beginners, and for invertebrate tanks.

Vertebrata; Actinopterygii; Perciformes; Pomacentridae
Black Damselfish　　　　　　　　*Neoglyphidodon melas*
13 cm (5.1 in.)　　　　　　　　　　　　Indo-Pacific

■ **Feeding** Eats soft corals in the wild, but readily accepts meaty and algae-based substitute foods.
■ **Compatibility** Not reef safe. May eat corals. Aggressive toward other fishes. Juveniles can be kept in groups, but adults become extremely aggressive. Keep singly or in mated pairs.

Hardy but aggressive species. This genus has juveniles that are stunningly attractive, but that grow into dull-looking, brownish black adults that will bully most other fishes in a home aquarium.

Vertebrata; Actinopterygii; Perciformes; Pomacentridae
Golden Damselfish   *Amblyglyphidodon aureus*
10 cm (3.9 in.)   Indo-west-Pacific

■ **Aquascaping** Acts most natural with abundant hiding places, such as dense coral growths.
■ **Feeding** Eats plankton in the wild; accepts most substitute foods.
■ **Compatibility** Reef safe. Can be aggressive toward other fishes. May eat small shrimps. Juveniles do well in groups, but adults become aggressive toward their own species.

A hardy damselfish that keeps its lemon-yellow coloration, but grows large and can be somewhat aggressive. Keep with other robust fishes.

Vertebrata; Actinopterygii; Perciformes; Pomacentridae
Giant Damselfish   *Microspathodon dorsalis*
26 cm (10.1 in.)   Eastern Pacific

■ **Aquascaping** Should have many good hiding places.
■ **Feeding** Readily accepts meaty and algae-based foods.
■ **Compatibility** Reef safe. Fairly peaceful toward other fishes, but likely to eat small crustaceans and not to be fully trusted with corals. Juveniles may do well in groups, but adults become aggressive toward their own species and should be kept singly.

Quite attractive as juveniles (photo), but adults become dull, grayish brown in overall coloration. Keep with other robust fishes.

Vertebrata; Actinopterygii; Perciformes; Cirrhitidae
Redspotted Hawkfish   *Amblycirrhitus pinos*
8 cm (3.1 in.)   Caribbean

■ **Feeding** Carnivore; readily accepts most meaty foods.
■ **Compatibility** Reef safe. Will eat any fish or crustacean small enough to swallow. Tends to bully other fishes; do not keep with sensitive, docile species. Particularly aggressive toward other hawkfishes.

Fascinating behavior, as it sits perching like a hawk on corals or rocks, waiting for prey. Hardy but extremely voracious.

Vertebrata; Actinopterygii; Perciformes; Cirrhitidae
Pixy Hawkfish   *Cirrhitichthys oxycephalus*
9 cm (3.5 in.)   Indo-Pacific, Eastern Pacific, Red Sea

■ **Feeding** Carnivore; readily accepts most meaty foods.
■ **Compatibility** Reef safe. Will eat any fish or crustacean small enough to swallow. Tends to bully other fishes; do not keep with sensitive, docile species. Particularly aggressive toward other hawkfishes, especially its own species. Keep singly or in mated pairs.

A commonly seen hawkfish, interesting to watch and very hardy, but not to be trusted with small fishes and crustaceans, which it can attack and swallow with amazing speed.

Vertebrata; Actinopterygii; Perciformes; Cirrhitidae
Swallowtail Hawkfish   *Cyprinocirrhites polyactis*
14 cm (5.5 in.)   Indo-Pacific

■ **Feeding** Carnivore; accepts most meaty foods offered as zooplankton substitutes.
■ **Compatibility** Reef safe. Much more placid than other hawkfishes, but may eat small ornamental shrimps and may bully delicate
fishes. Several specimens may be kept together if they are of nearly
identical size and introduced simultaneously.

The only plankton-feeding hawkfish, it will hover in strong currents.
Excellent for the reef aquarium, provided suitable food is available.

Vertebrata; Actinopterygii; Perciformes; Cirrhitidae
Flame Hawkfish   *Neocirrhites armatus*
9 cm (3.5 in.)   Western Pacific

■ **Feeding** Easily fed on all meaty foods.
■ **Compatibility** Reef safe with corals, but will eat any fish, snail,
or crustacean small enough to swallow. May bully timid fishes.
Keep singly, unless a mated pair.

The bright red color and prominent eyes of this fish make it an eye-
catching favorite of many aquarists. Fascinating to watch, it perches
like a hawk on corals or rocks, ever alert for passing prey. Hardy but
extremely voracious. Do not keep with small, delicate tankmates.

Vertebrata; Actinopterygii; Perciformes; Cirrhitidae
Freckled Hawkfish   *Paracirrhites forsteri*
22 cm (8.6 in.)   Indo-Pacific

■ **Feeding** Preys on small fishes and crustaceans in the wild.
Accepts a variety of substitute meaty foods in the aquarium.
■ **Compatibility** Reef safe, but will eat any fish or crustacean small
enough to swallow. Has a tendency to bully fishes; do not keep with
docile species. Keep singly, unless a mated pair.

One of the larger hawkfishes, attractive and interesting but growing
too large for most reef tanks. Hardy but extremely voracious.

Vertebrata; Actinopterygii; Perciformes; Cirrhitidae
Longnose Hawkfish   *Oxycirrhites typus*
10 cm (3.9 in.)   Indo-Pacific

■ **Feeding** Preys on small fishes and crustaceans in the wild.
Accepts many substitute foods.
■ **Compatibility** Reef safe. Will eat any fish or crustacean small
enough to swallow. Harmless to corals and sessile invertebrates.
Aggressive toward its own and related species. Keep singly, unless
a mated pair.

A favorite of many aquarists, it may perch on corals awaiting passing
food items. Hardy but predatory on smaller fishes.

Vertebrata; Actinopterygii; Perciformes; Opistognathidae
Yellowhead Jawfish   *Opistognathus aurifrons*
10 cm (3.9 in.)   Caribbean

■ **Aquascaping** Requires a deep sand bed (10 cm [3.9 in.] or deeper) for burrowing, and pieces of mollusk shell for tunneling.
■ **Feeding** Carnivorous; accepts a variety of meaty foods.
■ **Compatibility** Reef safe. Somewhat sensitive and shy. Keep with peaceful fishes. May be kept singly or in groups.

A fascinating fish that is excellent for a reef aquarium. Often difficult to acclimate in community tanks. Has a tendency to jump out of the tank, particularly during the first few weeks.

Vertebrata; Actinopterygii; Perciformes; Opistognathidae
Bluespotted Jawfish   *Opistognathus rosenblatti*
10 cm (3.9 in.)   Eastern Pacific

■ **Aquascaping** Must have a thick bed (10 cm [3.9 in.] or deeper) of mixed coral sand, and rubble or mollusk shells for its tunnel building.
■ **Feeding** Carnivorous; accepts a variety of meaty foods.
■ **Compatibility** Reef safe, but may eat small shrimps. Keep with peaceful fishes. Best kept singly or in mated pairs; intraspecific aggression can be a problem.

Excellent fish for a reef aquarium. Tends to jump out of the tank, particularly during the first few weeks. Provide good cover.

Vertebrata; Actinopterygii; Perciformes; Opistognathidae
Dusky Jawfish   *Opistognathus whitehurstii*
10 cm (3.9 in.)   Caribbean

■ **Aquascaping** Must have a thick bed (10 cm [3.9 in.] or deeper) of mixed coral sand, and rubble or mollusk shells for its tunnel building.
■ **Feeding** Carnivorous; accepts a variety of meaty foods.
■ **Compatibility** Reef safe, but may eat small shrimps. May be kept in groups if adequate sandy bottom is available. Each fish will require an area with a radius of about 15 cm (5.9 in.)

Excellent fish for the reef aquarium. Has a tendency to jump out of the tank, particularly during the first few weeks. Provide good cover.

Vertebrata; Actinopterygii; Perciformes; Labridae
Yellowtail Wrasse   *Anampses meleagrides*
21 cm (8.2 in.)   Indo-Pacific, Red Sea

■ **Aquascaping** Should have a large area of fine sand (4-5 cm [1.6-2 in.] or deeper) for digging. Needs well-established live rock to thrive.
■ **Feeding** Carnivorous. Very difficult to adapt to substitute meaty foods. Live food is often necessary to induce feeding.
■ **Compatibility** Reef safe. Several females may be kept together, but only one male per tank. Does best with peaceful tankmates.

Part of a challenging genus known as the tamarin wrasses that are difficult to adapt to aquarium life. For experienced aquarists only.

Vertebrata; Actinopterygii; Perciformes; Labridae
Redtail Tamarin Wrasse *Anampses chrysocephalus*
17 cm (6.6 in.) Hawaii and Midway Islands

■ **Aquascaping** Should have a large area with fine sand (4-5 cm [1.6-2 in.] or deeper) for digging. Needs well-established live rock with a healthy population of microfauna to thrive.
■ **Feeding** Carnivorous. Very difficult to adapt to substitute meaty foods. Live food is often necessary to induce feeding.
■ **Compatibility** Reef safe. Several females may be kept together, but only one male per tank. Does best with peaceful tankmates.

A true beauty, but a fish that requires expert care and feeding.

Vertebrata; Actinopterygii; Perciformes; Labridae
Lyretail Hogfish *Bodianus anthioides*
21 cm (8.2 in.) Indo-Pacific; Red Sea

■ **Aquascaping** Juveniles need good hiding places. Provide a large sand zone and ample swimming space.
■ **Feeding** Carnivorous; readily accepts a variety of meaty foods.
■ **Compatibility** Reef safe, but will eat most small, free-living invertebrates. Fairly peaceful for a hogfish, but may bully more sensitive and delicate fishes. Likely to eat fishes small enough to swallow.

A very beautiful and reasonably hardy species. Juveniles are shy, but adults become too aggressive for most community tanks.

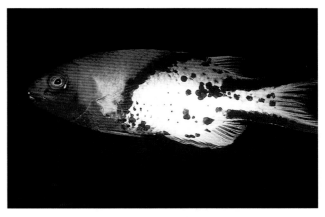

Vertebrata; Actinopterygii; Perciformes; Labridae
Twinspot Hogfish *Bodianus bimaculatus*
10 cm (3.9 in.) Indo-west Pacific

■ **Feeding** Carnivorous; readily accepts a variety of meaty foods.
■ **Compatibility** Reef safe, but will feed on most small, free-living invertebrates. Reasonably peaceful, but more sensitive and delicate fishes might be bullied. Several specimens may be kept together in large tanks if introduced simultaneously. In tanks less of than 500 liters (130 gal.) it is better kept singly.

This is a very nice wrasse for a reef aquarium, but it may be too competitive for small and sensitive fishes.

Vertebrata; Actinopterygii; Perciformes; Labridae
Spanish Hogfish *Bodianus rufus*
40 cm (15.6 in.) Tropical Western Atlantic

■ **Aquascaping** Juveniles need good hiding places. Provide a large sand zone and open swimming space.
■ **Feeding** Carnivorous; readily accepts a variety of meaty foods.
■ **Compatibility** Reef safe, but will feed on most small, free-living invertebrates; but corals are generally left undisturbed. Aggressive toward more-docile species and predatory on small fishes.

Too large for the average home aquarium, but an interesting show fish for tanks of 1,000 liters (260 gal.) or more.

Vertebrata; Actinopterygii; Perciformes; Labridae
Coral Hogfish   *Bodianus mesothorax*
19 cm (7.4 in.)   Western Pacific

■ **Aquascaping** Juveniles need good hiding places. Provide a large sand zone and open swimming space.
■ **Feeding** Carnivorous; readily accepts a variety of meaty foods.
■ **Compatibility** Reef safe, but will feed on most small, free-living invertebrates; corals are generally left undisturbed. Aggressive toward more-docile species and predatory on small fishes.

Very beautiful and a reasonably hardy species. Adults are too aggressive for most reef tanks. Better suited to a large community fish tank.

Vertebrata; Actinopterygii; Perciformes; Labridae
Redheaded Fairy Wrasse   *Cirrhilabrus solorensis*
13 cm (5.1 in.)   Indo-Australian Archipelago

■ **Aquascaping** Needs many hiding places. Provide a large sand zone where it can bury itself at night and good swimming space.
■ **Feeding** Carnivorous; readily accepts a variety of meaty foods.
■ **Compatibility** Reef safe. Quite peaceful, and leaves all but the smallest invertebrates alone. Several females may be kept together, but only one male per tank.

An excellent reef aquarium species, extremely beautiful and compatible with virtually all corals and motile invertebrates.

Vertebrata; Actinopterygii; Perciformes; Labridae
Twinspot Coris   *Coris aygula*
70 cm (27 in.)   Indo-Pacific

■ **Aquascaping** Needs stable decor that cannot be overturned by the fish and a large sand bed where it will bury itself completely when frightened and at night.
■ **Feeding** Carnivorous; readily accepts a variety of meaty foods.
■ **Compatibility** Corals will be ignored, but this species is too big and predatory for most reef aquariums.

A classic case of exotic juveniles (photo) turning into plain-looking adults that are simply unkeepable in the average home system.

Vertebrata; Actinopterygii; Perciformes; Labridae
Formosan Coris   *Coris frerei*
60 cm (23 in.)   Western Indian Ocean

■ **Aquascaping** Needs stable decor that cannot be overturned by the fish and a large sand bed where it will bury itself completely when frightened and at night.
■ **Feeding** Carnivorous; readily accepts a variety of meaty foods.
■ **Compatibility** Corals will be ignored, but this species is too big and predatory for most reef aquariums. (*Adult male at left.*)

A stunning show fish for large fish tanks. (Previously known as *C. formosa*.) Too large and aggressive for most home aquariums.

Vertebrata; Actinopterygii; Perciformes; Labridae
Harlequin Tuskfish   *Choerodon fasciatus*
30 cm (11.7 in.)   Western Pacific

■ **Aquascaping** Needs caves or other rocky hiding places.
■ **Feeding** Carnivorous; readily accepts a variety of meaty foods.
■ **Compatibility** Reef safe with corals. Likely to feed on most free-living invertebrates and fishes small enough to swallow. May be aggressive toward more docile fishes.

An exceptionally colorful wrasse—even its teeth are blue—and a hardy, interesting addition to a large fish tank with robust tankmates. Too large and predatory for most reef aquariums.

Vertebrata; Actinopterygii; Perciformes; Labridae
Bird Wrasse   *Gomphosus varius*
30 cm (11.7 in.)   Indo-Pacific

■ **Aquascaping** Needs hiding places and open swimming space.
■ **Feeding** Carnivorous; readily accepts a variety of meaty foods.
■ **Compatibility** Reef safe, but will eat most small free-living invertebrates and may harass or attack small fishes. Several females may be kept together, but only one male per tank. (Males are green; females, brown.)

An active fish with a swooping swimming style. The male is very attractive and can easily be paired with a female. Quite easy to keep.

Vertebrata; Actinopterygii; Perciformes; Labridae
Dusky Wrasse   *Halichoeres marginatus*
17 cm (6.6 in.)   Indo-west-Pacific

■ **Aquascaping** Should have a large area with fine-grained sand at least 5 cm thick. Will bury completely when frightened and at night.
■ **Feeding** In the wild, eats benthic invertebrates, but can be difficult to adapt to substitute meaty foods.
■ **Compatibility** Reef safe. Will eat most small free-living invertebrates. Can be aggressive toward smaller and more-docile fishes.

A species with subtle beauty that is sometimes introduced to prey on flatworms that can occur in plague-like proportions in an aquarium.

Vertebrata; Actinopterygii; Perciformes; Labridae
Cleaner Wrasse   *Labroides dimidiatus*
10 cm (3.9 in.)   Indo-Pacific

■ **Feeding** Nearly impossible to feed. A specialized feeder that lives as a cleaner of other fishes, it Ingests parasites, as well as mucus, scales, and fin fragments from the host fish. May accept finely minced meaty foods, brine shrimp, and worms.
■ **Conservation** Very low survival rates. Collection and sale of cleaner wrasses should not be encouraged.

Very difficult to adapt to aquarium life. Should be reserved for experienced aquarists able to provide advanced husbandry techniques.

Vertebrata; Actinopterygii; Perciformes; Labridae
Hawaiian Cleaner Wrasse   *Labroides phthirophagus*
12 cm (4.7 in.)   Hawaii

■ **Feeding** Nearly impossible to feed. A specialized feeder that lives as a cleaner of other fishes, it Ingests parasites, as well as mucus, scales, and fin fragments from the host fish. May accept finely minced meaty foods, brine shrimp, and worms.
■ **Conservation** Very low survival rates. Collection and sale of cleaner wrasses should not be encouraged.

This lovely species is nearly impossible to keep and is avoided by all responsible aquarists.

Vertebrata; Actinopterygii; Perciformes; Labridae
Leopard Wrasse   *Macropharyngodon meleagris*
15 cm (5.9 in.)   Indo-west-Pacific

■ **Aquascaping** Must be housed with well-established live rock that will provide important living food organisms.
■ **Feeding** Will starve in a new or sterile aquarium. Live adult brine shrimp can be a supplementary food source.
■ **Compatibility** Reef safe.

Under prolific conditions, in a large tank with plenty of live rock providing varied microfauna for its constant foraging, this species can live happily. Members of this genus all require experienced care.

Vertebrata; Actinopterygii; Perciformes; Labridae
Sixline Wrasse   *Pseudocheilinus hexataenia*
7.5 cm (2.9 in.)   Indo-Pacific, Red Sea

■ **Aquascaping** Secretive species that needs many hiding places.
■ **Feeding** Grazes on small benthic invertebrates. Accepts various meaty foods.
■ **Compatibility** Reef safe. Quite peaceful, but may eat very small shrimps (e.g., *Periclimenes* spp.). Several specimens may be kept in large tanks (300 liters [78 gal.] or larger).

This is a very hardy, peaceful, and beautiful species for reef aquariums. Can help eliminate excessive populations of flatworms and snails.

Vertebrata; Actinopterygii; Perciformes; Labridae
Moon Wrasse   *Thalassoma lunare*
25 cm (9.8 in.)   Indo-Pacific, Red Sea

■ **Aquascaping** Requires open swimming space as it grows.
■ **Feeding** Carnivorous; will accept most meaty foods.
■ **Compatibility** Reef safe with corals, but small fishes and free-moving invertebrates are likely to be eaten. Several females may be kept together, but allow only one male per tank.

A vibrantly colored, active fish that is hardy and suitable for large tanks with robust tankmates. Juveniles are rather plain looking, assuming ever more beautiful coloration as they mature.

Vertebrata; Actinopterygii; Perciformes; Labridae
Bluehead Wrasse   *Thalassoma bifasciatum*
18 cm (7 in.)   Caribbean, Tropical Western Atlantic

■ **Aquascaping** Needs hiding places and open swimming space.
■ **Feeding** Carnivorous; will accept most meaty foods.
■ **Compatibility** Reef safe, but will eat small invertebrates, including serpent stars. Can be aggressive toward smaller, more docile fishes. can be kept in groups of one male and several females.

A Caribbean beauty with electric colors, but a potential threat to most other invertebrates in a reef tank. Fairly easy to keep.

Vertebrata; Actinopterygii; Perciformes; Scaridae
Bicolor Parrotfish   *Cetoscarus bicolor*
80 cm (31 in.)   Indo-Pacific, Red Sea

■ **Feeding** Primarily herbivorous, scraping algae from the substrate with its beaklike mouth. Accepts a variety of substitute foods, but needs substantial quantities of algae to thrive.
■ **Compatibility** Likely to bite chunks of stony corals, otherwise safe with most fishes and invertebrates, including soft corals. Aggressive toward its own species and related fishes.

Far too big for all but very large home aquariums. Adult color phases are completely unlike the juvenile shown, but also attractive.

Vertebrata; Actinopterygii; Perciformes; Pinguipedidae
Redspotted Sand Perch   *Parapercis schauinslandi*
14 cm (5.5 in.)   Indo-Pacific

■ **Aquascaping** A large sand zone is obligatory for this family.
■ **Feeding** Carnivorous; accepts a variety of meaty foods.
■ **Compatibility** Reef safe, but crustaceans and fishes small enough to swallow are likely to be eaten. May become aggressive toward other fishes as it ages.

This is an attractive and hardy fish that makes an excellent bottom-dweller for reef tanks. Beware that small free-living invertebrates and some fishes are potential prey.

Vertebrata; Actinopterygii; Perciformes; Pholidichthyidae
Convict Blenny   *Pholidichthys leucotaenia*
35 cm (13.7 in.)   Indo-west-Pacific

■ **Aquascaping** Needs caves and crevices for hiding and deep sand for burrowing. May topple rocks if they are not firmly situated.
■ **Feeding** Omnivore; readily accepts most foods.
■ **Compatibility** Reef safe, but do not combine with fishes, crustaceans, or invertebrates small enough to be swallowed whole.

This hardy but very secretive species constantly digs and may bury corals in sand. Its coloring changes to an attractive vertical stripe pattern as it ages (photo is a juvenile). Has spawned in captivity.

Vertebrata; Actinopterygii; Perciformes; Blenniidae
Bicolor Blenny *Ecsenius bicolor*
10 cm (3.9 in.) Indo-Pacific

■ **Aquascaping** Needs established live rock for algal grazing.
■ **Feeding** Herbivore that scrapes microalgae from hard substrate. Accepts substitute foods, but is difficult to keep without algae.
■ **Compatibility** Usually reef safe and generally peaceful, but may occasionally eat corals and bite clams and other invertebrates. May be aggressive toward conspecifics and related species.

This is an interesting and generally commendable species for reef tanks. Some specimens may develop troublesome habits.

Vertebrata; Actinopterygii; Perciformes; Blenniidae
Red Sea Mimic Blenny *Ecsenius gravieri*
8 cm (3.1 in.) Red Sea, Gulf of Aden

■ **Aquascaping** Needs established live rock for algal grazing.
■ **Feeding** Herbivore that scrapes microalgae from hard substrate. Accepts substitute foods, but is difficult to keep without algae.
■ **Compatibility** Usually reef safe and generally peaceful, but may eat corals and bite clams and other invertebrates. May be aggressive toward conspecifics and related species.

Mimics the venomous Blackline Fang Blenny, *Meiacanthus nigrolineatus*. Good reef species, but with occasional problem specimens.

Vertebrata; Actinopterygii; Perciformes; Blenniidae
Midas Blenny *Ecsenius midas*
13 cm (5.1 in.) Indo-Pacific, Red Sea

■ **Feeding** Carnivorous; eats zooplankton and substitutes such as *Mysis* and brine shrimp. Feed several times daily. A varied, vitamin-enriched diet is necessary for good health and vivid color.
■ **Compatibility** Reef safe. Generally peaceful, but may become aggressive toward similar-looking fish species.

An excellent reef aquarium species, and the only planktivore in its genus. Will often swarm together in mixed schools with *Pseudanthias* spp.

Vertebrata; Actinopterygii; Perciformes; Blenniidae
Highfin Blenny *Atrosalarias fuscus*
14.5 cm (5.7 in.) Western Pacific

■ **Aquascaping** Needs established live rock for algal grazing.
■ **Feeding** Herbivore that scrapes microalgae from hard substrate. Accepts substitute foods, but is very difficult to keep without good algae-foraging opportunities in the aquarium.
■ **Compatibility** Reef safe and peaceful, although some specimens may nip at stony corals.

This is a good reef aquarium species with several color variations, from blackish brown to yellow.

Vertebrata; Actinopterygii; Perciformes; Blenniidae
Leopard Blenny   *Exallias brevis*
14.5 cm (5.7 in.)   Indo-Pacific

■ **Feeding** Feeds almost exclusively on the polyps of small-polyped stony corals. Hardly possible to keep alive on substitute foods.
■ **Compatibility** Not reef safe. Will eat most stony corals.
■ **Conservation** The majority of imported specimens starve to death shortly after importation because of a lack of suitable foods.

This is a beautiful fish, but one most aquarists must shun. Don't buy it unless you have the skill, time, and resources to invest in experimental husbandry techniques.

Vertebrata; Actinopterygii; Perciformes; Blenniidae
Redlip Blenny   *Ophioblennius atlanticus*
12 cm (4.7 in.)   Tropical Western Atlantic

■ **Aquascaping** Needs established live rock for algal grazing.
■ **Feeding** Herbivore that scrapes microalgae from hard substrate. Accepts substitute foods, but is very difficult to keep without good algae-foraging opportunities in the aquarium.
■ **Compatibility** Reef safe. Some specimens may nip at stony corals and clams. May be aggressive toward conspecifics.

An appealing Caribbean species and an excellent algae eater for reef aquariums. Hardy and fairly peaceful.

Vertebrata; Actinopterygii; Perciformes; Blenniidae
Jeweled Blenny   *Salarias fasciatus*
13 cm (5.1 in.)   Widespread in the Indo-Pacific

■ **Aquascaping** Needs established live rock for algal grazing.
■ **Feeding** Herbivore that scrapes microalgae from hard substrate. Accepts substitute foods, but is very difficult to keep without good algae-foraging opportunities in the aquarium.
■ **Compatibility** Usually reef safe. May be aggressive toward conspecifics and more-timid fishes, especially other small herbivores.

Among the very best algae grazers for reef tanks. Extremely efficient, but will usually starve when all the algae has been eaten.

Vertebrata; Actinopterygii; Perciformes; Blenniidae
Bluestriped Fang Blenny   *Plagiotremus rhinorhynchos*
12 cm (4.7 in.)   Indo-Pacific

■ **Feeding** Feeds on the scales and body mucus of other fishes. Difficult to adapt to substitute foods.
■ **Compatibility** Aggressive predator that will harm other fishes. Has also been reported to attack invertebrates.

Part of a noteworthy group known as the fang blennies or sabretooth blennies that are not appropriate for most home aquariums. To be kept properly, they require an experienced aquarist and a specially dedicated system.

Vertebrata; Actinopterygii; Perciformes; Blenniidae
Cleaner Mimic   *Aspidontus taeniatus*

11.5 cm (4.5 in.)   Indo-Pacific, Red Sea

■ **Feeding** Carnivorous; feeds on the scales and body mucus of other fishes, as well as fish eggs and polychaete worm tentacles. Difficult to adapt to substitute foods.
■ **Compatibility** Generally reef safe, but will aggressively prey upon other fishes in the aquarium.

This species mimics the Cleaner Wrasse, *Labroides dimidiatus*, allowing it to sneak up on unsuspecting victims. Not recommended to most aquarists, but it could be kept in a specialized predator display.

Vertebrata; Actinopterygii; Perciformes; Blenniidae
Blackline Fang Blenny   *Meiacanthus nigrolineatus*

9.5 cm (3.7 in.)   Red Sea, Gulf of Aden

■ **Feeding** Carnivorous planktivore; accepts a variety of meaty foods.
■ **Compatibility** Generally peaceful, but may bite other fishes (or the aquarist) if provoked.
■ **Hazards** Has a mildly venomous bite that may cause swelling and irritation in humans.

The venomous bite of this species is believed to be a means of defense against predators. It is a good fish for the reef aquarium, but not among the easiest to keep.

Vertebrata; Actinopterygii; Perciformes; Blenniidae
Striped Fang Blenny   *Meiacanthus grammistes*

12 cm (4.7 in.)   Indo-west Pacific

■ **Feeding** Carnivorous planktivore; accepts a variety of meaty foods.
■ **Compatibility** Generally peaceful, but may bite other fishes (or the aquarist) if provoked.
■ **Hazards** Has a mildly venomous bite that may cause swelling and irritation in humans.

This is a good and hardy fish for the reef aquarium. Aquarists who are sensitive to animal stings should note that it has a mildly venomous bite and may nip humans if provoked.

Vertebrata; Actinopterygii; Perciformes; Callionymidae
Spotted Mandarinfish   *Synchiropus picturatus*

7 cm (2.7 in.)   Indo-west Pacific

■ **Aquascaping** Must be housed with plenty of live rock to supply a varied, rich supply of tiny, live food organisms.
■ **Feeding** Carnivorous; feeds on minute benthic organisms. May accept brine shrimp, mysid shrimp, and other meaty foods.
■ **Compatibility** Reef safe. Needs a peaceful, noncompetitive aquarium. Do not keep with active or aggressive fishes or large crustaceans. Keep only one male per tank.

A wonderful fish for the established reef tank with rich microfauna.

Vertebrata; Actinopterygii; Perciformes; Callionymidae
Green Mandarinfish *Synchiropus splendidus*
10 cm (3.9 in.) Indo-west Pacific

■ **Aquascaping** Must be housed with plenty of live rock to supply a varied, rich supply of tiny, live food organisms.
■ **Feeding** Carnivorous; feeds on minute benthic organisms. May accept brine shrimp, mysid shrimp, and other meaty foods.
■ **Compatibility** Reef safe. Needs a peaceful, noncompetitive aquarium. Do not keep with aggressive fishes or large crustaceans. Keep only one male (with elongated first dorsal spine) per tank.

A true beauty for a quiet, established reef aquarium.

Vertebrata; Actinopterygii; Perciformes; Callionymidae
Scooter Dragonet *Synchiropus ocellatus*
6 cm (2.3 in.) Western Pacific

■ **Aquascaping** Must be housed with plenty of live rock to supply a varied, rich supply of tiny, live food organisms.
■ **Feeding** Carnivorous; feeds on minute benthic organisms. May accept brine shrimp, mysid shrimp, and other meaty foods.
■ **Compatibility** Reef safe. Needs a peaceful, noncompetitive aquarium. Do not keep with active or aggressive fishes or large crustaceans. Keep only one male per tank.

An interesting little fish for a quiet reef tank with rich microfauna.

Vertebrata; Actinopterygii; Perciformes; Gobiidae
Orangespotted Shrimp Goby *Amblyeleotris guttata*
8 cm (3.1 in.) Indo-west Pacific

■ **Aquascaping** Provide a large area of sand flat, at least 5 cm (2 in.) thick, consisting of fine sand and coral rubble.
■ **Feeding** Carnivorous; accepts a variety of meaty foods.
■ **Compatibility** Reef safe, but may eat tiny shrimps.

This is one a of group of specialized gobies that live in burrows with pistol shrimps (*Alpheus* spp.). When paired with a commensal shrimp, these gobies are fascinating aquarium specimens, especially in sand-zone biotopes. Good choice for a biotope tank.

Vertebrata; Actinopterygii; Perciformes; Gobiidae
Spottail Shrimp Goby *Amblyeleotris latifasciata*
13 cm (5.1 in.) Indo-Pacific

■ **Aquascaping** Provide a large area of sand flat, at least 8 cm (3.1 in.) thick, consisting of fine sand and coral rubble.
■ **Feeding** Carnivorous; accepts a variety of meaty foods.
■ **Compatibility** Reef safe, but may eat tiny shrimps.

This is another commensal goby that lives in a burrow with a pistol shrimp (*Alpheus* spp.). When paired with a lifelong partner shrimp, these gobies are fascinating aquarium specimens, especially in sand-zone biotopes. Good choice for a biotope tank.

Vertebrata; Actinopterygii; Perciformes; Gobiidae
Pinkspotted Shrimp Goby *Cryptocentrus leptocephalus*
10 cm (3.9 in.)   Indo-Pacific

■ **Aquascaping** Provide a large area of sand flat, at least 8 cm (3.1 in.) thick, consisting of fine sand and coral rubble.
■ **Feeding** Carnivorous; accepts a variety of meaty foods.
■ **Compatibility** Reef safe. Extremely aggressive toward other bottom-dwelling fishes. Likely to eat small shrimps.

A very attractive shrimp goby but large enough to be a threat to others that compete with it for space and food. It is an excellent species for a reef tank, particularly a sand-zone aquarium.

Vertebrata; Actinopterygii; Perciformes; Gobiidae
Yellow Watchman Goby *Cryptocentrus cinctus*
7 cm (2.7 in.)   Indo-west Pacific

■ **Aquascaping** Provide a large area of sand flat, at least 5 cm (2 in.) thick, consisting of fine sand and coral rubble.
■ **Feeding** Carnivorous; accepts a variety of meaty foods.
■ **Compatibility** Likely to eat small shrimps, and may attack other shrimp goby species. Otherwise peaceful and harmless. Best kept singly or in mated pairs.

A beautiful, common species that is seen in two very distinct color morphs: uniformly bright yellow, or gray.

Vertebrata; Actinopterygii; Perciformes; Gobiidae
Blackray Shrimp Goby *Stonogobiops nematodes*
4 cm (1.6 in.)   Indonesia and the Philippines

■ **Aquascaping** Provide a large area of sand flat, at least 3 cm (1.2 in.) thick, consisting of fine sand and coral rubble.
■ **Feeding** Carnivorous; accepts a variety of meaty foods.
■ **Compatibility** Reef safe. Needs a peaceful community tank, otherwise very shy. May be aggressive toward other bottom-dwelling fishes. Best kept in pairs. Two males will always fight.

Lives in burrows with a pistol shrimp, usually *Alpheus randalli*. Excellent species for reef tanks, particularly, sand-zone aquariums.

Vertebrata; Actinopterygii; Perciformes; Gobiidae
Brownbarred Goby *Amblygobius phalaena*
15 cm (5.9 in.)   Indo-Pacific

■ **Aquascaping** Provide a large area of sand flat consisting of fine sand and coral rubble.
■ **Feeding** Digs in the sand for benthic invertebrates and detritus. Also grazes on algae. Accepts a variety of substitute foods.
■ **Compatibility** Reef safe. Prone to being harassed by active and aggressive fishes. Best kept singly or in mated pairs.

Does not associate with shrimps, as others in its genus, but a great fish for a sand-zone reef aquarium. Will keep bottom substrate loose.

Vertebrata; Actinopterygii; Perciformes; Gobiidae
Rainford's Goby *Amblygobius rainfordi*
6.5 cm (2.5 in.) Western and Central Pacific

■ **Aquascaping** Provide plenty of live rock and sand for grazing.

▧ **Feeding** Omnivorous; eat filamentous algae and will dig in the sand for benthic invertebrates and detritus. Accepts a variety of substitute meaty foods, but needs some algae in order to do well.

■ **Compatibility** Reef safe. Prone to being harassed by aggressive fishes. Keep singly, except in a large system.

Excellent reef aquarium fish; peaceful and colorful. Often starves in newly set up tanks without rich and diverse microfauna and -flora.

Vertebrata; Actinopterygii; Perciformes; Gobiidae
Signal Goby *Signigobius biocellatus*
7 cm (2.7 in.) Western Pacific

▧ **Aquascaping** Requires well-established live rock and a deep sand bed to provide live microfauna that serve as food for the fish.

■ **Feeding** Hunts for benthic invertebrates in the sand. Difficult to adapt to substitute foods.

■ **Compatibility** Reef safe, but may eat shrimps and worms. Best kept in pairs, as it occurs in nature.

A lovely species with two ocelli (false eyespots), but prone to starving in the aquarium. Best reserved for experienced aquarists.

Vertebrata; Actinopterygii; Perciformes; Gobiidae
Yellowheaded Sleeper Goby *Valenciennea strigata*
18 cm (7 in.) Indo-Pacific

▧ **Aquascaping** Requires well-established live rock and a deep sand bed to provide live microfauna that serve as food for the fish.

▧ **Feeding** Digs for benthic invertebrates in the sand. Difficult to provide with sufficient food. Accepts a variety of substitute foods, but can starve unless live food is available.

▧ **Compatibility** Reef safe. May eat shrimps and small fishes.

A wonderful fish for a sand-zone reef aquarium, but a challenge to feed properly. Not a good choice for inexperienced aquarists.

Vertebrata; Actinopterygii; Perciformes; Gobiidae
Orangespotted Sleeper Goby *Valenciennea puellaris*
14 cm (5.5 in.) Indo-west-Pacific

▧ **Aquascaping** Requires well-established live rock and a deep sand bed to provide live microfauna that serve as food for the fish.

■ **Feeding** Digs for benthic invertebrates in the sand. Difficult to provide with sufficient food. Accepts a variety of substitute foods, but can starve unless live food is available.

▧ **Compatibility** Reef safe. May eat shrimps and small fishes.

A beautiful fish for a well-established sand-zone reef aquarium, but prone to starving in most other systems. For experienced keepers only.

Vertebrata; Actinopterygii; Perciformes; Gobiidae
Ornate Goby   *Istigobius ornatus*
10 cm (3.9 in.)   Indo-Pacific, Red Sea

■ **Aquascaping** Should have caves and rocky hiding places close to a sandy substrate.
■ **Feeding** Carnivorous; readily accepts a variety of meaty foods.
■ **Compatibility** Reef safe, but shy and not capable of competing for food with larger or more aggressive fishes. May eat worms and small shrimps. Peaceful toward most fishes, except its own species and close relatives.

A fascinating and hardy fish for a reef tank. (*Female shown.*)

Vertebrata; Actinopterygii; Perciformes; Gobiidae
Neon Goby   *Gobiosoma oceanops*
3.5 cm (1.4 in.)   Tropical Western Atlantic

■ **Aquascaping** Does best in a tank with live rock and live sand.
■ **Feeding** Serves as a cleaner of other fishes, eating parasites and probably mucus from the host fish. Accepts various meaty foods (shrimp meat, brine shrimp, worms) of an appropriate size.
■ **Compatibility** Reef safe and peaceful, but can fall prey to predators. Can be aggressive with its own kind, particularly in small tanks.

A wonderful little fish for peaceful coral reef tanks. Will function as a cleaner fish in an aquarium and even clean the aquarist's hands.

Vertebrata; Actinopterygii; Perciformes; Gobiidae
Citron Clown Goby   *Gobiodon citrinus*
7 cm (2.7 in.)   Indo-Pacific, Red Sea

■ **Aquascaping** Does best with live *Acropora* coral, its natural host.
■ **Feeding** Carnivorous; accepts a variety of meaty foods.
■ **Compatibility** Reef safe. Likely to nip *Acropora* polyps in conjunction with spawning preparations, but causes little damage. Best kept in quiet communities, with groups of several specimens.

A marvelous fish when combined with *Acropora* coral. Fascinating spawning behavior can be observed in captivity. Hardy, peaceful, and decorative fish species.

Vertebrata; Actinopterygii; Perciformes; Gobiidae
Yellow Clown Goby   *Gobiodon okinawae*
3.5 cm (1.4 in.)   Indo-Pacific

■ **Aquascaping** Does best with live *Acropora* coral, its natural host.
■ **Feeding** Carnivorous; accepts a variety of meaty foods.
■ **Compatibility** Reef safe. Best kept in groups of several specimens. Among branching coral colonies, pairs will form and disperse among the corals. Avoid housing with large, aggressive fishes.

Like other members of its genus, an excellent fish for combination with *Acropora* corals. Fascinating spawning behavior can be observed in the aquarium. Hardy, peaceful, and attractive.

Vertebrata; Actinopterygii; Perciformes; Gobiidae
Green Clown Goby   *Gobiodon rivulatus*
3.5 cm (1.4 in.)   Western Pacific

■ **Aquascaping** Does best with live *Acropora* coral, its natural host.
■ **Feeding** Carnivorous; accepts a variety of meaty foods.
■ **Compatibility** Reef safe. Best kept in groups of several specimens. Among branching coral colonies, pairs will form and disperse among the corals. Avoid housing with large, aggressive fishes.

A small beauty and a perfect fish for combination with *Acropora* corals. Fascinating spawning behavior can be observed in the aquarium. Hardy, peaceful, and attractive.

Vertebrata; Actinopterygii; Perciformes; Microdesmidae
Purple Firefish   *Nemateleotris decora*
8 cm (3.1 in.)   Indo-Pacific

■ **Aquascaping** Needs rocky crevices or coral rubble for hiding.
■ **Feeding** Carnivorous. Accepts a variety of plankton substitutes, such as mysid shrimp and brine shrimp, preferably vitamin-enriched, that it will pluck out of the water column.
■ **Compatibility** Reef safe. Peaceful and harmless species. Avoid keeping with large and competitive species. Rather aggressive toward conspecifics. Best kept singly or in mated pairs.

An eyecatching fish for the reef aquarium. Hardy, if properly fed.

Vertebrata; Actinopterygii; Perciformes; Microdesmidae
Firefish   *Nemateleotris magnifica*
8 cm (3.1 in.)   Indo-Pacific

■ **Aquascaping** Needs rocky crevices or coral rubble for hiding.
■ **Feeding** Carnivorous. Accepts a variety of plankton substitutes, such as mysid shrimp and brine shrimp, preferably vitamin-enriched, that it will pluck out of the water column.
■ **Compatibility** Reef safe. Peaceful and harmless species. Avoid keeping with large and competitive species. Rather aggressive toward conspecifics. Best kept singly or in mated pairs.

A beautiful fish for quiet reef tanks. Hardy, if provided suitable foods.

Vertebrata; Actinopterygii; Perciformes; Microdesmidae
Scissortail Dartfish   *Ptereleotris evides*
12 cm (4.7 in.)   Indo-Pacific

■ **Aquascaping** Needs rocky crevices or coral rubble for hiding.
■ **Feeding** Carnivorous. Accepts a variety of plankton substitutes.
■ **Compatibility** Reef safe. A peaceful and harmless species. Avoid combination with large and aggressive species. Juveniles do well in large groups, but adults tend to live in pairs.

An excellent fish for the reef aquarium. Less prone to hide than most other dartfishes. Tends to try to escape by fleeing; will jump from uncovered aquariums, so tank must have a good cover.

Vertebrata; Actinopterygii; Perciformes; Acanthuridae
Achilles Surgeonfish   *Acanthurus achilles*
24 cm (9.4 in.)   Central Pacific

■ **Aquascaping** Should have plenty of swimming space.
■ **Feeding** Herbivorous. Needs live and dried algae, algae-based food mixtures, leaf lettuce, zucchini, and/or broccoli.
■ **Compatibility** Generally reef safe. Very aggressive toward its own kind and other surgeonfishes. Best kept singly. Prone to parasites.

One of the more delicate and hard-to-keep surgeonfishes. Best reserved for experienced aquarists. Needs a lot of space—a minimum system size of 500 liters (130 gal.) or larger.

Vertebrata; Actinopterygii; Perciformes; Acanthuridae
Atlantic Blue Tang   *Acanthurus coeruleus*
35 cm (13.7 in.)   Tropical Western Atlantic

■ **Aquascaping** Should have plenty of swimming space.
■ **Feeding** Herbivorous. Needs live and dried algae, algae-based food mixtures, leaf lettuce, zucchini, and/or broccoli.
■ **Compatibility** Generally reef safe. May be kept in groups in tanks 1,000 liters (260 gal.) or larger, otherwise best kept singly or in mated pairs.

Among the more hardy *Acanthurus* spp.—excellent for large Caribbean reef tanks. Juveniles are bright yellow, adults are blue.

Vertebrata; Actinopterygii; Perciformes; Acanthuridae
Powder Blue Surgeonfish   *Acanthurus leucosternon*
30 cm (11.7 in.)   Indian Ocean

■ **Aquascaping** Should have plenty of swimming space.
■ **Feeding** Herbivorous. Needs live and dried algae, algae-based food mixtures, leaf lettuce, zucchini, and/or broccoli.
■ **Compatibility** Generally reef safe. Normally does well with unsimilar looking species, but is very aggressive toward other surgeonfishes. Should be kept singly, except in large systems.

Extremely beautiful and sought after, but a delicate and hard-to-keep surgeonfish. Very susceptible to white-spot disease (marine ich).

Vertebrata; Actinopterygii; Perciformes; Acanthuridae
Orangeshoulder Surgeonfish   *Acanthurus olivaceus*
35 cm (13.7 in.)   Indo-Pacific

■ **Aquascaping** Should have plenty of swimming space.
■ **Feeding** Herbivorous. Feeds on diatoms, detritus, and filamentous microalgae. Accepts a variety of substitute foods.
■ **Compatibility** Reef safe. Generally peaceful toward fishes, even other surgeonfishes. Small groups may be kept together in large tanks. May be attacked by more aggressive surgeonfishes.

One of the best surgeonfishes for a reef tank. Fairly hardy and less aggressive than others in its family. Juveniles are yellow.

Vertebrata; Actinopterygii; Perciformes; Acanthuridae
Mimic Surgeonfish   *Acanthurus pyroferus*
25 cm (9.8 in.)   Indo-west-Pacific

■ **Aquascaping** Should have plenty of swimming space.
■ **Feeding** Herbivorous. Needs live and dried algae, algae-based food mixtures, leaf lettuce, zucchini, and/or broccoli.
■ **Compatibility** Generally reef safe. Best kept singly. Varying aggression toward fishes; normally does well with unsimilar species.

Fairly hardy; suitable for reef tanks 300 liters (78 gal.) or larger. Juveniles are colorful mimics of some pygmy angelfishes (*Centropyge vroliki* and *C. flavissimus*), but adults (photo) are brownish.

Vertebrata; Actinopterygii; Perciformes; Acanthuridae
Clown Surgeonfish   *Acanthurus lineatus*
38 cm (14.8 in.)   Indo-Pacific

■ **Aquascaping** Should have plenty of swimming space.
■ **Feeding** Herbivorous. Needs live and dried algae, algae-based food mixtures, leaf lettuce, zucchini, and/or broccoli.
■ **Compatibility** Generally reef safe. Extremely aggressive toward its own species and any other fishes with behavioral or morphological resemblances. Will often harass target fishes until they are killed.

Rather difficult to keep and very belligerent. Best reserved for experienced aquarists. Needs a large tank of at least 1,000 liters (260 gal.).

Vertebrata; Actinopterygii; Perciformes; Acanthuridae
Hawaiian Bristletooth   *Ctenochaetus hawaiiensis*
25 cm (9.8 in.)   Central Pacific

■ **Aquascaping** Needs well-established live rock to provide natural grazing surfaces. Needs plenty of open swimming space.
■ **Feeding** Herbivorous. Scrapes detritus, diatoms, and other unicellular algae off macroalgae, coral bases, and rocks. Needs a variety of dried algae and algae-based foods.
■ **Compatibility** Reef safe. Aggressive toward conspecifics.

A fairly hardy fish suitable for a larger reef aquarium. Juveniles are very colorful and prized by aquarists, but adults are dull brownish overall.

Vertebrata; Actinopterygii; Perciformes; Acanthuridae
Striped Bristletooth   *Ctenochaetus striatus*
22 cm (8.6 in.)   Indo-Pacific

■ **Aquascaping** Needs well-established live rock to provide natural grazing surfaces. Needs plenty of open swimming space.
■ **Feeding** Herbivorous. Scrapes detritus, diatoms, and other unicellular algae off macroalgae, coral bases, and rocks. Needs a variety of dried algae and algae-based foods.
■ **Compatibility** Reef safe. Peaceful toward unsimilar fishes.

A reasonably hardy, if unspectacular, surgeonfish, suitable for a 350-liter (90 gal.) or larger reef tank.

Vertebrata; Actinopterygii; Perciformes; Acanthuridae
Palette Surgeonfish   *Paracanthurus hepatus*
30 cm (11.7 in.)   Indo-Pacific

■ **Aquascaping** Juveniles are shy and require plenty of hiding places, such as branching corals. Needs open swimming space.
■ **Feeding** Omnivorous; feeds mostly on zooplankton, but also algae. Needs a balanced, nutritious diet to avoid deficiency diseases.
■ **Compatibility** Reef safe. Juveniles do best in groups. Adults can be aggressive toward each other, except in very large systems.

This is an atypical surgeonfish, because of its zooplankton needs. Susceptible to ich and nutritional deficiencies. Not a beginner's fish.

Vertebrata; Actinopterygii; Perciformes; Acanthuridae
Yellow Tang   *Zebrasoma flavescens*
18 cm (7 in.)   Central Pacific

■ **Aquascaping** Needs room to swim; 250 liters (65 gal.) or more.
■ **Feeding** Herbivorous. Needs live and dried algae, algae-based food mixtures, leaf lettuce, zucchini, and/or broccoli.
■ **Compatibility** Reef safe. Often aggressive toward fishes it perceives as competitive. Keep singly, except in large tanks.

One of the best and most popular surgeonfishes. Excellent algae grazer for medium- and large-sized tanks. Very hardy, but too aggressive for small aquariums.

Vertebrata; Actinopterygii; Perciformes; Acanthuridae
Brown Tang   *Zebrasoma scopas*
20 cm (7.8 in.)   Indo-Pacific

■ **Aquascaping** Needs room to swim; 250 liters (65 gal.) or more.
■ **Feeding** Herbivorous. Needs live and dried algae, algae-based food mixtures, leaf lettuce, zucchini, and/or broccoli.
■ **Compatibility** Reef safe. Often aggressive toward fishes it perceives as competitive. Keep singly, except in large tanks, where groups should be introduced simultaneously.

This is a fish with subdued coloration, but a good algae grazer for medium- and large-sized tanks.

Vertebrata; Actinopterygii; Perciformes; Acanthuridae
Sailfin Tang   *Zebrasoma veliferum*
40 cm (15.6 in.)   Indo-west Pacific

■ **Aquascaping** Should have plenty of swimming space.
■ **Feeding** Mostly herbivorous. Needs live and dried algae, algae-based food mixtures, leaf lettuce, zucchini, and/or broccoli.
■ **Compatibility** Reef safe. Often very aggressive toward fishes with behavioral or morphological resemblances. Best kept singly, except in very large tanks of 3,000 liters (780 gal.) or larger.

An elegant, hardy, and efficient algae grazer. Due to its large adult size, it may outgrow tanks less than 1,000 liters (260 gal.). See *Z. desjardinii*.

Vertebrata; Actinopterygii; Perciformes; Acanthuridae
Indian Ocean Sailfin Tang   *Zebrasoma desjardinii*
40 cm (15.6 in.)   Red Sea, Indian Ocean

■ **Aquascaping** Should have plenty of swimming space.
■ **Feeding** Herbivorous. Needs live and dried algae, algae-based
food mixtures, leaf lettuce, zucchini, and/or broccoli.
■ **Compatibility** Reef safe. Often very aggressive toward fishes with
behavioral or morphological resemblances. Best kept singly, except
in very large tanks of 3,000 liters (780 gal.) or larger.

A very hardy and appealing algae grazer. It may outgrow tanks of
less than 1,000 liters (260 gal.). Very similar to *Z. veliferum.*

Vertebrata; Actinopterygii; Perciformes; Acanthuridae
Purple Tang   *Zebrasoma xanthurum*
25 cm (9.8 in.)   Red Sea, Arabian Gulf

■ **Aquascaping** Should have plenty of swimming space.
■ **Feeding** Herbivorous. A varied, nutritious diet, rich in live and dried
algae, is necessary to maintain health and coloration.
■ **Compatibility** Reef safe. Often very aggressive toward fishes it
perceives as competitors. Best kept singly, except in very large tanks
of 3,000 liters (780 gal.) or larger.

Prized for its color and algae grazing, this is a reef aquarium favorite
for medium- and large-sized tanks (350 liters [90 gal.] or more).

Vertebrata; Actinopterygii; Perciformes; Acanthuridae
Orangespine Unicornfish   *Naso lituratus*
45 cm (17.6 in.)   Indo-Pacific

■ **Aquascaping** Needs ample swimming space (1,000 liters [260
gal.] or more).
■ **Feeding** Must have brown macroalgae, like *Sargassum* and
Dictyota. Provide similar algae (fresh, frozen, or dried) to thrive.
Soaked nori (dried sushi seaweed) is a good alternative.
■ **Compatibility** Reef safe. Aggressive toward conspecifics and re-
lated species. Keep singly.

This is a great reef aquarium fish, colorful and active, for large tanks.

Vertebrata; Actinopterygii; Perciformes; Siganidae
Virgate Rabbitfish   *Siganus virgatus*
30 cm (11.7 in.)   Indo-Pacific

■ **Feeding** Mostly herbivorous. Accepts a variety of substitute foods
in the aquarium, but live and dried or frozen algae is essential.
■ **Compatibility** Reef safe and fairly peaceful toward most fishes.
Aggressive toward conspecifics and closely related species. Best
kept singly.
■ **Hazards** All rabbitfishes have venomous fin spines. Stings can
be painful—sometimes with serious side effects. Handle with care.

Very hardy and a constant algae grazer for the reef aquarium.

Vertebrata; Actinopterygii; Perciformes; Siganidae
Magnificent Rabbitfish   *Lo magnificus*
23 cm (9 in.)   Thailand

■ **Feeding** Mostly herbivorous. Accepts a variety of substitute foods in the aquarium, but live and dried or frozen algae is essential.
■ **Compatibility** Reef safe and fairly peaceful toward most fishes. Aggressive toward conspecifics and closely related species.
■ **Hazards** All rabbitfishes have venomous fin spines. Stings can be painful—sometimes with serious side effects. Handle with care.

A beautiful and durable algae grazer for reef aquariums. (Some authors lump the genus *Lo* with *Siganus*.)

Vertebrata; Actinopterygii; Perciformes; Siganidae
Foxface Rabbitfish   *Lo vulpinus*
25 cm (9.8 in.)   Western Pacific

■ **Feeding** Mostly herbivorous. Accepts a variety of substitute foods in the aquarium, but live and dried or frozen algae is essential.
■ **Compatibility** Reef safe and fairly peaceful toward most fishes. Aggressive toward conspecifics and closely related species.
■ **Hazards** All rabbitfishes have venomous fin spines. Stings can be painful—sometimes with serious side effects. Handle with care.

A great beginner's fish—colorful, hardy, and an active algae grazer that makes a good community member.

Vertebrata; Actinopterygii; Perciformes; Zanclidae
Moorish Idol   *Zanclus cornutus*
22 cm (8.9 in.)   Indo-Pacific
■ **Aquascaping** Well-established live rock is essential to supply some of the desired live food organisms this species grazes upon.
■ **Feeding** Most specimens are very reluctant to feed in captivity. Its natural diet may include sponges, bryozoans, hydroids, polychaete worms, and algae—at least for some populations.
■ **Compatibility** May nip at corals and other sessile invertebrates.
■ **Conservation** The vast majority of imported specimens starve.

A marine icon, but extremely difficult to keep in most cases. For experienced aquarists only.

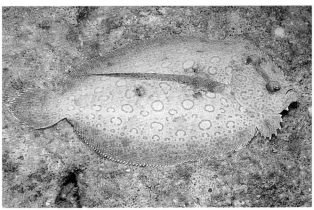

Vertebrata; Actinopterygii; Pleuronectiformes; Bothidae
Peacock Flounder   *Bothus lunatus*
46 cm (17.9 in)   Caribbean

■ **Aquascaping** Requires ample areas of open sandy bottom.
■ **Feeding** Carnivorous. Offer a variety of meaty foods.
■ **Compatibility** Reef safe with corals, but a threat to fishes and crustaceans small enough for it to attack and swallow.

Flounders are ambush predators and not the easiest fishes to keep in a typical reef aquarium. A large, sand-bottom biotope would be an appropriate setting. *B. mancus* is the Indo-Pacific Peacock Flounder.

Vertebrata; Actinopterygii; Tetraodontiformes; Balistidae
Clown Triggerfish *Balistoides conspicillum*
50 cm (19.5 in.) Indo-Pacific

■ **Feeding** Carnivorous. Small juveniles are difficult to adapt to aquarium foods. Subadults and adults readily accept all meaty foods.
■ **Compatibility** Not safe with invertebrates; fishes also at risk.
■ **Hazards** Unpredictable biter; may seriously damage aquarists' fingers, heaters, and electrical wires.

A magnificent-looking fish for very large aquariums with large, robust tankmates. It often develops a nasty, dangerous disposition, even though it may be initially peaceful.

Vertebrata; Actinopterygii; Tetraodontiformes; Balistidae
Undulate Triggerfish *Balistapus undulatus*
30 cm (11.7 in.) Indo-Pacific

■ **Feeding** Carnivorous. Readily accepts most meaty foods.
■ **Compatibility** Not safe with invertebrates; fishes also at risk.
■ **Hazards** Unpredictable biter; may seriously damage aquarists' fingers, heaters, and electrical wires.

A very handsome species with a notorious reputation for attacking and killing its tankmates. Should only be kept in very large fish-only aquariums with other big, robust species—better yet in an aquarium of its own.

Vertebrata; Actinopterygii; Tetraodontiformes; Balistidae
Niger Triggerfish *Odonus niger*
40 cm (15.6 in.) Indo-Pacific

■ **Feeding** Carnivorous; accepts most meaty foods.
■ **Compatibility** Harmless with corals, but sponges and free-living invertebrates are at risk. Several specimens may be kept together if approximately the same size and introduced simultaneously.
■ **Hazards** May inflict nasty bites on aquarists' fingers.

This is a triggerfish with relatively mild manners, suitable for sizable reef tanks. It does, however, eventually attain a size requiring a large aquarium and companions large enough to avoid being eaten.

Vertebrata; Actinopterygii; Tetraodontiformes; Balistidae
Sargassum Triggerfish *Xanthichthys ringens*
25 cm (9.8 in.) Tropical Western Atlantic

■ **Feeding** Omnivorous; readily accepts most meaty foods, but also eats live and dried algae (*Sargassum*).
■ **Compatibility** Harmless to corals, but shrimps and some free-living invertebrates are likely to be eaten. Usually not aggressive toward other fishes. Unlike most triggerfishes, this species can be kept in groups.

This is a fairly peaceful triggerfish, hardy, and a possible candidate for the reef aquarium.

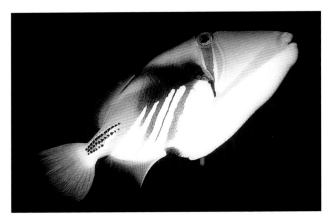

Vertebrata; Actinopterygii; Tetraodontiformes; Balistidae
Picasso Triggerfish   *Rhinecanthus aculeatus*
25 cm (9.8 in.)   Indo-Pacific

■ **Feeding** Carnivorous; readily accepts most meaty foods.
■ **Compatibility** Not safe with most invertebrates and smaller fishes. May be kept in groups if introduced simultaneously.
■ **Hazards** May inflict painful bites on aquarists' fingers, and is likely to damage heaters and electrical wires.

One of several flamboyantly colored triggerfishes, but a species that should be kept in a fish-only aquarium with other large, robust species.

Vertebrata; Actinopterygii; Tetraodontiformes; Balistidae
Queen Triggerfish   *Balistes vetula*
55 cm (21 in.)   Tropical Atlantic

■ **Feeding** Carnivorous; readily accepts most meaty foods.
■ **Compatibility** Not safe with invertebrates; fishes also at risk. Becomes more aggressive as it matures.
■ **Hazards** A notorious biter; may seriously damage aquarists' fingers, heaters, and electrical wires.

This is an impressive fish with beauty and a formidable personality. It is appropriate only for large fish-only aquariums with other big, robust species—or a tank of its own.

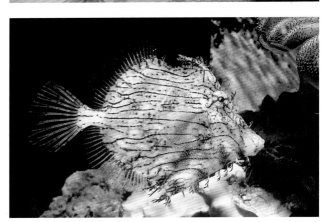

Vertebrata; Actinopterygii; Tetraodontiformes; Monacanthidae
Tasseled Filefish   *Chaetodermis penicilligera*
30 cm (11.7 in.)   Indo-Pacific

■ **Feeding** Omnivorous; eats algae and most meaty foods.
■ **Compatibility** Except for the most noxious and strong stinging anemones and soft corals, corals should not be considered safe with this fish. Will not bother other fishes, but may be harassed by active and aggressive species.

A fascinating, curious-looking species that is a valuable addition to special aquariums, but not safe in most reef tanks. Grows very quickly.

Vertebrata; Actinopterygii; Tetraodontiformes; Monacanthidae
Longnose Filefish   *Oxymonacanthus longirostris*
12 cm (4.7 in.)   Indo-Pacific

■ **Aquascaping** Requires a large aquarium filled with live *Acropora* spp. corals that can withstand constant polyp harvesting.
■ **Feeding** Eats only *Acropora* polyps in the wild. Rarely accepts substitute foods, and is likely to starve shortly after being imported.
■ **Compatibility** Not reef safe. Does best in small groups.
■ **Conservation** Must generally be considered impossible to keep without its natural food source.

An alluring fish, but extremely difficult to keep. For experts only.

Vertebrata; Actinopterygii; Tetraodontiformes; Ostraciidae
Longhorn Cowfish   *Lactoria cornuta*
45 cm (17.6 in.)   Indo-Pacific

■ **Feeding** Carnivorous. Accepts a variety of meaty foods.
■ **Compatibility** Not reef safe. Should not be kept with aggressive
fishes. May release the potent poison ostracitoxin if the animal is
injured, stressed, or dying. The toxin is particularly lethal to fishes.

Although very cute at the small size when it is usually purchased, this
is a problematic fish suitable only for special aquariums.

Vertebrata; Actinopterygii; Tetraodontiformes; Ostraciidae
Spotted Boxfish   *Ostracion meleagris*
16 cm (6.2 in.)   Indo-Pacific

■ **Feeding** In the wild, it feeds on various invertebrates (poly-
chaetes, mollusks, crustaceans, sponges). Difficult to adapt to
substitute foods. Often starves in the aquarium.
■ **Compatibility** Not safe with any invertebrates. Must not be kept
with aggressive fishes. Likely to release a deadly (to fishes) toxin if
the animal is injured, stressed, or dying.

A most appealing fish, but very hard to keep and a toxic time bomb,
only suitable for special aquariums. Males are blue, females brown.

Vertebrata; Actinopterygii; Tetraodontiformes; Tetraodontidae
Golden Puffer   *Arothron meleagris*
50 cm (19.5 in.)   Indo-Pacific, Eastern Pacific

■ **Feeding** Omnivorous; eats various invertebrates, including corals
and algae. Offer a variety of meaty and algae-based foods.
■ **Compatibility** Not safe with invertebrates.

This is a huge, greedy fish that demands plenty of food and a very large
aquarium with efficient filtration. Several color forms are known, including the popular yellow morph shown. A brownish, whitespotted
morph is often sold as the Guinea Fowl Puffer.

Vertebrata; Actinopterygii; Tetraodontiformes; Tetraodontidae
Saddled Toby   *Canthigaster valentini*
10 cm (3.9 in.)   Indo-Pacific

■ **Feeding** Omnivorous; accepts a variety of meaty and algae-based
foods. Should be fed several times daily.
■ **Compatibility** Not safe with invertebrates. Generally safe with
large fishes, but may nip fins. Keep singly or in male-female pairs.

This and other tobies, or sharpnose puffers, are interesting little fishes
with an innocuous appearance, but they are predators on many invertebrates and are likely to nip the fins of other fishes. Recommended for fish-only systems with larger tankmates, or a species tank.

CHAPTER 7

REEF ALGAE

The Healthiest Reefs Have Algae. So Will Your Reef Aquarium.
Why Not Make it Beautiful?

LGAE ARE NOT NEARLY AS CONSPICU-OUS in coral reef ecosystems as they are in the large seaweed and kelp beds of more northerly waters. Nor are the huge blossomings of planktonic algae regular seasonal events as they are in colder ocean areas. The fact that algae do not dominate and grow rampantly over the aquascape is testament to the stability of the coral reef environment and the lack of dissolved nutrients in the water.

Still the importance of algae in the ecology of the tropical coral reef has long been grossly underestimated. When we actually look for them, algae are easily found almost everywhere on the reef. The popular image of the coral reef as some sort of "plantless community" is simply a myth. Coral reefs could not exist without a very large algae component acting as primary producers car-

A luxuriant growth of *Halimeda* calcareous algae, **left**, makes a striking display in a reef aquarium. **Above**, encrusting purple calcareous algae attractively spreads over a piece of reef rock.

rying out the vital reaction of photosynthesis. Some scientists have even argued that the term "algal reef" is more appropriate than "coral reef."

INCONSPICUOUS BUT VITAL

THE MOST TYPICAL AND ABUNDANT FORM of algae growth on a reef is the short, turflike cover found at the bases of corals, on dead coral branches and boulders, and on hard rubble. There are many different species and genera of algae that grow together to form this interwoven bed of algae, appropriately named **turf algae**, or periphytonic overgrowth. Here, representatives of all the major taxonomic groups are found, such as diatoms, flagellates, brown algae, red algae, and green algae. Turf algae are short and inconspicuous because they are constantly grazed on by a multitude of herbivorous animals. This is in itself proof of the enormous importance of the algae. They grow at a tremendous pace, but there are so many animals fully dependent on this turf for nutrition that it never gets a chance to grow luxuriantly or

Marine aquarium "gardening" is growing in popularity as reef aquarists discover the beauty and vibrant colors of marine plants, such as this red cluster of *Halymenia* sp. macroalgae. Forming a green backdrop is a growth of *Caulerpa* sp. algae that thrives in many systems.

to dominate an area. The algae-eating animals maintain a vital regulating function by continuously grazing on the algae—never eliminating it, but preventing it from taking over.

TYPES OF ALGAE

GREEN CALCAREOUS ALGAE of the genus *Halimeda* and various other macroalgae, e.g., *Ulva*, *Cladophora*, and *Hypnea*, are among the larger and more conspicuous algae groups and are also essential for the total productivity of the coral reef. The green calcareous algae species of the genus *Halimeda* are especially important, as their hardened skeletons are an important component of coral sand.

In smaller patches, one may also find large populations of **fleshy algae**, such as the brown algae *Sargassum* spp. and *Lobophora* spp., as well as the various types of *Caulerpa* spp. green algae. The encrusting and leaf shaped red **coralline algae** of the Family Corallinaceae cover large areas of the rocky substrates of coral reefs. They are also common and much appreciated in reef aquariums, where they are introduced with live rock. The actual contribution of these calcium-binding algae in the total production of the reef still remains to be determined, but they play a most important part in the reef-building process.

In some locations, often near the geographical distribution limits of coral reefs, fleshy leaflike algae as well as encrusting coralline algae dominate completely over corals. Here scattered corals grow among a diverse flora of macroalgae.

The unicellular **phytoplankton**, or planktonic algae, that drift over the reef, following the water flow, are traditionally believed to be scarce and account for only a very small part of the total production of the reef. New research has, however, shown that phytoplankton are ecologically more important than previously thought and can occur in high concentrations, at least seasonally. Phytoplankton are important as food for some specialized planktivorous invertebrates, e.g., certain soft corals.

On the other hand, another group of single-celled algae is of enormous importance for reef production: the dinoflagellates known as **zooxanthellae** live in the cells of many invertebrate animals, including the majority of coral species. These symbiotic algae partners are directly responsible for the success of corals in tropical waters, and account for both nutrient and oxygen production that is directly utilized by their host coral. One can safely say that without these tiny zooxanthellate algae, there would be no coral reefs as we know them today.

Even though the various types of algae are relatively inconspicuous in a healthy reef, they are responsible for the greater part of the production of nutrients and energy. It may actually be appropriate to compare their role with that of the trees of the rainforest. If the algae were to disappear altogether, corals, fishes, and a huge array of algae-eaters would starve. It is the continuous growth of algae that is so vital. The fact that they are almost immediately grazed down does not detract from the importance of their productivity. The grazing rapidly conveys the energy from the algae's growth into the nutrient chain, while at the same time preventing the algae from ousting other organisms on the reef.

ALGAE IN THE AQUARIUM

As ALGAE ARE SUCH AN IMPORTANT biological component of coral reefs, it is a bit strange that they are not usually seen to be vital to the biology of the coral reef aquarium as well. It would be fair to say that algae are often portrayed as the enemy in reef systems, but the reality its that various algae will always be a part of a reef aquarium. Indeed, they *must* be there if the system is alive and well.

Nutrients, which are added to the aquarium water in food and excrement from the animals, will never be completely removed by protein skimmers or other technical equipment. The biochemical processes of bacteria in the system break them down into simpler compounds, but a closed (not open to the sea) aquarium system will always tend toward nutrient accumulation. Algae will aid in rendering these nutrients harmless by recirculating them in the nutrient chain through photosynthesis. In order to achieve this, it is not sufficient that algae simply be present, but rather that there be significant growth of algae in the well-functioning aquarium.

We believe that a healthy, well-maintained coral reef aquarium will normally display an ample selection of

An eye-catching growth of encrusting calcareous algae has developed from a piece of live rock over time in a reef aquarium, where it flourishes in the calcium-rich conditions.

Two species of green *Codium*—a hardy genus that may sprout from live rock—sometimes appearing many months after the rock was purchased. *Codium* may require periodic hand harvesting.

A beautiful example of a Dutch planted reef that houses an outstanding display of fleshy macroalgae and soft corals. Such algae effectively scavenge dissolved nutrients from the water.

different algae, but none should be allowed to dominate to such an extent that it becomes a threat to other organisms. As on the reef, most algae should be found merely as a short matting of turf algae. However, red encrusting coralline algae may be allowed to spread over a wider area. The coralline red algae are highly decorative and will only rarely conflict with corals and other animals. Besides, they have a marvelous capability to displace less-desirable algae, including the notorious green filamentous forms, which tend to be an ongoing nightmare for some aquarists.

Larger macroalgae, such as *Caulerpa* spp., kelplike brown algae, and leaflike red algae, may—as in nature—be allowed to establish themselves in lesser areas of the aquarium, where they absorb nutrients, add to the natural look of the reefscape, and pose no threat to sessile invertebrates. The question then remains: how can reefkeepers control algae overgrowth and keep it from dominating their corals or even taking over the whole aquarium?

GRAZING HELPERS

A new aquarium will nearly always develop various blooms of algal growth as the system stabilizes. Patience is needed, but adding herbivorous snails, small hermit crabs, and perhaps an algae-grazing fish or two will also help.

■ ■ ■

ALGAE CONTROL

EXCESSIVE ALGAE GROWTH in an aquarium is an indication that something is wrong with the captive environment. You can manipulate the nutrient supply to the system to get more or less algae growth, but if the algae gets out of hand, it may take some time to regain control of the situation.

Like all plants, algae need nutrients, particularly nitrogen and phosphorous that are normally absorbed as nitrates and phosphates. Healthy coral reefs are generally poor in these nutrients, and unless you have a desire to grow a lot of algae, it is important to keep the aquarium water virtually free of nitrates and phosphates. If nutrient levels rise, algae are among the first life forms to take advantage of the abundance, and their growth can practically explode. Among the factors that most strongly influence nutrient levels are the efficiency of the filtration system, the quality of the source water (freshwater), the organic load from decorative material (live rock and/or a thick sand bed),

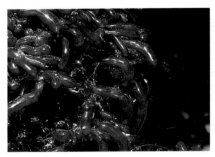

Water-filled *Valonia sp.* bubble algae is both a curiosity and a potential nuisance.

Green filamentous algae may plague a system with high nutrient levels.

Green cyanophyta (blue-green algae) can completely overgrow an aquascape.

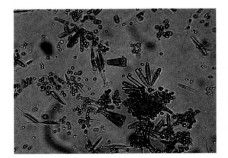

Magnified view of large diatoms and smaller flagellates from an aquarium wall.

Delicate *Dictyota* spp. brown algae can sometimes spread over live rock.

Round *Valonia* sp. bubbles and *Caulerpa nummularia* completely engulf a rock.

TABLE 7-1

COMMON ALGAE GRAZERS FOR THE MARINE AQUARIUM

COMMON NAME	SCIENTIFIC NAME	MAIN FOOD PREFERENCES
Striped Bristletooth	*Ctenochaetus striatus*	Diatoms and other microscopic algae; detritus.
Orangeshoulder Surgeonfish	*Acanthurus olivaceus*	Diatoms, detritus, short filamentous algae.
Orangespine Unicornfish	*Naso lituratus*	Kelplike brown algae such as *Sargassum* and *Dictyota*.
Powder Blue Surgeonfish	*Acanthurus leucosternon*	Filamentous algae and fleshy green algae.
Sailfin Tang	*Zebrasoma veliferum*	Filamentous algae and fleshy green algae.
Yellow Tang	*Zebrasoma flavescens*	Filamentous algae and fleshy green algae.
Foxface Rabbitfish	*Lo vulpinus*	Filamentous algae and fleshy green algae.
Bicolor Blenny	*Ecsenius bicolor*	Short filamentous algae.
Jeweled Blenny	*Salarias fasciatus*	Short filamentous algae.
Neritid snails	*Nerita* spp.	Very short filamentous algae as well as microscopic algae.
Astraea snails	*Astraea* spp.	Very short filamentous algae as well as microscopic algae.
Hermit crabs	*Calcinus* spp., *Clibanarius* spp., *Paguristes cadenati*, *Phimochirus operculatus*	Very short filamentous algae as well as microscopic algae.
Sea urchins	*Echinometra* spp., *Diadema* spp., *Echinothrix* spp., *Mespilia globulus*, *Tripneustes gratilla*	All kinds of short algae, including coralline red algae.

the animal population (which generates wastes), and the foods introduced by the aquarist.

Normally, biological filtration causes a long-term increase in the nutrient concentration in the aquarium water. Therefore, a biologically based filtration system, such as the once very popular Dutch mini-reef that uses a trickle-type or wet/dry filter, is particularly suitable if you want to specialize in growing macroalgae, but not especially good for maintaining a coral reef aquarium. Many algae, like the beautiful green *Caulerpa* spp., the red *Halymenia* spp., and the brown *Sargassum* spp., need eutrophic (nutrient-rich) conditions to grow in abundance.

Efficient protein skimming combined with live rock and vigorous water motion—what we prefer to call a semi-biological system—has turned out to be the best filtration setup for reef aquariums in which corals are more important than algae. (In some literature, this has been frequently, and a bit misleadingly, called the Berlin Method.)

It is also necessary to have a light source that gives the correct cold-temperature white or bluish light to which reef organisms are accustomed. According to common experience, a light source color temperature of 6,000 to 10,000 degrees Kelvin is generally optimal in

The beauty of marine algae is shown in the variety of green, brown, and red macroalgae growing on the shallow reef flat of Rarotonga in the South Pacific. This small patch includes several genera: red *Galaxaura*, brown *Turbinaria*, and green *Halimeda* and *Caulerpa*.

avoiding algae problems, while at the same time securing good growth conditions for corals. A very warm (yellowish) light (less than 6,000 degrees Kelvin) has a high percentage of red and/or yellow light rays, which are easily absorbed by the common color pigments in algae, and it can contribute to increased algae problems.

Low salinity has also, over and over again, proven to be a direct cause for an uncontrollable growth of filamentous algae. If you have an algae problem, check and double check the salinity, and be sure that it is within the range of 32-36 parts per thousand.

Other key factors include the number of animals and the intensity of feeding. If these are pushed beyond the limits of the system size and filtration capacity, problem algae will be seen. As systems age and young fishes grow into large, pollution-generating "show specimens," nutrient levels may rise. Increased protein skimming and more frequent water changes may be necessary.

Herbivores (algae eaters) are another answer, and too many aquarists underestimate their absolutely essential

role in the aquarium—despite the fact that the natural coral reef would soon be overgrown without them.

Too often, a single surgeonfish is purchased as a token algae eater, and the rest of the livestock budget goes toward other, more enticing animals. To avoid ending up with a hopelessly overgrown aquarium, we often need a number of different algae eaters that target different forms of algae. Some herbivores prefer to eat green algae; some choose brown algae or coralline algae, while still others specialize in scraping away the filmy diatoms and other microscopic algae species. Some algae eaters will devour large, fully grown algae, but the majority prefer young growth that is tender and readily digestible. Snails are experts at grazing the tiniest algae, which spread as a thin coating on rocks and aquarium surfaces.

Certain herbivores have algae as their predominant, or even exclusive, food item. Such species are capable of eating huge quantities of algae in a short time. On the other hand, several of the fish species we know as algae eaters, for example, will often eat other foods (dried or

Powder Blue Surgeonfish (*Acanthurus leucosternon*) in the Indian Ocean normally forage singly or in pairs, but sometimes form large feeding swarms to graze in the safety of a pack. Without such herbivorous fishes, wild reefs become overgrown with algae.

frozen rations) as well, if they are readily available.

To achieve adequate algae control in the aquarium, it is necessary to keep several different kinds of algae eaters, fishes, and invertebrates. It is also important to introduce enough total herbivores to keep pace with normal algae growth. Among the many animals that appear regularly in the trade, there are quite a few that primarily or secondarily eat algae (see Table 7-1, page 213).

Be sure that algae eaters are among the very first organisms that are introduced in a new aquarium, soon after the live rock. Together with detritus feeders, these herbivores are unquestionably the most important animals we need to establish and keep a successful reef aquarium.

PATIENCE — PATIENCE — PATIENCE

REMEMBER TO GIVE YOUR NEW AQUARIUM time to stabilize. Nearly all marine aquariums will have uncontrolled algal growth in the initial phases. Within the first few months after setup, the aquarist will nearly always observe considerable changes in the growth of algae. The normal succession of algae growth will start with brown diatoms and blue-green algae, which may grow considerably for a period of 20-25 days. Thereafter, filamentous algae, such as the green *Derbesia* and *Bryopsis* species, will take over and frequently dominate the tank for some months. At the same time as these begin to decline, more welcome algae, like coralline red algae, will start to spread. This is a natural course of events in the aquarium and no reason to panic.

The best response is to start adding herbivores, be sure that your skimmer is working, and check to be sure that you aren't polluting the tank with food or nutrient-contaminated source water. We suggest patience, rather than rearranging the aquascape, changing light, altering water flow, trying new maintenance routines, or instituting any other measures that only serve to prolong the break-in period. Chances are that the impatient aquarist who tries to hurry things along too much will end up with more nuisance algae rather than less.

CHAPTER 8

FOODS & FEEDING

*The Science and Learned Arts of Keeping
Your Aquarium Inhabitants Well Nourished*

ALL ORGANISMS NEED NUTRIENTS IN SOME form or another. The reef is actually one of the most interesting biotopes for observing this, as there are so many different ways in which reef organisms meet their energy needs. As interesting as the feeding process may be, it also provides the aquarist with certain tricky challenges. Unlike in the average goldfish pond, you cannot just throw some flake food into the reef aquarium every now and then and expect the animals to live happily and healthy forevermore.

Coral reefs are generally regarded as ecosystems with precious few available nutrients in the water column. Nevertheless, they contain a very high diversity and biomass of living organisms. How is it possible that these plants and animals can sustain themselves in such a com-

Rasping food from a rock, this surgeonfish needs a herbivorous diet to thrive in the aquarium. **Above,** a Coral Hind allows a cleaner wrasse to search for food between its teeth.

petitive and nutrient-poor system? We now know that nutrients are recycled very efficiently and that all forms of nutrients are absorbed or consumed as quickly as they become available. The nutrient situation in a reef aquarium is, however, very different from that in the wild.

The majority of animals available in the aquarium trade will give the reasonably experienced aquarist few difficulties with feeding and maintaining an adequate food supply. With some practice, most aquarists develop a routine and some intuitive feeling for how much food is needed, but beginners often find the whole subject of feeding somewhat intimidating.

Unless you know what you are doing, or you have an experienced advisor to call upon, the risk is that you will end up starving some animals to death. This is a result of feeding too little too infrequently—as well as buying animals that are not easy to keep nourished. Before buying any new fish or invertebrate, two essential questions must be asked and answered: 1) What does it eat? 2) Will I able to supply it with the foods it needs?

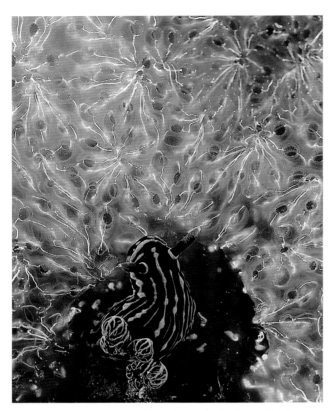

Mowing through a sponge, this nudibranch displays a highly specialized feeding habit that makes it a challenge to keep alive.

NUTRITION BASICS

ANIMALS EAT TO PROVIDE themselves with a steady supply of carbohydrates, proteins, fats, minerals, and vitamins that are used to build and maintain the body of the animal, plus supplying it with energy for its various life functions. The nutrients taken in are broken down in the organism's digestive system, transported to the cells, and converted into chemical energy in a process known as **cellular respiration** (see page 19). In this process, carbohydrates are acted on by enzymes to produce chemical energy (ATP); atmospheric oxygen (entering the body via lungs, gills, or diffusion directly through the tissue) combines with hydrogen to form water; and carbon dioxide is released as a waste product. Nutrients can roughly be divided into the following groups:

Carbohydrates: In general these are celluloses, starches, and sugars that are all products of photosynthesis. Cellulose is nearly impossible to utilize for most animals, but some can digest it through the help of certain bacteria that decompose these particular molecules. For other animals, cellulose may be of importance as a fiber source that helps in the digestion of other nutri-

ents. Starches and sugars are the most important energy sources for many animals. They are easily digested and rapidly broken down into simple molecules like water and carbon dioxide, so that the energy is available very shortly after eating the carbohydrate.

Proteins: Proteins are complex nitrogenous substances composed mainly of amino acids. Many different proteins are extremely important for the building of animal cells. Most animals are able to synthesize several amino acids directly, but some amino acids—known as essentials—must be supplied through food. These essential amino acids vary somewhat for different animal species, but the lack of the right amino acids can have severely negative effects on any organism.

For most aquarium animals, proteins originating from shrimps, mussels, and marine fishes will generally provide most essential amino acids, while proteins from mammals or plants are of relatively little use. Any surplus of proteins may be used by the organism as an energy source or can be stored in the form of fat.

Fats: This is a very important group of naturally occurring nutrients. They are an essential component of most animal diets, and are needed for energy and to maintain the health of body tissues. Chemically, fats are glycerides of fatty acids (the composition of the different acids is responsible for the properties of individual fats). Fat from mammals contains saturated fatty acids, which are virtually indigestible for aquarium animals, while fats from plants and marine fats (from fish, for example) are unsaturated and more readily digestible. Fatty acids are extremely important nutrients for most marine animals, particularly those in critical growth stages, such the tiny fry of fishes. Additionally, the essential vitamins A, D, E, and K are soluble in fat only.

Minerals: Seawater contains an almost endless supply of dissolved minerals as macroelements and trace elements (see page 28). Many of the mineral requirements of aquarium animals can thus be absorbed directly from the surrounding water. However, it is not known to what extent additional mineral uptake via food is of importance to various animals. What we do know, however, is that the average mineral content in most available food sources of marine origin is very high and varied, and presumably sufficient for most organisms.

Vitamins: Even though most organisms take up only minute traces of most vitamins, it has been proven beyond doubt that these organic compounds are required for good health. They must be present in the food, and deficiency syndromes will be seen if they are lacking. Such problems are curable only by administering the appropriate vitamin. Partial vitamin deficiencies may cause minor ill effects or less-well-defined health problems. Aquarium animals may take up the water-soluble vitamins (B and C) directly from the aquarium water, while the fat-soluble vitamins must come from food.

WHAT DO ORGANISMS EAT?

A TYPICAL REEF AQUARIUM is filled with different organisms displaying wildly differing approaches to staying well-nourished. Some animals, including most fishes and many crustaceans, actively search for food, while others, including most sessile or sedentary animals, are much more passive and able to gather only nutrients that are brought to them by the water currents. In this chapter we describe some selected feeding requirements, but details on specialized feeding demands for particular organisms can be found in the Stocking Guide (pages 98-207). Also see Table 8-1 on the following page.

Many fishes have obvious food requirements that are easily satisfied. For example, the majority of surgeonfishes are algae eaters and quite helpful in maintaining a successful aquarium. The Yellow Tang (*Zebrasoma flavescens*) is a commonly kept herbivore, and as long as algae are available, the feeding of this species should not be a problem. As with many surgeonfishes, it will also greedily take frozen and dried foods as well. This species is typical of many other marine aquarium fishes that are practically omnivorous and eat nearly everything that comes their way, be it zooplankton or dry foods.

Other fishes can be very difficult to feed. Specialized plankton feeders, such as the fairy basslets of the genus *Pseudanthias*, seem to have fast metabolisms and will not thrive without a frequent supply of plankton or a good plankton substitute throughout the day. In our own experience, the automatic, near-continuous addition of a live plankton substitute such as brine shrimp (*Artemia*) is the only reliable way to feed many of these delicate fishes. Without this sort of intensive feeding plan, these beautiful but constantly hungry fishes will usually starve to death.

Hand feeding a seahorse is not required, but these animals do need high quality live or frozen food, such as *Mysis* shrimp.

> ## SPACED MEALS
>
> Most marine fishes will benefit from several small feedings per day, rather than one large meal. Automatic feeders can be useful for feeding species that require frequent offerings.
>
> ■ ■ ■

Mandarinfishes (*Synchiropus* spp.) were long considered very difficult to keep. We now understand that this stems from their specialized feeding requirements. For one thing, mandarinfishes are very slow feeders. It seems they always need to have a second look or thought before deciding on whether or not to eat a certain piece of food. Often, they will not be interested in food that does not move. Thus it was previously difficult to find suitable foods for them. Today, in an aquarium with well-established live rock and coarse sand or coral rubble, there is a continuous supply of many different small invertebrates that make excellent foods for mandarinfishes.

Some other fishes need the same sorts of live food that is bred in the reef aquarium itself. The small benthic pipefishes of the genus *Corythoichthys*, for instance, also depend on being able to pick tiny invertebrates from live rock. If you want to keep such fishes, you must remember not to keep more specimens than the tank can support. (Always

TABLE 8-1

AQUARIUM ORGANISMS with PARTICULAR FOOD PREFERENCES

GROUP	COMMON NAME	SCIENTIFIC NAME	FOOD PREFERENCES
FISHES	Fairy basslets	*Pseudanthias* spp.	Zooplankton in continuous supply. Will, however, normally accept substitutes.
	Longnose Filefish	*Oxymonacanthus longirostris*	Polyps of small-polyped stony corals, preferentially *Acropora* spp. Substitutes are only very rarely accepted.
	Mandarinfishes	*Synchiropus* spp.	Tiny live organisms from live rock.
	Multibarred Angelfish	*Centropyge multifasciatus*	Unknown, but probably selective on small invertebrates and therefore very difficult to keep.
	Orangespine Unicornfish	*Naso lituratus*	Brown algae
	Pipefishes	Many species in Family Syngnathidae	Tiny live organisms from live rock.
CNIDARIA	Strawberry corals	*Dendronephthya* spp.	Phytoplankton
CRUSTACEA	Boxing Shrimp	*Hymenocera picta*	Sea stars
ECHINODERMATA	Feather stars	Order Crinoidea	Need an almost continuous flow of minute live plankton.

avoid stocking too many competing fishes that target this same limited resource.)

Feeding fishes is one problem, but what about feeding invertebrates? As explained earlier, many corals, giant clams, and related organisms receive a large portion of the nutrients they need from their symbiotic algae, or zooxanthellae. As long as these animals are placed under sufficient and appropriate lighting, no intentional feeding is necessary for many of the common species.

There are, however, cnidarians—like the nonphotosynthetic gorgonians—that lack symbiotic algae and are therefore totally dependent upon feeding. Suitable foods can include live and frozen plankton or various plankton substitutes. For many nonphotosynthetic corals, it is often difficult to find a food that is sufficient to keep them alive. This is particularly true for the colorful soft corals of the genus *Dendronephthya*, frequently named strawberry corals, which seem to be heavily dependent on phytoplankton (suspended microalgae) for food. Cultured phytoplankton is now commercially available, and expert aquarists may yet find ways to satisfy the nutrition needs of these very appealing corals.

Turning to mollusks, most snails that are kept in aquariums are more or less obligate algae grazers and need no special feeding. On the other hand, the naked snails (nudibranchs) are, for the most part, almost impossible to feed. The majority of these beauties are highly specialized, depending on such hard-to-get foods as live sponges, bryozoans, colonial anemones (zoanthids), or corals. The very similar-looking sea slugs (Saccoglossa) are mainly specialized obligate algae eaters. Often, a given species will eat only one or a few species of algae.

Feeding time in the magnificent 15,000 L (3,900 gal.) reef aquarium of Klaus Jansen. A huge, well-established system such as this offers its own sources of live foods—algae, microfauna, and even hatches of zooplankton—but frequent feeding is also required by the owner.

Inexperienced aquarists attracted to these often colorful mollusks will undoubtedly regret their purchase as it almost always results in the untimely death of the animal.

FEEDING IN THE AQUARIUM

ONE WAY OF COPING with so many different feeding strategies in the aquarium is to divide the animals into main groups such as herbivores, carnivores, and omnivores—for those that, respectively, eat plants, animals, or "everything." (In practice, however, nothing is so simple as in even the best theories.)

Few species are absolute in their preferences, and even though they may prefer one food item, or group of food items, it is common for many animals to accept or even seek out other foods. In nature, animals often switch food sources depending on availability. The animals we keep in our tanks are often offered foods very different from those they were used to eating in nature, but a remarkably high percentage adapt to these alternate foods.

Many types and brands of marine aquarium foods are available in the market today, and most of them have reasonably high nutrient quality. There are very good dry foods (in the forms of flakes, grains, or pellets), and protein-rich freeze-dried organisms (such as krill, various zooplankton, or shrimps) also make excellent foods. A huge array of frozen marine foods are offered in better aquarium shops, with choices ranging from mixed rations to specific food items, such as *Mysis* shrimp, krill in various sizes, plankton, and even marine sponges. Cultures of live plankton, such as *Artemia* or rotifers, are available in various sizes. And aquarists living close to the sea have the opportunity to collect their own live marine plankton. Anyone who has seen an aquarium regularly fed with live marine plankton will know what vivid colors and natural behaviors, including reproductive displays, high-quality live foods can bring out.

We believe the best policy is to vary the diet you offer your fishes and to observe their reactions. But take care not to overfeed: too much food will cause nutrients to accumulate, often resulting in an increased growth of filamentous algae. Smaller amounts, fed more often, is always a sound approach.

CHAPTER 9

FRIENDS
OF THE REEF

Animal Welfare, Reef Conservation, and the Informed Marine Aquarist

WE ARE ENTHUSIASTIC AQUARISTS. We do everything within our powers to keep our marine animals in good condition. We think of the aquarium hobby as a sound and worthwhile pursuit, educational not only for us but for the many people who visit and view our reef systems. Unfortunately, not everyone shares our view. In recent years, various groups have called for an end to the marine aquarium hobby, asking for a ban on the collection and sale or purchase of reef organisms, including fishes, corals, and live rock.

Much of the criticism is focused on environmental issues, while arguments about animal welfare sometimes are heard. Although many of the criticisms aimed at the aquarium trade turn out to be triggered by a lack of facts, they gain attention because many coral reefs are in trou-

Captivated by a public display at the Dallas World Aquarium, children get a firsthand view of the coral realm. **Above**, coral bleaching, a worldwide threat to the future of reef ecosystems.

ble throughout the Tropics. Reefs are disappearing because of pollution, mining, erosion from the cutting of rainforests, shoreline development, overexploitation, and destructive fishing practices. Most worrisome, massive coral bleaching events, in which extremely warm water conditions cause corals to lose their zooxanthellae and die, have occurred from the west coast of Africa through the Indian Ocean, in various places in the Pacific, and in the Caribbean Sea. Many scientists now fear that global warming is becoming a threat to the very future of coral reefs. Foes of marine aquariums have argued that collection for this trade is just another unnecessary pressure on reefs that are already in trouble.

To the contrary, we believe that the aquarium hobby is emerging as an important force for the good of coral reefs. However, we must also admit that the trade and hobby is not without fault. Some serious abuses have occurred in the past and are still taking place in some regions. Things could surely be better. We must acknowledge that reefkeeping, like most human activities,

Newly caught reef fishes being sorted at a trading facility in the Philippines, an important source of marine fishes and invertebrates. Efforts are underway to teach local fishermen net fishing and proper handling of livestock to ensure maximum survivability of livestock.

has its share of negative impacts. Still, we believe that the benefits far outweigh the costs, and the responsible aquarist can play a role in minimizing the problems.

A HOBBY & A LIVELIHOOD

AQUARIUM KEEPING is the spare-time pursuit of millions of people worldwide, many of them passionate about a hobby that goes back many, many centuries. At the same time, for several hundred thousand individuals, the aquarium trade is a livelihood—a way to make a living by catching, farming, or trading aquarium organisms.

The aquatic trade is particularly important as a source of income in many Third World countries, where whole local communities can be dependent on the capture or aquaculture of ornamental fishes and invertebrates. In the Philippines alone, there are an estimated 7,000 aquarium fish collectors, many of them supporting large families. According to a UNESCO report, the number of people in Sri Lanka directly involved in the export of reef animals is an overwhelming 50,000.

The FAO (Food and Agriculture Organization of the United Nations) reported that the export value of ornamental fishes and invertebrates in 1996 was more than US $200 million. In excess of 60 percent of that money, some US $130 million, went directly into the economies of developing countries.

Ornamental fish trade experts at the FAO and other international organizations, such as the International Center for Living Aquatic Resources Management (ICLARM), point out that by increasing income and curbing environmental degradation, the aquarium industry contributes significantly to local food security. Marine aquarium organisms are, in fact, one of the most lucrative "value-added products" that can be harvested sustainably from coral reefs. That is, they bring a higher economic return than most other reef activities.

For example, in 1994, the Maldives exported less than 250 kg of ornamental fishes to the United Kingdom and received, in terms of net weight of fish, more than US $496,000 per ton. In contrast, food fish harvested from the wild in the Seychelles was exported at a value of just US $6,000 per ton. In a report published by UNEP's World Conservation Monitoring Center, live coral in the aquarium trade is estimated to be worth about US $7,000 per ton, while the use of harvested coral for lime production yields only about US $60 per ton.

Nevertheless, the aquarium hobby and trade occasionally receive bad press from environmental groups as well as animal welfare activists. Some of the issues that are raised should be—and are—of concern to those of us who care about the future of reefs and reefkeeping.

Such is the case with the continuing battle against **cyanide fishing**. Even after more than two decades of efforts to stop the practice, cyanide is still used in parts of the world to stun fishes for easy capture. It is done on a large scale with food fishes, and it is done with ornamentals for sale to marine aquarium hobbyists. Not only do a large percentage of the fishes caught this way end up dying prematurely—often soon after they are purchased—the reef corals sprayed with cyanide are seriously damaged or killed.

Even though one safely can say that most marine fishes captured in the wild today are harvested using hand-held nets that do little or no harm to the reefs, cyanide fishing continues to be an unfortunate stain on the aquarium trade. It is bad for nature, it is bad for the consumer, and it is bad for the whole aquarium hobby.

Similarly, there have been some reports of local overharvesting of prized fishes and popular corals in certain collection areas. At various times, the aquarium trade has been accused of overcollecting Queen Angels in the Caribbean, Yellow Tangs around Hawaii, and of severely reducing some local populations of Clown Triggerfishes and Elegance Corals—as a few examples—in areas of the Pacific.

DOING BETTER

FORTUNATELY, SOME INTERESTING constellations have been forming in recent years between trade and conservation groups that are now working in a common effort to preserve reefs by establishing collection and production for the aquarium trade as a sustainable activity for Third World peoples.

One of the most promising developments was the formation, in 1998, of the Marine Aquarium Council (MAC). The Council began as an ambitious initiative by a cross section of organizations representing marine

Local fishing village on Santiago Island, Philippines, where sustainable harvests from the reef are vital to the native population—and an increasing concern of environmentalists.

Feather stars (*Himerometra robustipinna*) await shipping from a holding facility. Collectors need to be educated to avoid animals, such as these, that almost never survive in captivity.

Giant clams (*Tridacna* spp.), farmed in the Solomon Islands, are an example of successful aquaculture that is supplying the aquarium trade and providing income to Third World villages.

hobbyists, the aquarium industry, conservation groups, international organizations, government agencies, public aquariums, and scientists.

MAC is now established as an independent institution whose goal is to transform the marine aquarium industry into one that is based on quality and sustainability. MAC is working to make this happen by developing standards for quality products and sustainable practices; establishing a system to certify compliance with these standards and to label the results; and creating consumer demand for certification and labeling.

Simply put, MAC is going to track marine livestock from the reef to the home aquarium, through the entire chain of custody—including collectors, brokers, exporters, importers, distributors, and local fish stores. Live fishes and other organisms that are collected properly and sustainably (no cyanide, no overharvesting) and shipped according to high standards, will be sold as "MAC Certified."

The Council believes that this will create consumer demand for quality and sustainability in the collection, culture, and commerce of marine ornamentals. Research has shown that fishes caught, handled, and shipped properly show much lower mortality and arrive in the consumer's tanks in a much healthier state.

MAC will develop into a largely self-financed system based on improved economic return for the collectors from certified marine aquarium organisms, from industry willingness to pay for certification—and, most important, from the hobbyist's willingness to pay for marine ornamentals of verifiable quality that are more robust and longer-lived. (Read more on MAC's website: www.aquariumcouncil.org.)

MARINE AQUACULTURE

AT THE SAME TIME, the captive propagation of fishes, corals, and other invertebrates is growing rapidly. Many animals, such as giant clams (*Tridacna* spp.), that were nearly wiped out in many reef areas by overcollection for the Asian restaurant trade, are now being propagated by many tropical island nations.

> ## BEST CHOICES
>
> More reef animals will gradually become available with certification, assuring that they have been harvested and handled in a sustainable fashion. Such livestock is of superior quality and helps provide a livelihood for rural communities in the Third World.
>
> ■ ■ ■

Brownish and dull-colored clams are destined to be eaten—locally or in distant gourmet restaurants—but breeders are also actively selecting for the bright colors and patterns desired by aquarists. Captive-bred animals are now normally more beautiful, and thus in more demand, than most wild-collected clams.

Coral farms that produce small, started colonies of numerous species are also appearing in many places in the world. Some of these farms are even involved in projects to restock reefs that have been damaged by bleaching events and other natural or manmade disasters. Even live rock, our favorite and indispensable decoration material, is being "farmed" more and more often.

An increasing number of fish species are becoming available as "captive-bred" or "tank-raised," and the elusive knowledge needed to accomplish this successfully is starting to accumulate after decades of work by struggling researchers.

While the majority of animals that enter the aquarium trade—and hobbyists' tanks—still are wild-caught, this is changing. From several perspectives, this is definitely an advantage: captive breeding can lead to animal stocks that are better adapted to life in a captive environment, it can produce animals with more desirable qualities in terms of shape and coloration, and it can defuse some of the criticism that aquarists are contributing to the destruction of wild reefs.

On the other hand, unlike net fishing or hand-collection from the wild, farming of marine organisms creates fewer local jobs and demands higher financial investments. So far, most of the commercial captive breeding facilities are either geographically situated in rich countries close to the consumer markets, or are financed from such countries.

Will captive propagation hurt the livelihoods of local people in the countries that have reefs? Do we risk the possibility that they will lose an important income source from sustainable use of reef resources, and that they might turn to less fortunate ways of exploiting their reefs?

Without sustainable uses of coral reefs—such as the responsible collection of aquarium organisms—reefs are almost certain to be more vulnerable to more destruc-

TABLE 9-1

SPECIES of CONCERN: CONSERVATION & ANIMAL WELFARE

NOTE: This table lists selected animals whose capture, trade, and/or keeping in aquariums raises particular animal welfare or conservation issues. It includes only those groups that, to the authors' knowledge, appear with some regularity in the aquarium trade. All keepers of reef animals have a responsibility to know the basic needs of any species kept and to provide the best possible care.

TAXONOMIC GROUP	PROBLEM	RECOMMENDATION
FISHES		
Most sharks and rays, Elasmobranchii	With a limited number of exceptions, most of these animals are far too active and/or grow far too large to be suitable for a home aquarium.	Study the characteristics and needs of the species in question, and plan carefully before buying any shark or ray.
Seahorses, *Hippocampus* spp.	Considerable concern has been raised about the fate of seahorses worldwide. As a group they appear to be very vulnerable, and in many areas are threatened by extinction due to habitat destruction and overexploitation for several purposes. Seahorses are delicate, hard-to-keep aquarium animals with particularly challenging nutritional needs. Far too many captive seahorses ultimately starve to death because of aquarists' inexperience and lack of knowledge.	Although we do not believe that the trade in seahorses for the aquarium hobby is of significant proportions, there is reason to believe that collection can add to the problem in certain areas. Do not buy a seahorse unless you are certain that you have the qualifications to keep it successfully. Look for captive-bred specimens.
Butterflyfishes, *Chaetodon* spp.	Most butterflyfishes are spectacular, exquisitely beautiful animals. Unfortunately, although there are some very valuable aquarium species among them, the majority are extremely difficult to keep, mainly because of highly specialized food requirements. Many are obligate coral feeders that never will learn to accept anything but live coral polyps. Because the appropriate food is difficult to provide, many starve to death in aquariums.	Do not buy any butterflyfish without first studying the requirements of the species to make sure that you can provide the necessary food.The following species are so difficult to keep that they probably should not be offered in regular trade: *austriacus, baronessa, bennetti, capistratus, guentheri, guttatissimus, larvatus, lunulatus, rainfordi, meyeri, octofasciatus, ornatissimus, plebeius, speculum, triangulum, trifascialis, trifasciatus.*
Multibarred Angelfish, *Paracentropyge multifasciata*	Although experiences with this species vary, it appears that the vast majority die shortly after importation, probably from malnutrition.	Do not buy this species unless you are an experienced aquarist and willing to put a great deal of effort into experimental husbandry techniques.
Moorish Idol, *Zanclus cornutus*	The spectacular beauty of this fish makes it sought after by far more aquarists than those who have the qualifications to keep it successfully. It is extremely difficult to feed, despite scattered reports of some specimens eating everything from algae to flake food. Most imported specimens starve to death.	Don't buy this species unless you are an experienced aquarist and willing to put a great deal of effort into experimental husbandry techniques.
Longnose Filefish, *Oxymonacanthus longirostris*	This is a true jewel of a fish, with exotic colors and an intriguing shape. Unfortunately, it is a very specialized feeder—in the wild it eats nothing but the polyps of *Acropora* corals. Although there are occasional reports of specimens eating substitute foods, and some aquarists succeed in keeping it with its natural food source, the vast majority of imported specimens starve to death shortly after importation.	Don't buy this species unless you are an experienced aquarist and willing to put a great deal of effort into experimental husbandry techniques.

(continued on next page)

TABLE 9-1

SPECIES of CONCERN: CONSERVATION & ANIMAL WELFARE (CONT.)

TAXONOMIC GROUP	PROBLEM	RECOMMENDATION
CNIDARIANS Nonphotosynthetic soft corals, e.g., *Dendronephthya*, *Chironephthya*, and *Scleronephthya*	These very colorful corals do not contain symbiotic algae. They require weak to moderate light and have no protection against UV-radiation. Very little is known about their feeding requirements or husbandry demands in general. Their glorious colors make them popular and fairly common in the trade, but they are extraordinarily difficult to keep. Most colonies collapse rapidly in an aquarium.	Sooner or later, we expect that the full secret for keeping these corals will be understood. Until this happens, only the most experienced and dedicated aquarists should attempt to keep them.
Most nonphotosynthetic gorgonians, e.g., members of the family Ellisellidae	These gorgonians do not contain symbiotic algae. They require weak to moderate light and have no protection against UV-radiation. For most species, very little is known about their feeding requirements or husbandry demands in general. Most colonies collapse rapidly in an aquarium.	Sooner or later, we expect that the full secret for keeping these corals will be understood. Until this happens, only the most experienced and dedicated aquarists should attempt to keep them.
MOLLUSKS Nudibranchs, Nudibranchia	Several colorful nudibranch snails, e.g., members of the genera *Chromodoris*, *Jorunna*, and *Phyllida*, are occasionally found in the trade. All are food specialists, primarily eating specific species of sponges only. The same is true for the large, bright red and white Spanish Dancer, *Hexabranchus sanguineus*. Without their exact food requirements, they are doomed.	Do not buy any nudibranchs unless you are absolutely sure that you will be able to provide sufficient amounts of the food necessary to their survival (in most cases this will be impossible).
Sea slugs, Cephalaspidea, Saccoglossa, Anaspidea, and Notaspidea	Most sea slugs are food specialists, often feeding on one specific group or species of algae. A few species (e.g., *Elysia crispata*, formerly *Tridachia crispata*) are reasonably hardy, but not one of them can be kept unless the right alga is growing in the aquarium. Sometimes carnivorous sea slugs (e.g., *Chelidonura* spp. and *Philinopsis* spp.), which prey selectively on other invertebrates, are imported. Without their natural prey, they will eventually starve to death in an aquarium.	Do not buy sea slugs unless you are absolutely sure that you will be able to provide unlimited amounts of the necessary food. For all but some herbivorous species, that will be very difficult or even impossible.
ECHINODERMS Feather stars, Crinoidea	Several species of feather stars are found in the trade, although irregularly. They are very delicate, fragile animals, and many are severely damaged during transport. Those that do survive to reach the home hobbyist usually die shortly thereafter. We have found no documented cases of feather stars surviving in aquariums for more than a period of months.	Feather stars should not be collected or bought by most amateur aquarists. The care of these animals is suited only to those aquarists who are willing to put a great deal of effort into experimental husbandry techniques.

tive uses. This can take the form of destructive fishing by outsiders who have no stake in the future of the local reefs, or it could be by desperate local fishers themselves.

SAYING "NO"

BEYOND SUPPORTING GLOBAL EFFORTS to build a sustainable aquarium trade, there are also immediate actions we can take on a more personal level:

It is a fact of marine aquarium keeping that certain species of reef animals are more delicate than others. Some are difficult to maintain without special feeding and care; others are close to impossible to keep alive for any length of time, even by the most advanced hobbyist. A perfect illustration is the Longnose Filefish (*Oxymonacanthus longirostris*), an impossibly beautiful fish that is an obligate corallivore—a species that must eat live coral polyps to survive. Although the occasional specimen will learn to accept substitute fare, the sad fact is that an estimated 98 or 99 percent of these fish starve to death in the aquarium.

We believe that few hobbyists would buy such a fish if they knew the animal (and their money) were about to be sacrificed. When you are aware—either from reading, discussions with other aquarists, or by personal trial and error—that a particular animal offered for sale is likely to succumb under the conditions you can offer, *please* do not buy it. There are so many other choices that it is utterly unnecessary to encourage the continued collection of these animals by paying to watch them die in your tank.

Certainly, the degree of difficulty of keeping marine animals is ever-changing. Less than two decades ago, stony corals of the genus *Acropora* were unanimously considered impossible to keep—even by professional aquarists and university-funded biologists. Today we hold them as some of the best and hardiest animals one can keep in a reef aquarium. In a modern aquarium with good lighting and water conditions, many *Acropora* species will grow so prolifically that the aquarist must harvest and pass the surplus to other hobbyists. What a change: just a few years ago, any *Acropora* colony imported was destined for rapid death.

Possibly threatened by overcollection in the wild, the Banggai Cardinal is an ideal species for home aquarists to breed and sell.

There are many examples like this. Therefore, we do not advocate banning the collection or trade in a species simply because it is difficult to keep at the present time. However, we do consider it the aquarium trade's responsibility to give sound advice to its customers, and the individual aquarist's duty to avoid species that have very poor survival records. We hope this book will serve as one tool in helping you make those responsible choices.

So far, there are no known cases where the aquarium trade has been responsible for extinguishing any species. However, there are examples of population declines in local areas because of collection for the trade. Still, negative long-term effects have so far not been shown, and studies have demonstrated that local populations quickly rebound if collection is done on a rotating basis. Efforts are now underway to

> ## ACT RESPONSIBLY
>
> Concerned hobbyists can aid the cause of reef protection by choosing sustainably harvested, certified, and aquacultured marine livestock.
>
> ■ ■ ■

collect the data necessary to begin setting reasonable catch or take limits on fishes and corals to ensure that the harvest is kept at a sustainable level. The assembly of objective records on the local effects of animal collecting is just one of the very important areas that MAC and others are targeting.

Some species of animals are probably more at risk from collection for the aquarium trade than others. Over the last few years we have seen an outcry about the Banggai Cardinalfish (*Pterapogon kauderni*) which is found only in a very small area in Indonesia, and we have learned that seahorses (*Hippocampus* spp.) appear to be very vulnerable because of many forms of human impact on their habitats as well as massive trade in dead specimens for folk medicine in Asian cultures. Luckily, both cardinalfishes and seahorses have turned out to be reasonably easy to propagate in captivity, and alternatives to wild collection are developing rapidly.

Table 9-1 on pages 227-228 provides a list of animals that need our particular concern in the areas of animal welfare and nature conservation. Please also note our recommendations in the presentation of individual species in the Stocking Guide section of this book.

AQUARIUM KEEPING & CONSERVATION

WE WOULD LIKE TO THINK that reef aquarium keeping is here to stay. The body of knowledge and success at keeping, growing, and even propagating marine animals have increased tremendously in a very few years. The marine aquarium hobby is currently full of excitement and positive change. Compare aquariums shown in photos in this book with aquariums in books from

Breathtakingly beautiful, wild reef environments are threatened and will need all the help they can get in the coming century.

15 years ago, and you will quickly see for yourself that a revolution has taken place. This new age is not just the result of easier access to animals and better equipment. It is primarily a result of our discovering how technique and biology work together in an aquarium. The remarkable work of aquarists in creating living reef microcosms has even captured the attention of marine scientists. We are getting results and demonstrating ways of observing reef animals in a way that can increase the potential sources of knowledge about reef biology—in a time when more and more reefs are being degraded by human and climatic factors.

The trade and husbandry of ornamental reef organisms is beneficial to many parties through the whole "**chain of custody**" from collectors to hobbyists. We believe the aquarium trade has potential for being a very "green" and environmentally friendly trade, making sustainable use of natural resources and providing high income to tropical island peoples through low-impact activities.

Perhaps just as important, this is a hobby that raises the environmental awareness of those who keep aquariums as well as those who come into contact with them. Reef aquariums—both public and private—play an enormously positive role in raising public awareness about what coral reefs are and what problems they face.

Coral reefs are going to need all the friends they can find in the coming century. The reef aquarium is a constant learning experience for those of us who keep one, as well as all who come to visit. It is a living connection to wild reefs and, we hope, a beautiful and powerful tool in helping to protect them.

FURTHER READING

THE FOLLOWING BOOKS ARE RECOMMENDED to the serious aquarist who is seeking further reef secrets. The list contains scientific as well as popular titles. Some are directly aimed at the interests of aquarium hobbyists, while others are more general natural history texts.

CORAL REEF BIOLOGY: GENERAL

Byatt, A., A. Fothergill & M. Holmes. 2001. *The Blue Planet*. BBC Worldwide Ltd., London, UK.

Cannon, L. & M. Goyen. 1989. *Exploring Australia's Great Barrier Reef—a World Heritage Site*. The Watermark Press, Surry Hills, NSW, Australia.

Davidson, O.G. 1998. *The Enchanted Braid: Coming to Terms with Nature on the Coral Reef*. John Wiley & Sons, Inc., NY.

Dubinsky, Z. (ed.). 1990. *Ecosystems of the World, Vol. 25, Coral Reefs*. Elsevier, NY.

Gray, W. 1993. *Coral Reefs & Islands: The Natural History of a Threatened Paradise*. David & Charles, Brunel House Newton Abbot Devon, UK.

Holliday, L. 1989. *Coral Reefs*. Salamander Books Ltd., London, UK.

Mather, P. & I. Bennett. 1993. *A Coral Reef Handbook, 3rd ed.* Surrey Beatty & Sons Pty. Ltd., Chipping Northon, NSW, Australia.

Sorokin, Y.I. 1995. *Coral Reef Ecology*. Springer Verlag, Berlin, Germany.

Wood, R. 1999. *Reef Evolution*. Oxford University Press, NY.

THE CORAL REEF AQUARIUM

Delbeek, C. & J. Sprung. 1994. *The Reef Aquarium, Vol. 1*. Ricordea Publishing, Coconut Grove, FL.

Fenner, R.M. 2001. *The Conscientious Marine Aquarist*. Microcosm/T.F.H. Publications, Inc., Neptune City, NJ.

Fosså, S.A. & A.J. Nilsen. 1996. *The Modern Coral Reef Aquarium Vol. 1*. Birgit Schmettkamp Verlag, Bornheim, Germany.

Paletta, M.S. 2001. *The New Marine Aquarium*. Microcosm/T.F.H. Publications, Inc., Neptune City, NJ.

Sprung, J. & C. Delbeek. 1997. *The Reef Aquarium, Vol. 2*. Ricordea Publishing, Coconut Grove, FL.

ALGAE

Cribb, A.B. 1996. *Seaweeds of Queensland. A Naturalist's Guide (Handbook No. 2)*. The Queensland Naturalist's Club, Inc., Brisbane, Australia.

Littler, D.S., M.M. Littler, K.E. Bucher & J.N. Norris. 1989. *Marine Plants of the Caribbean. A Field Guide from Florida to Brazil*. Airlife Publishing Ltd., Shrewsbury, UK.

Payri, C.E., A.D.R. N'Yeurt & J. Orempuller. 2000. *Les algues de Polynésie française / Algae of French Polynesia*. Au Vent de Îles, Tahiti, Polynesia.

INVERTEBRATES
(GENERAL TEXTS AND BOOKS COVERING SEVERAL TAXONOMIC GROUPS)

Allen, G.R. & R. Steene. 1994. *Indo-Pacific Coral Reef Field Guide*. Tropical Reef Research, Singapore.

Colin, P. & C. Arneson. 1995. *Tropical Pacific Invertebrates*. Coral Reef Press, CA.

Fosså, S.A. & A.J. Nilsen. 2000. *The Modern Coral Reef Aquarium, Vol. 3*. Birgit Schmettkamp Verlag, Bornheim, Germany.

Fosså, S.A. & A.J. Nilsen. 2002. *The Modern Coral Reef Aquarium, Vol. 4*. Birgit Schmettkamp Verlag, Bornheim, Germany.

Gosliner, T.M., D.W. Behrens & G.C. Williams. 1996. *Coral Reef Animals of the Indo-Pacific*. Sea Challengers, Monterey, CA.

Humann, P. 1994. *Reef Creatures, 4th ed.* New World Publications, Inc., FL.

Ruppert, E.E. & R.D. Barnes. 1994. *Invertebrate Zoology, 6th ed.* Saunders College Publishing, Fort Worth, TX.

Shimek, R. (publication in progress). *PocketExpert Guide: Marine Invertebrates.* Microcosm/T.F.H. Publications, Inc., Neptune City, NJ.

Vine, P. 1986. *Red Sea Invertebrates.* Immel Publishing, London, UK.

CORALS

Borneman, E.H. 2001. *Aquarium Corals: Selection, Husbandry, and Natural History.* Microcosm/T.F.H. Publications, Inc., Neptune City, NJ.

Fabricus, K. & P. Alderslade. 2001. *Soft Corals and Sea Fans.* Australian Institute of Marine Science (AIMS), Townsville, Queensland, Australia.

Fosså, S.A. & A.J. Nilsen. 1998. *The Modern Coral Reef Aquarium,Vol. 2.* Birgit Schmettkamp Verlag, Bornheim, Germany.

Green, E.P. & F. Shirley. 1999. *The Global Trade in Coral.* World Conservation Monitoring Centre. World Conservation Press, Cambridge, UK.

Humann, P. 1993. *Reef Coral Identification.* New World Publications, Jacksonville, FL.

Veron, J.E.N. 1995. *Corals in Space & Time. The Biogeography and Evolution of the Scleractinia.* Comstock/Cornell, London, UK.

Veron, J.E.N. 2000. *Corals of the World, Vol. 1–3.* Australian Institute of Marine Science (AIMS), Townsville, Queensland, Australia.

Wallace, C. 1999. *Staghorn Corals of the World. A Revision of the Genus Acropora.* CSIRO Publishing, Collingwood, Australia.

MOLLUSKS

Andrews, J. 1994. *A Field Guide to the Shells of the Florida Coast.* Gulf Publishing Company, Houston, TX.

Debelius, H. 1998. *Nudibranchs and Sea Snails. Indo-Pacific Field Guide.* IKAN—Unterwasserarchiv, Frankfurt, Germany.

Knop, D. 1996. *Giant Clams: A Comprehensive Guide to the Identification and Care of Tridacnid Clams.* Dähne Verlag GmbH, Ettlingen, Germany.

Wells, F.E. & C.W. Bryce. 1988. *Seashells of Western Australia.* Western Australian Museum, Perth, Australia.

Wells, F.E. & C.W. Bryce. 1993. *Seaslugs of Western Australia.* Western Australian Museum, Perth, Australia.

Wilson, B. 1993/1994. *Australian Marine Shells, Vol. 1–2.* Odyssey Publishing, Kallaro, Western Australia.

CRUSTACEANS

Debelius, H. 1999. *Crustacea Guide of the World.* IKAN—Unterwasserarchiv, Frankfurt, Germany.

Jones, D. & G. Morgan. 1994. *A Field Guide to the Crustaceans of Australian Waters.* Reed, Chatswood, NSW, Australia.

ECHINODERMS

Hendler, G., J.E. Miller, D.L. Pawson & P.M. Kier. 1995. *Sea Stars, Sea Urchins, and Allies.* Smithsonian Institute Press, Washington, D.C.

FISHES

Allen, G. 2000. *Marine Fishes of South-East Asia.* Periplus Editions (HK) Ltd., Western Australian Museum, Perth, WA, Australia.

Fautin, D.G. & G.R. Allen. 1992. *Field Guide to Anemonefishes and their Host Sea Anemones.* Western Australian Museum, Perth, WA, Australia.

Humann, P. 1994. *Reef Fish Identification.* New World Publications Inc., Jacksonville, FL.

Michael, S. 2001. *Reef Fishes, Vol. 1. A Guide to their Identification, Behavior, and Captive Care.* Microcosm/T.F.H. Publications, Inc., Neptune City, NJ.

Michael, S. (publication in progress). *Reef Fishes, Vol. 2. A Guide to their Identification, Behavior, and Captive Care.* Microcosm/T.F.H. Publications, Inc., Neptune City, NJ.

Michael, S. 2001. *PocketExpert Guide: Marine Fishes.* Microcosm/T.F.H. Publications, Inc., Neptune City, NJ.

Randall, J.E., G.R. Allen & R.C. Steene. 1990. *Fishes of the Great Barrier Reef and Coral Sea.* Crawford House Press, Bathurst, Australia.

Wilkerson, J.D. 2001. *Clownfishes.* Microcosm/T.F.H. Publications, Inc., Neptune City, NJ.

DANGEROUS ANIMALS

Halstead, B.W., P.S. Auerbach & D.R. Campbell. 1990. *A Color Atlas of Dangerous Marine Animals.* CRC Press, Inc., Boca Raton, FL.

Marsh, L. & S. Slack-Smith. 1986. *Sea Stingers.* Western Australian Museum, Perth, WA, Australia.

Vine, P. 1986. *Red Sea Safety.* Immel Publishing, London, UK.

PHOTOGRAPHY CREDITS

(The letters A, B, C, D following a page number refer to photo positions from top to bottom on pages 98-207.)

BIOQUATIC PHOTO—ALF JACOB NILSEN
E-mail: ajnilsen@online.no
Fax: 004738372351
11, 12, 13, 15, 17, 19, 21, 27, 29, 30, 32, 33, 36, 38, 46, 52, 53, 55(Top Left, Top Right, Bottom Center, Bottom Right), 56, 64, 66, 67(Top), 68, 69, 70, 72, 73, 77, 78(Top, Center), 86(Bottom), 88(Center, Bottom), 97(Top), 98(A, C), 99(A, B, C), 101(A, B, C), 102(A, B, C), 103(A, B, D), 104, 105(A, B, D), 106, 107(B, C, D), 109, 110(B, C), 111(A, B, C), 112(B, C), 114(B, C, D), 115(A, B, C), 116(A, B, C), 117(D), 118(C), 119(A, B, C), 120(B, D), 121(A, B, C), 122(A), 123(A, C, D), 124(A, B, C), 125(A), 126(A, C), 127(B, C, D), 128(A, B), 129(A, B), 131(A, B), 132, 133(A), 135(C, D), 136(A, C, D), 137(A, C), 139(B, C, D), 140(B), 141(D), 143(A, C, D), 144(A, C), 145(A, D), 146(B), 148(A, B, D), 149, 150(B, C, D), 151(A, C), 152(A, D), 153, 154(C), 155(C), 156, 157(A, B, C), 158(C), 160(A, B), 161(D), 162(A), 164(C), 165(A, B, D), 167(C, D), 168(B, D), 171(B, C), 172(B), 173(A, D), 175(C), 176(A, B), 177(A, C), 178(B, C), 179(A, C, D), 180(A, B), 182(B), 185(B), 188(B), 189(B, C), 190(C, D), 192(A, B), 193(B, C), 194(D), 196(B), 197(B, D), 198(C), 199, 200(D), 201(D), 202(A, D), 203(B, C), 206(D), 208, 210, 211(Top, Center), 212, 214, 215, 219, 221, 222, 225(Center, Bottom), 229, 240(Left)

SVEIN A. FOSSÅ 49, 55(Top Center, Bottom Left), 78(Bottom), 86(Top, Center), 94, 96(Bottom), 97(Center, Bottom), 98(B, D), 99(D), 100(B, C), 105(C), 107(A), 113(D), 114(A), 115(D), 116(D), 117(C), 120(C), 122(D), 126(B), 127(A), 130(D), 136(B), 137(D), 138(A), 142(C, D), 144(D), 145(B), 147(C), 154(A, D), 156, 158(B), 159(C, D), 160(D), 161(A, B, C), 162(D), 163(A, B, D), 164(B), 165(C), 166(A, D), 167(A, B), 168(A), 169(C), 170(C, D), 171(A), 172(A, C, D), 174, 175(A, B), 176(C), 178(A), 181(B, C), 183(A, C), 184(B, C, D), 185(C, D), 186(B), 187(B, C, D), 188(A, D), 189(A, D), 191(C), 192(C), 194(C), 195, 196(A), 197(A), 198(A), 200(C), 201(A), 202(B, C), 204(A, B), 205(A, C), 206(A, B, C), 207(A, C, D), 240(Right)

SCOTT W. MICHAEL 100(D), 101(D), 102(A), 108, 110(A), 117(B), 118(A), 120(A), 122(B, C), 123(B), 124(D), 125(B), 128(C, D), 129(C), 130(B, C), 131(C), 133(B, D), 134(A, C, D), 135(B), 137(B), 138(C, D), 140(A, C, D), 141(A, B, C), 142(A, B), 143(B), 144(B), 146(A, C), 147(A), 151(B), 152(C), 154(B), 155(A, B), 157(D), 158(A, D), 159(A, B), 162(B, C), 163(C), 164(A, D), 166(B, C), 168(C), 169(A, B, D), 170(A, B), 171(D), 173(B, C), 175(D), 176(D), 177(B, D), 178(D), 179(B), 180(D), 181(D), 182(A, C, D), 183(B, D), 184(A), 185(A), 186(A, C, D), 187(A), 188(C), 190(A, B), 191(A, B, D), 192(D), 193(A, D), 194(A, B), 196(C, D), 197(C), 198(B, D), 200(A, B), 201(B, C), 203(A, D), 204(C, D), 205(B, D), 207(B)

JANINE CARINS MICHAEL 100(A), 103(C), 111(D), 112(A, D), 113(A, C), 117(A), 118(B, D), 119(D), 121(D), 125(C, D), 126(D), 131(D), 133(C), 134(B), 135(A), 138(B), 145(C), 146(D), 147(B, D), 151(D), 152(B), 155(D)

DENISE NIELSEN TACKETT 8, 48, 57, 58, 61, 67(Bottom), 74, 75, 83, 84, 95, 96(Top, Center), 148(C), 209, 216, 230

OCEAN PHOTO / ERLING SVENSEN 10, 16, 65, 88(Top), 110(D), 130(A)

LARRY TACKETT 14, 20, 42, 60, 217, 218

PAUL HUMANN 113(B), 139(A), 150(A), 180(C)

A. FLOWERS AND L. NEWMAN 9, 26, 129(D)

JAN CARLÉN 160(C), 181(A)

PAUL HOLTHUS 224, 225(Top)

DR. BRUCE CARLSON 223

TRACY GRAY 23

JAN HARBERS 211(Bottom)

ED LOVELL 54

TORSTEN LUTHER 50

JEFFERY A. TURNER/REEF AQUARIA DESIGN, INC. 62

JOSHUA HIGHTER All illustrations

INDEX

ABOUT THE AUTHORS

ALF JACOB NILSEN is a biologist, teacher, and author of many articles and books, including *The Modern Coral Reef Aquarium* series, which he has coauthored with Svein A. Fosså in both German and English.

Alf Jacob was born and bred in Kirkehamn, a small fishing village on the island of Hidra, situated on the coastline of southern Norway. Growing up along the North Sea, he says that the oceans have always been a natural part of his life, and he and his family continue living on this beautiful island.

Alf Jacob holds a degree in Pedagogic Science from  the Teaching Academy of Stavanger and a degree in biology from the University of Bergen. At the present time he works as a teacher in Natural History and Mathematics in the local school, where he also teaches students who have learning disabilities.

He has been a marine aquarist since 1979, and has published numerous articles on the subject of reefkeeping and invertebrate biology in a number of magazines in Europe and North America. He speaks frequently on the same topics at international conferences and gatherings of reef aquarists.

Alf Jacob is a member of the International Society for Reef Studies (ISRS), and as a certified scuba diver he has visited and photographed coral reefs in many parts of the world. He is the founder of Bioquatic Photo, a natural history photo library that spans his interests in aquariums, marine biology, the seas, foreign travel, and astronomy.

SVEIN A. FOSSÅ is an ichthyologist, co-author of the *The Modern Coral Reef Aquarium* series, and a leading international voice for responsible and sustainable practices in the aquarium trade.

He has been an aquarist since early childhood and possesses a wide range of experiences with freshwater and marine aquarium keeping. He holds a degree in biology from the University of Bergen, specializing in systematic ichthyology.

Svein, who resides with his wife and two children in the small, picturesque town of Grimstad on the south coast of Norway, has been involved with the aquatics trade since 1986. Since 1992, he has worked as an independent author and advisor on aquarium techniques, ichthyology, and pet trade policies and legislation worldwide. He lectures regularly in many countries, and has authored several articles, reports and other publications, including a number of previous works on reef aquarium keeping and reef animals with Alf Jacob Nilsen.

Svein is a consultant on Public and International Affairs to the Norwegian Pet Trade Organization (NZB), secretary of the Scandinavian Pet Trade Union (SPTU), European liaison director for the Marine Aquarium Council (MAC), and president of Ornamental Fish International (OFI).

Besides his passionate interest in nature and aquatic biology, Svein is an ardent traveler with a keen interest in geography, history and human culture, including gastronomy and food history.